Resort Spatiality

This book theorises resorts as distinct kinds of urban milieux, capturing the complexity of destinations famous for 'sun, sand and sex' mass tourism. Drawing on qualitative field research (participant observation, interviews and photography), the book discusses examples from six international resort destinations spread across four continents: the Gold Coast, Australia; Phuket and Koh Phangan, Thailand; Cancún, Mexico; Miami, USA; and Ibiza, Spain.

The book reviews the material and symbolic production of lived spaces in these resorts, considering the mutually constitutive, mutually transformative relations between their spatial formations, built environments, popular imaginaries, representations, narratives of identity, rhythms, and the experiences and practices of both tourists and locals. In doing so, it argues for more nuanced ways of conceptualising tourism, globalisation and spatiality, reimagining how these phenomena unfold in lived spaces.

Taking a cultural studies approach to urban analysis, the book demonstrates the value in embracing complexity, fluidity, partiality and uncertainty. It will be of interest to students and researchers of tourism, geography, cultural studies, development studies, anthropology and sociology.

Zelmarie Cantillon is a Postdoctoral Research Fellow in the School of Humanities, Languages and Social Science at Griffith University, Gold Coast, Australia. She is co-editor of *The Routledge Companion to Popular Music History and Heritage* (2018) and has contributed to numerous edited collections and journals.

New Directions in Tourism Analysis

Series editors:

Dimitri Ioannides, E-TOUR, Mid Sweden University, Sweden

Although tourism is becoming increasingly popular both as a taught subject and an area for empirical investigation, the theoretical underpinnings of many approaches have tended to be eclectic and somewhat underdeveloped. However, recent developments indicate that the field of tourism studies is beginning to develop in a more theoretically informed manner, but this has not yet been matched by current publications.

The aim of this series is to fill this gap with high quality monographs or edited collections that seek to develop tourism analysis at both theoretical and substantive levels using approaches which are broadly derived from allied social science disciplines such as Sociology, Social Anthropology, Human and Social Geography, and Cultural Studies. As tourism studies covers a wide range of activities and sub fields, certain areas such as Hospitality Management and Business, which are already well provided for, would be excluded. The series will therefore fill a gap in the current overall pattern of publication.

Suggested themes to be covered by the series, either singly or in combination, include: consumption; cultural change; development; gender; globalisation; political economy; social theory; and sustainability.

Performing Cultural Tourism
Communities, Tourists and Creative Practices
Edited by Susan Carson and Mark Pennings

Advances in Social Media for Travel, Tourism and Hospitality
New Perspectives, Practice and Cases
Edited by Marianna Sigala and Ulrike Gretzel

Being and Dwelling through Tourism
An Anthropological Perspective
Catherine Palmer

Resort Spatiality
Reimagining Sites of Mass Tourism
Zelmarie Cantillon

For more information about this series, please visit www.routledge.com/New-Directions-in-Tourism-Analysis/book-series/ASHSER1207

Resort Spatiality
Reimagining Sites of Mass Tourism

Zelmarie Cantillon

Routledge
Taylor & Francis Group

LONDON AND NEW YORK

First published 2019 by Routledge

2 Park Square, Milton Park, Abingdon, Oxon OX14 4RN
605 Third Avenue, New York, NY 10017

Routledge is an imprint of the Taylor & Francis Group, an informa business

First issued in paperback 2022

British Library Cataloguing-in-Publication Data
A catalogue record for this book is available from the British Library

Library of Congress Cataloging-in-Publication Data
A catalog record has been requested for this book

ISBN: 978-1-138-54174-0 (hbk)
ISBN: 978-1-03-233883-5 (pbk)
DOI: 10.4324/9781351010337

Typeset in Times New Roman
by Taylor & Francis Books

Contents

Figures

Tables

Acknowledgements

This book would not have come to fruition without the guidance and friendship of my two wonderful mentors, Patricia Wise and Sarah Baker. I want to express my deepest gratitude for all of your feedback and your unwavering confidence in my abilities over the years. You have both taught me so much about being a well-rounded academic – not just about critical thinking, researching, writing and publishing, but also about the importance of being kind, generous, humble and empathetic. Many thanks also to Ben Highmore and Rob Shields, whose encouragement provided the impetus for me to pursue this book.

I wish to acknowledge the support I have received from Griffith University, in the form of scholarships and grants as well as fostering my professional development. The School of Humanities, Languages and Social Science saw me through my beginnings as an overwhelmed, unsure undergraduate all the way through to the completion of my PhD. Thank you to all the academic and administrative staff for educating me, giving me advice, and showing genuine interest in the progression of my studies. In the post-PhD phase of my career, I owe particular thanks to the Griffith Centre for Social and Cultural Research, which generously provided me with the office space where this book was completed.

I am incredibly appreciative for the team at Routledge – including Dimitri Ioannides, Emma Travis and Carlotta Fanton – for enthusiastically embracing this project from the outset and offering me assistance along the way.

I would also like to acknowledge that some text and images from the following journal article appear in several chapters throughout this book:

- Cantillon, Z 2015, 'Polyrhythmia, heterogeneity and urban identity: intersections between "official" and "unofficial" narratives in the socio-spatial practices of Australia's Gold Coast', *Journal of Urban Cultural Studies*, vol. 2, no. 3, pp. 253–274.

On a personal note, special thanks to my dear friends in and outside of academia: Serena Malone, Anneliese Martinu, Laura Rodriguez Castro, Kristy Seymour, Ashleigh Watson, Maryanne Hereijgers, Bob Buttigieg, Takeshi Ashenden, Josh Clough, and all the PhD students and postdoctoral fellows I have had the pleasure of meeting over the last several years. Thank you all for the much-needed lunch dates, coffee breaks and wine time. My sincere thanks to my family: my brother, JJ, who has always been so supportive and proud; and my mother, Marion, who has always been there for me. Above all, thank you to my partner and best friend, Rogan Sharpe, for your love, warmth, intellect and understanding.

Lastly, to each person who agreed to be interviewed for this project: thank you for sharing your time and invaluable insights with me.

Zelmarie Cantillon
Gold Coast, Queensland, Australia

1 Introduction

Spatiality and mass tourism

Introduction

Living on the Gold Coast, Australia, I have often felt out of place in my own city. I am asked 'Where are you from?' in the most mundane moments – waiting at my tram stop to go to work, buying jeans at my local shopping centre, eating with friends at a restaurant. When I reply with my suburb, fellow Gold Coasters respond apologetically – 'Sorry, I thought you were a tourist!' – while visitors respond with fascination – 'Oh wow, you *live* here? You are so lucky!' It has always seemed strange to me that I am assumed, by default, to be from elsewhere. This is not an uncommon experience, however, in a city whose public spaces – especially its leisure spaces – are seen to belong to tourists rather than residents.

The Gold Coast has long been dominated by tourism in its image, economy and development. It is famous for a particular brand of 'sun, sand and sex' mass tourism, boasting long stretches of sandy beaches, family-friendly theme parks and a lively nightlife scene. Being largely geared towards the desires and demands of tourists, the city has created a peculiar context for the lives of locals. It is from my own everyday experiences living on the Gold Coast that the inspiration for this book emerged. In 2009, when I moved to the Gold Coast from its hinterland, I quickly became accustomed to a set of popular, localised attitudes towards the city that I picked up from interactions with new friends, neighbours and strangers. We complain about tourists, calling them annoying and rude, and deride and (try to) avoid the tourist hub, Surfers Paradise, especially when major events are on. We say the Gold Coast only cares about tourism dollars, and express disdain for the city's supposed superficiality, tackiness and lack of culture.

However, these attitudes are marked by ambivalence. Many of us have jobs in tourism-related industries such as hospitality, retail and construction, and thus rely on tourism for income. We also inevitably end up spending time in Surfers Paradise, given that it is the city's major entertainment and nightlife precinct. Further, even though we say the Gold Coast does not have 'culture' (an ambiguous and problematic notion, at best) in the ways that Melbourne or Sydney do, we have witnessed an increasing number of arts festivals, boutique bars and trendy cafes popping up all over the city. Despite our criticisms, many of us enjoy living on the Gold Coast, and for the very same reasons that lure tourists: the weather, the beaches and the lifestyle.

In my time living on the Gold Coast, I have grown especially interested in the attitudes outlined above, and in the spatial context in which I am immersed. In the initial stages of this project, it struck me that the Gold Coast was a unique kind of place, different from other Australian cities. At the same time, it has parallels with other places around the world – other beachside mass tourism destinations that I call resorts. It was also obvious to me that the way these places were written and talked about – in scholarly work, in the media, and more informally – seemed to be lacking, often falling back on simplistic, well-worn stereotypes regarding the perils of mass tourism development.

The objective of this book is to capture some of the complexity of resorts, theorising them as distinct kinds of urban milieux. Drawing on qualitative field research (participant observation, interviews and photography), I discuss examples from six international resort destinations spread across four continents: the Gold Coast, Australia; Phuket and Koh Phangan, Thailand; Cancún, Mexico; Miami, USA; and Ibiza, Spain. Examining localised expressions of globalised processes, I attend to the commonalities that delineate resorts as particular types of places, but also the differences that set them apart. Each chapter considers the dynamics between the material and symbolic (Highmore 2005), or real and imagined (Soja 1996; Lefebvre 1991 [1974]), aspects of spatiality. I explore the mutually constitutive relations between the representations, imaginaries and materialities of resorts, and how they are perceived and experienced differently by tourists and locals. In doing so, the book argues for more nuanced ways of conceptualising tourism, globalisation and spatiality, reimagining how these phenomena unfold in lived spaces. Taking a cultural studies approach to urban analysis, the book demonstrates the value in embracing complexity, fluidity, partiality and uncertainty.

In this chapter, I set the scene for the analysis that follows. I provide an overview of the existing literature on resorts, and how this book extends this research to develop fresh insights. The chapter then discusses some of the key theoretical and conceptual frameworks underpinning my approach to conceptualising spatiality and mass tourism. Lastly, I briefly outline the fieldwork process and my methodological perspectives. First, however, I offer a working definition of resorts and explain the factors informing my choice of sites on which to focus.

Resorts: a definition

Although the term 'resort' has also been applied to ski towns and elaborate hotels, the places examined in this book are, specifically, beachside destinations which are sites of intensified mass tourism development of the sun, sand and sex[1] variety. Further, I have chosen to refer to these destinations as 'resorts' (rather than resort cities or resort towns) to encompass their diverse forms – as cities and towns, but also islands and regions.

Resorts share a number of symbolic and material commonalities that distinguish them as particular kinds of places. Most obviously, their economies have long been dependent on the tourism industry, which has created unique historical, social and spatial conditions (Pons, Crang & Travlou 2009). They are known for their warm weather and beautiful beaches, but also for nightlife and events like Spring Break in Miami and Cancún, Schoolies on the Gold Coast, Full Moon Parties in Koh Phangan, and the summertime clubbing season in Ibiza (see Chapter 3). As such, resorts attract visitors seeking family vacations, romantic getaways and clubbing or partying holidays alike. Each resort examined in this book is an international destination with established tourism-related infrastructure, services and amenities, including natural and built attractions; numerous accommodation options (from backpacker hostels to five-star hotels); restaurants, bars and nightclubs; shopping malls and precincts; gyms and spas; and tour operators.

On top of these material qualities, resorts also share similarities in terms of their popular imaginaries, myths, tourism narratives and representations, being perceived and marketed as places associated with escapism, fantasy, hedonism, spectacle and excess (see Chapter 3). Simultaneously, as a result of the dominance of mass tourism, they are frequently stereotyped and disparaged as being overdeveloped, tacky tourist traps; as banal, transient, depthless and fake; and as representative of the 'worst' aspects of globalisation and mass consumption, which are seen to enforce cultural homogeneity and destroy local cultures (see Chapter 4). Therefore, although tourism has been important in forming the economic base of these places, and although it continues to generate employment and substantial revenue, the industry has also had negative social and environmental impacts (see Chapters 5 and 6).

Resorts are examples of tourism urbanisation, defined by Mullins (1992) as 'the process whereby urban areas, particularly large cities, are *specially developed* for the production, sale, and consumption of goods and services providing pleasure' (p. 188, original emphasis). Mullins (1992, 1991) suggests that this trend gained traction due to the same series of post-World War II social and economic changes in the West that gave rise to the emergence of mass tourism – technological advancements, greater disposable incomes, paid holidays, and so on. Unlike the conventional modern metropolis, which has its roots in 'the agglomeration of manufacturing industry, trade, and administration' (Gladstone 1998, p. 3), sites of tourism urbanisation are characteristically postmodern, based on leisure and consumption rather than the production and exchange of commodities (Pons, Salamanca & Murray 2014; Mullins 1991).

Consequently, resorts may not feature some of the spatial qualities that we expect from traditional cities, such as central business districts (CBDs). While they may have zones where legal, financial and administrative services are concentrated (such as the downtown regions of Miami and Cancún), these do not serve as singular, dominant centres. Indeed, the 'business' of resorts has more to do with tourism-related industries than any other kinds of commercial activities typically associated with CBDs. Much like Soja's (1996) exopolis, resorts tend to be de-centred urban areas, featuring multiple, scattered centres and peripheries with different functions for tourists and residents (see Chapter 2). Perhaps more significant and recognisable than any kind of CBD are recreational business districts (RBDs) (Meyer-Arendt 1990; Butler 1980; Pigram 1977; Stansfield & Rickert 1970; Stansfield 1969) or tourism business districts (Getz 1993). Usually located along the coastline, these districts are tourist-oriented hubs of entertainment and leisure, densely occupied by restaurants, food stalls, hotels, apartment buildings, souvenir shops, pedestrian malls and other tourist facilities. Often, the most developed centres in resorts are these recreation and tourism districts, which are designed to cater for transient tourist populations rather than to serve the needs of residents (Mullins 1992; Meyer-Arendt 1990). This raises important questions about local senses of belonging and who has rights to urban space (see Chapter 6).

In addition to sharing certain commonalities, each resort is also different. Resorts have their own 'local specificity' (Massey 1998, p. 122) or 'urban spatial specificity' (Soja 2000, p. 8), which refers to their unique geographical, social, political and cultural contexts, histories, trajectories, materialities and imaginaries. Like all places, resorts have different landscapes, architectural styles, demographics, social and political issues, cultural practices, and so on. There are multiple sources of local specificity, which not only originate internally, but are shaped by external forces as well – places are constituted by a mixture of the local *and* the global (Massey 2007, 1994). Resorts are products of (and contributors to) global trends in mass tourism, but these trends manifest differently depending on each place's local specificity (see Chapters 3 and 4). Further, as Massey (2007) observes, '[a]ctions in one place affect other places' (p. 15). Thus, to conceptualise the spatiality and local 'character' of a resort, we must notice its relations with what is beyond, both in terms of how it is influenced by and how it influences other localities (Massey 2007, 1994). In Massey, Allen and Pile's (1999) words, 'it is impossible to tell the story of any individual city without understanding its connections to elsewhere' (p. 2). These ideas underpin the comparative, multi-sited approach of this book (Falzon 2016 [2009]; Saukko 2003; Marcus 1995). Such an approach allows me to elucidate patterns and connections in how particular global phenomena play out across various local sites, while still attending to discontinuities and idiosyncrasies (Saukko 2003).

The resorts examined in this book were selected based on my initial impressions of both their similarities and their differences. Miami has been frequently compared to the Gold Coast, most notably due to their similar skylines, high-end waterfront real estate, weather and tourism industries, with some making claims that the Gold Coast was deliberately modelled on Miami Beach (see Scott, Gardiner & Dedekorkut-Howes 2016; Griffin 1998; Pigram 1977). However, Miami is also particularly valuable as an example because of its maturity as a destination, having experienced several periods of ebb and flow in its popularity over the past century. Cancún, like Miami, attracts university students during Spring Break, but quite unlike the other resorts I chose, its development as a destination was fairly recent, being a purpose-built resort – a 'planned utopia' (Murray 2007, p. 340) – initiated in the mid-1970s. Just as Cancún, Phuket and Koh Phangan are imagined as 'exotic' destinations for Western tourists, fusing beach activities and cultural experiences. These Thai resorts are especially popular among young Australians, being in close proximity to Australia and relatively affordable. Ibiza is, similarly, an appealing vacation spot for young people due to its reputation as a global mecca for mainstream dance music culture. Ibiza's imaginaries epitomise the 'sex' aspect of sun, sand and sex mass tourism, involving not only sexual pursuit, but partying, drinking and other adult activities.

(Re)imagining resorts: the existing literature

Although the terms 'resort', 'resort city' and 'resort town' are not uncommon in the literature, these kinds of places have not been extensively theorised. In particular, with the exception of tourism urbanisation, there is little scholarly work on resorts from the perspectives of urban cultural studies (Fraser 2015; Highmore 2005) or cultural geography in the same vein as conceptualisations of urban formations like the exopolis (Soja 2000, 1996), fantasy city (Hannigan 1998), edge city (Garreau 1991) or post-industrial city (Gospodini 2006; Mommaas 2004; Hall 1997).

In tourism literature, the most notable and influential studies on resorts have been those of British seaside resorts (Agarwal 2002, 1997; Shaw & Williams 1997; Walvin 1978; Hern 1967; Barrett 1958), especially Blackpool and Brighton (Webb 2005; Urry 2002; Meethan 1996; Shields 1991; Bennett 1986, 1983; Gilbert 1949). These early resorts are significant in that they 'set the dominant patterns for mass tourism' (Meethan 2001, p. 9) that persist today. Few studies, however, take a comparative approach, and fewer still draw explicit parallels between the particular contemporary resorts on which I focus. Exceptions include fleeting comparisons made by Gladstone (1998), who mentions the Gold Coast, Miami Beach and Cancún as examples of tourism urbanisation; D'Andrea (2007), who lists Ibiza and Koh Phangan as sites for nomadic dance countercultures; and Tutenges (2012), who names Cancún, Koh Phangan, Ibiza and the Gold Coast as examples of nightlife resorts.

On the basis of some of the earliest research on seaside resorts – especially by Gilbert (1949) and Barrett (1958), who identified some common phenomena among such places – the concept of 'resort morphology' was developed (see Andriotis 2003; Meyer-Arendt, Sambrook & Kermath 1992; Jeans 1990; Meyer-Arendt 1990; Pigram 1977; Lavery 1974; Stansfield 1969). Resort morphology examines the spatial formation of (usually seaside/beachside) tourism destinations in an attempt to illustrate the relations between form, function and development (Liu & Wall 2009). By identifying similarities between resorts, resort morphology highlights the distinctiveness of these types of places as urban formations. Researchers have observed that the form of resorts reflects their function as sites for tourist consumption: development is most intensified near the beach, expanding along the coastline in a linear fashion while also sprawling inland (Andriotis 2003; Pigram 1977; Stansfield 1969). In this development pattern, the beachfront is commonly tourist-focused, dominated by the attractions, amenities and accommodation which constitute the RBD – a concept which originated in resort morphology literature (Getz 1993; Meyer-Arendt 1990; Pigram 1977; Stansfield & Rickert 1970; Stansfield 1969). Residents' housing, institutions and services, on the other hand, are more likely to occupy areas further inland, but wealthier residents tend to live closer to the beach than other locals (Stansfield 1969). These general trends are evident in the urban formations of the resorts this book investigates, but in each case with important variations (see Chapter 2).

Closely related to resort morphology is a body of literature that theorises how these sites develop and change over time. This is grounded in Butler's (2006, 1980) tourism area life cycle (TALC), Smith's (1992, 1991) work on beach resort evolution, and Prideaux's (2009, 2004) resort development spectrum. Each model identifies a pattern of development that tracks resorts from their quiet, small town beginnings to their evolution into large, international mass tourism destinations and, often, into cities with increasingly diverse economic activities. These models outline various stages or phases that resorts may go through, defined by criteria relating to population growth, tourist arrivals and overnight visitors, accommodation types, local participation and resident attitudes, environmental impacts, and more. For example, Butler's (2006) TALC outlines that destinations start out as relatively unknown and undeveloped, attracting alternative tourists seeking something off the beaten path. As visitors increase, locals in the area respond by developing touristic infrastructure and amenities, which attracts even more visitors. As tourist arrivals continue to grow, partly due to focused marketing efforts, multinational corporations and chains occupy more spaces, and the area solidifies itself as a popular mass tourism destination. After this point, the destination stagnates before either losing popularity and declining, or rejuvenating itself by reorientating or restructuring its attractions and marketing tactics. Such predictive models on resort evolution have been particularly relevant to the planning, development and management of resort destinations (see Prideaux 2009; Mill 2008; Agarwal & Shaw 2007).

The literature on resort evolution, resort morphology and tourism urbanisation tends to focus on the materiality of resorts – their landscapes, built environments, attractions, developments over time, and the flows and activities of tourists and residents. Inspired by the works of Lefebvre (2004 [1992], 1991 [1974]) and Soja (2000, 1996), this book differs from the existing literature in that I aim to conceptualise the spatiality of resorts not only in terms of the 'real', but also the imagined and the lived. I consider how resorts, as distinct urban milieux, are produced and reproduced from both macro- and micro-level perspectives. I examine the material aspects of resorts referred to above; their symbolic existence (their popular imaginaries, representations and narratives of identity); and the lived experiences of tourists and locals in social spaces (which draw together elements of the material and the symbolic). Below, I outline some of the key concepts underpinning these understandings of spatiality and how they relate to tourism.

Space, place and assemblage

Scholarly work has increasingly recognised the significance of the spatial dimensions of culture and everyday life, a movement which is referred to as 'the spatial turn'. The centrality of space to everyday life means that how we think about space, and how we demarcate it, represent it, regulate it, construct it and move within it, has powerful social, political and historical effects. Considerations of spatiality are particularly important to understanding the sites and practices of tourism, which is an inherently spatial phenomenon (Minca 2000). Tourists depart from their everyday spatial contexts to visit destinations with unfamiliar socio-spatial qualities – attractions, landscapes, climates and cultures – and these places are, in turn, everyday spaces for those who live there.

In *For Space* (2005), Massey problematises traditional understandings of 'space', which has typically been defined in opposition to 'place'. She argues that space has often been theorised as global, natural, abstract and empty, a surface or void that is disconnected from cultures, histories and meaning. In contrast, place has been seen as that which is local, everyday, meaningful, authentic, closed and fixed. Massey (2005) rejects any strict separation between space and place, and offers three propositions which underpin a more productive approach to conceptualising spatiality:

> *First*, that we recognise space as the product of interrelations; as constituted through interactions, from the immensity of the global to the intimately tiny ... *Second*, that we understand space as the sphere of the possibility of the existence of multiplicity in the sense of contemporaneous plurality; as the sphere in which distinct trajectories coexist; as the sphere therefore of coexisting heterogeneity ... *Third*, that we recognise space as always under construction ... always in the process of being made. It is never finished; never closed. Perhaps we could imagine space as a simultaneity of stories-so-far. (p. 9, original emphasis)

In short, space is never empty nor static, but rather heterogeneous and always in process, produced through a multiplicity of interrelations and a plurality of trajectories. As such, it is anything but disconnected from cultures and histories: 'space does not exist prior to identities/entities and their relations ... [I]dentities/entities, the relations "between" them, and the spatiality which is part of them, are all constitutive' (Massey 2005, p. 10).

While the distinction between space and place (and the characteristics attributed to each) is false, the concept of 'place' nevertheless continues to be a significant framing device for how people perceive, use and regulate spaces. Therefore, following Massey's approach, I do not abandon the term 'place' in favour of 'space' or vice versa. Just as with the propositions about space outlined above, Massey (2007, 1994) stresses that we need to reconfigure our understandings of place, to develop a 'progressive' or 'global' sense of place. A place is thought of as somewhere that has been territorialised and named, and has become associated with a particular identity, culture, history, government, climate, landscape, and built environment. However, while places are indeed distinct and have their own local specificity, they are not coherent, unified or harmonious. That is, they are full of 'internal conflicts' (Massey 1994, p. 155), and can have multiple, contested identities, cultures, and so on.

Despite what maps, local government areas and zoning policies may infer, places do not have easily definable geographic boundaries. As Massey (2007) points out, 'places do not lend themselves to having lines drawn around them' (p. 13). Miami, for example, is imagined as a particular place, but it encompasses numerous other sprawling cities and neighbourhoods (which are in themselves places that are different from each other), so it is difficult to determine where Miami ends and the next place begins. Miami, as a *sense* of place, and somewhere that people can identify as living in or belonging to, emanates beyond rigidly demarcated city limits. Place, then, is not spatially bounded, fixed or closed, but fluid and open (Massey 2007, 1994). As discussed earlier, rather than being threatened by external forces, places are in fact always connected to, constituted by and influencing what exists outside of them. Places like resorts are 'specific nodes' (Massey 2007, p. 167) in a wider global network of international mass tourism destinations, and this network is always evolving, making and losing connections.

Places, spaces and networks can also be usefully conceptualised as 'assemblages' in Deleuze and Guattari's (2004 [1987]) terms. An assemblage is a collection of diverse elements that form a larger whole that 'expresses some identity and claims a territory' (Surin 2011, p. 91). What constitutes the assemblage is constantly shifting and changing in nature, with the 'whole' never actually being stable or complete. Just as Massey argued with regard to place, assemblages and the multiplicities that constitute them are largely defined relationally, including by relations both within and beyond[2] the assemblage. The assemblage is in a perpetual state of becoming, always being made and remade. Places are assemblages composed of multiplicities of bodies, mobilities, rhythms, representations, identities, histories, communities, cultures, signs, power relations, buildings, material objects, imaginaries, and affects. Tourism is also an assemblage, composed of an array of elements and performances: the actions and dispositions of 'hosts', such as hospitality staff, entertainers and tour guides; the images, representations and narratives of place disseminated by governments, tourism-related businesses, investors, news media and popular cultural representations; the existence of basic tourist amenities, such as public bathrooms, accommodation, and currency exchange services; and the staging of natural, cultural and built attractions to facilitate tourist consumption, such as through adding boardwalks, observation decks, directional signage and informational plaques, as well as landscaping and street cleaning.

Importantly, assemblages involve both order and disorder, multiplicities and hierarchies, mobilities and moorings (Hannam, Sheller & Urry 2006). Even though, in their lived actuality, places have a tendency to be messy, dynamic and connected to elsewhere, full of multiplicities and contested uses and meanings, they are also shaped by sedimented histories (Highmore 2005) and traditions. In this sense, they *do* have 'lines drawn around them' (Massey 2007, p. 13): they are regulated by policy and governance, carved up into zones, stratified in terms of class, race and gender, and subjected to meta-narratives of identity. This ordering is characteristic of world cities like resorts, which experience tensions and movements between 'the jarring of a territorialised politics with another geography of flows and connections' (Massey 2007, p. 14). These processes, and the unique ways in which they interact and manifest, are part of what constructs a place's local specificity and its spatiality.

Perceived, conceived and lived space

In *The Production of Space* (1991 [1974]), Lefebvre posits that spatiality can be thought of as a 'perceived-conceived-lived triad' (p. 40) of physical space, mental space and social space, which he also refers to as spatial practice, representations of space and representational spaces.[3] Physical space designates that which is 'real' or material, such as the built environment and landscape; mental space is the 'imagined', including representations, myths and imaginaries; while the 'real-and-imagined' of social space refers to lived experiences and practices (Soja 1996, pp. 5–6; Lefebvre 1991 [1974]). Lefebvre and Soja work against a long-standing convention of treating the perceived and the conceived as a binary. Soja (1996) argues that a 'thirding' of the spatial imagination functions not simply to undo this binary, but to restructure it, taking into account how space is sensed, felt and lived (see also Lefebvre 1991 [1974]).

The spatiality of resorts is constituted by the mutually transformative relations between imaginaries, representations, materialities and lived experiences. Imaginaries can be defined as mental, conceptual perceptions and mappings of particular places and events (Highmore 2005; Soja 2000). They involve not only ideas about how a place looks and how to navigate it, but also what kinds of people occupy it and what goes on there – its landscape, cultures, identities, norms, and so on. Imaginaries encompass both material and symbolic elements (Highmore 2005), and are formed at both a singular level, such as through subjective experiences and memories, and at a collective level, such as through representations, historical canons and other texts and myths. When these are widely held or understood, I refer to them as *popular* imaginaries – perceptions, stereotypes, narratives or reputations of a place that are based on its most iconic, well-known characteristics.

Imaginaries of resorts inform, and are informed by, representations of place in film and television, songs, literature, news reporting, social media, and travel brochures, guides and websites. These representations, and the narratives they put forth, can be conflicting – for example, a tourism campaign may depict a destination as being safe and family-friendly while news reports may focus on drug use and crime (see Chapter 3). Moreover, imaginaries will differ greatly between and among tourists and locals depending on their respective experiences and their exposure to certain representations, and how much value they assign to these. Locals, for instance, are more likely to imagine their city in terms of their everyday experiences than in terms of tourism promotions, although these factor into their understandings as well. Even for tourists, imaginaries are multiple, varied and contested (Urry 1995), although some are more pervasive than others.

Since representations significantly shape the imaginaries of tourists, there is a necessity for destinations to cultivate lived spaces that closely align with these expectations (Crang 2014; Crouch, Jackson & Thompson 2005; Urry 2002; MacCannell 2001). Tourists 'seek to experience "in reality" the pleasurable dramas they have already experienced in their imagination' (Urry 2002, p. 13), through, for example, gazing upon spectacle first-hand, feeling the humid air and the sun on their skin, experiencing fun and relaxation, and creating certain kinds of memories. Destinations, therefore, have the power to make fantasy into reality.

In this way (among others), representations and imaginaries have material consequences (Highmore 2005) in that they transform the real. One of the material effects of imaginaries and representations is that they establish 'normative agendas' (Crang 2014, p. 69) of what should be seen and done, as well as offering 'guides for action' (Shields 1991, p. 30) as to standard ways of behaving, dressing and interacting. Conceived space, then, becomes internalised, embodied and lived out, influencing spatial practices and social performances.[4] For example, numerous images in tourism promotions of the Gold Coast feature families at the beach and in nearby areas wearing swimwear and flip-flops, which indicates to future visitors that these are appropriate kinds of attire and activities.

If people perform as they are positioned to by the most dominant representations – exhibiting a kind of socio-spatial competence – then those narratives are reified and their associated norms are reaffirmed and perpetuated, implicitly encouraging others to perform in similar ways. In other words, a degree of coordination between imaginaries, representations and lived experiences is required for social spaces to be reproduced and naturalised (Shields 1991). However, any coordination is tentative and social spaces are always changing. The real, lived spaces of resorts will never be exactly as they are depicted or imagined. To an extent, representations and imaginaries are partial and reductive,[5] whereas lived spaces are infinitely complex, rich and dynamic. The *in situ* experience of space inevitably entails subversive performances, surprises, unexpected encounters, sights, smells, and so on – and this is why materiality matters. Traces of these actual uses of space feed back into popular imaginaries and representations, working to reinforce or transform them, or add another layer to the multiplicity.

The built environment also significantly shapes spatiality. Iconic landmarks and particular architectural styles, for instance, function as symbols of place in popular imaginaries and representations. Further, the built environment expresses something about how its creators (urban planners, developers, architects and interior designers) imagined the space to be used (Allen 1999). Therefore, like narratives and representations, the built environment and its significations can be used as a mechanism of control over bodies (Foucault 1991 [1977]), positioning people to enact particular spatial practices. Pathways and pedestrian crossings indicate where people are to walk; lighting contributes to a certain atmosphere; and observation decks and balconies encourage gazing upon and photographing visual spectacle.

Although spatial arrangements may act as structures of control, individuals can exercise agency from within them. The built environment 'organizes an ensemble of possibilities ... and interdictions' (de Certeau 2002 [1984], p. 387). City walkers can abide by and actualise these material spatial signifiers, reinforcing popular imaginaries about how the space is to be encountered, consumed and performed. Alternatively, they can reject or transform them through 'rebellious performances' (Edensor 2001, p. 60), by taking detours or otherwise disrupting the normative flows of people through spaces. Such micro-level transgressions have the potential to alter macro-level norms and popular imaginaries as well. This will inevitably occur since people within lived spaces are heterogeneous, with different cultural backgrounds, desires, imaginaries and purposes for being there (e.g. in resorts, in addition to tourists, there are locals engaging in everyday activities, leisure and paid labour). However, as mentioned above, for a resort to remain popular and satisfying to its visitors, a certain degree of coherence in performances is needed so that the experience and atmosphere of lived space aligns with representations and imaginaries of that space. In Sheller and Urry's (2004) words, 'if the performances by hosts and guests no longer happen then the place stops "happening"' (p. 7). Far from being separate entities, bodies and spaces form an assemblage, co-producing one another (Grosz 2002 [1992]; Lefebvre 1991 [1974]).

In Lefebvre's (2004 [1992]) terms, socio-spatial performances – informed by the relations between perceived, conceived and lived – manifest as particular *rhythms*. Lefebvre (2004 [1992], 1991 [1974]) broadly defines rhythms as the connections between space, time and energies. These rhythms can be linear or cyclical – linear being routine social activity and imposed structures of organisation, or 'the daily grind' (Lefebvre 2004 [1992], p. 30); cyclical being things in nature, such as day and night, seasons, tides, and bodily rhythms such as respiration, circulation and hunger. There would be no capacity to measure the linear without the cyclical, and the two 'exert a reciprocal action' (Lefebvre 2004 [1992], p. 8). Although places are always changing, their rhythms mark a degree of regularity and routine (Edensor 2010).

Urban rhythms consist of movements of people, such as tourists, shoppers, clubbers and those going to and coming from work or school; the effects of transport schedules and traffic lights; sensory elements such as smells, sounds and moods; as well as global flows of capital, ideas and trends (Edensor 2010; Highmore 2005; Lefebvre 2004 [1992]; Allen 1999). There exists a multiplicity of simultaneous, interwoven rhythms which intersect and interact, with some being more dominant than others. How these rhythms shift throughout the day and night alters the meanings made available in spaces, and thus how people act within them (Allen 1999). For example, in the transition between the cyclical rhythms of day and night, linear rhythms shift as well, since day and night are associated with different norms and activities. Therefore, although a rhythm is lived and material – and thus can be sensed and observed – it is also connected to the imaginary and the representational.

Tourism, globalisation and mobilities

Tourism, like urban spaces, is comprised of different rhythms and mobilities. It is also in itself a key form of mobility in contemporary society, being marked by multiple flows of people, objects and ideas across space (Hall 2008; Shaw & Williams 2004; Sheller & Urry 2006, 2004; Urry 2007, 2000). In this sense, tourism is both a process and product of globalisation. As an agent or process of globalisation, tourism enables people with different cultures, expectations, desires, habits and norms to travel to far off places relatively easily and afford-ably (at least for those with a certain degree of economic capital). Thus, international destinations like resorts have a constant – but always shifting and heterogeneous – presence of transient, culturally diverse visitors who transform the spatiality, sociality and local cultures of these places as they consume them. At the same time, experiences of these destinations make their mark on tourists as well, who carry new knowledges back home with them.

As a product of globalisation, tourism (whether regional, domestic or international) has been shaped significantly alongside global changes and tech-nological advances. International destinations are not only occupied by people from around the world, but also multi-national hotel chains, brand retailers and fast food outlets in addition to boutique local businesses and attractions (see Chapter 4). Wahab and Cooper (2001) argue that worldwide population growth, the increasing affluence of some nations, and technological innovations (such as in transport and computers) have bolstered tourism industries across the globe while simultaneously making destinations more competitive.

Those of us privileged enough to travel and to access new technologies can now see, learn about and form detailed imaginaries of places before ever visiting them, through engagements with representations found on the inter-net and in film and television. These feature multiple and often conflicting narratives and images, ranging from carefully crafted campaigns presented by local and national governments on official tourism websites to anecdotes from individuals on TripAdvisor. The internet has made it easy for us to research destinations, plan our own itineraries, search for the best deals, book our own holidays, leave reviews for others to take into account, and share our travel stories and photographs. As Buhalis (2001) suggests, this access to information has made (some) tourists more independent, sophisticated, discerning consumers, for whom destinations must cater in order to stay competitive.

Tourist types and motivations: from mass to alternative

Tourism – travelling for pleasure – has become a central practice in the lives of people across the globe. Scholars such as Urry (2002) suggest that tourists are motivated by a desire to experience *difference*, to gaze upon and engage with sites, cultures and objects that are not available at home, or to encounter familiar things in new contexts. These experiences come to play an important role in shaping one's self-identity and (auto)biographical narratives, as well as contributing to the accumulation of cultural capital (Crang 2014; Desforges 2000; Rojek 1993; Giddens 1991). However, such experiences, and what they reveal about the tourist to themselves and to others, vary greatly depending on the type of holiday being undertaken.

Tourism is often categorised into broad types such as 'mass tourism' and 'alternative tourism'. Mass tourism (also known as Fordist tourism) is typically defined as large-scale, standardised, predictable, inflexible and packaged forms of touristic consumption (Vainikka 2013; Kontogeorgopoulos 2009; Pons et al. 2009; Aguiló, Alegre & Sard 2005; Torres 2002; Urry 2002; Poon 1993). Mass tourism has been closely associated with the sun, sand and sex model of tourism exemplified by resorts, and thus also identified with spaces like crowded beaches, theme parks and nightclubs. Mass tourists are seen to be motivated by a desire to escape their everyday lives, roles and responsibilities, seeking difference and pleasure through intensified, collective experiences of fun, excitement or relaxation (Kontogeorgopoulos 2003; Re Cruz 2003; MacCannell 2001; Boissevain 1996; Poon 1993). They are assumed to value convenience, comfort, efficiency and familiarity (Kontogeorgopoulos 2004; Shaw & Williams 2004; Cohen 1972). In his typology of four main tourist roles, Cohen (1972) distinguishes between 'the organized mass tourist' and 'the individual mass tourist' (p. 167). For him, the former is unadventurous, sticks to the tourist hubs and opts for guided tours and packaged deals with neatly organised itineraries, whereas the latter desires greater novelty and agency, but still chooses to stay in established, mature destinations with a plethora of hotels, attractions and purpose-built tourist facilities. In these ways, the contrast between home and away may be considered less apparent for mass tourists (Rojek 1993).

Mass tourism, and mass tourists, are frequently deprecated in scholarly literature, the media and popular discourse. 'Tourist' has become a pejorative term (Westerhausen 2002; MacCannell 1999 [1976]), referring to visitors who are characteristically homogenous or 'robot-like' (Poon 1993, p. 4), lacking in 'taste',[6] vulgar, selfish, careless, obnoxious, loud, disrespectful and sometimes patronising or racist towards host communities (Pons et al. 2009; Konto-georgopoulos 2003; Poon 1993). As Rojek (1993) observes:

> Tourists are presented as lacking initiative and discrimination. They are unadventurous, unimaginative and insipid. For them, travel experience is akin to grazing – they mechanically consume whatever the tour operator feeds them. Their presence coarsens the quality of tourist sights. Mass tourism is often likened to a plague, which destroys the beauty and serenity of civilization. (p. 175)

In such constructions, mass tourism is perceived as a 'destructive force' (Vainikka 2013, p. 273) that erodes meaning, authenticity and difference through processes of mass production and consumption, which are seen to homogenise, standardise and Westernise tourist spaces to cater to the desires of mass tourists (see Chapter 4).

Alternative tourism (or post-Fordist tourism), on the other hand, refers to forms that reject the practices, tastes and motivations commonly associated with mass tourism. Although alternative, non- or anti-mainstream ways of doing tourism have long existed alongside mass tourism, they have become increasingly popular and widespread over the last several decades, as evidenced by the rise of tourism styles including ecotourism, cultural tourism, adventure tourism, rural tourism, heritage tourism and backpacker tourism (Vainikka 2013; Shaw & Williams 2004; Meethan 2001; Poon 1993). In contrast to mass tourists, alternative tourists are apparently experienced and discerning, favouring individualised or customised (rather than packaged and standardised) experiences tailored to their particular interests and lifestyles, and wanting greater independence, flexibility and opportunities for spontaneity (rather than predictability) (Vainikka 2013; Kontogeorgopoulos 2009; Shaw & Agarwal 2007; Aguiló et al. 2005; Prideaux 2004; Urry 2002; Buhalis 2001; Boissevain 1996; Poon 1993). To cater to the specific and varied desires and preferences of post-Fordist consumers, the tourism sector has become increasingly segmented, developing niche tourism products and marketing tactics aimed at different groups (Aguiló et al. 2005; Shaw & Williams 2004; Urry 2002; Meethan 2001; Poon 1993).

Post-Fordist tourists tend to prefer 'unique environmental, cultural or social landscapes' (Torres 2002, p. 88) and are assumed to be more respectful and environmentally conscious. Instead of seeking 'the simple aimless pleasures of mass tourism' (Meethan 2001, p. 128), alternative tourists – especially cultural tourists – are seen to be motivated by a desire for authenticity[7] (MacCannell 1999 [1976]) and self-improvement (Meethan 2001; Rojek & Urry 1997; Boissevain 1996; Rojek 1993). MacCannell (1999 [1976]) argues that, since modernity is supposedly alienating and shallow, authenticity is more readily found in 'traditional' or 'exotic' cultures and 'natural' or 'untouched' places (Chhabra, Healy & Sills 2003; Meethan 2001; Brown 1996). Through engagements with supposedly authentic people, places, practices and objects, alternative tourists expect to acquire insight, knowledge and more sophisticated tastes, returning home as 'better' versions of themselves (Kontogeorgopoulos 2003; Rojek 1993).

In the literature, these visitors are sometimes distinguished from tourists (taken to be mass tourists) by instead being called 'travellers' (Law, Bunnell & Ong 2007; Rojek 1993). As Rojek (1993) posits:

> The traveller is associated with refined values of discernment, respect and taste. Travel is seen as pursuing the ageless aristocratic principle of broadening the mind … travel experience is presented as a resource in the task of self-making. … It shakes you up in order to make you a more mature, complete person. (p. 175)

In Cohen's (1972) typology, the characteristics of the traveller are captured by 'the explorer' and 'the drifter' types: the former wants to get away from mass tourism spaces and to experience and connect with other cultures, but does not completely abandon basic comforts and scheduling, while the latter seeks out the most remote areas to get as far from his/her everyday life as possible and live among the host culture(s) for extended periods of time. For drifters, authenticity is associated with 'roughing it' – sacrificing material comforts, sometimes even shelter, electricity and running water – in places and cultures that have been minimally influenced by Western cultures (Kontogeorgopoulos 2003).

Despite definitional variations, what alternative tourists/travellers have in common is a desire to go beyond where the mass tourists go, to find solitude in 'hidden', 'untouched' or 'pristine' places (Law et al. 2007; Torres 2002; Westerhausen 2002; Rojek 1993). In this context, authenticity depends on an absence of anyone non-local, and especially the absence of mass tourists, who are seen to 'spoil' cultures and landscapes (Kontogeorgopoulos 2003; Rojek 1993). Of course, these alternative tourists are themselves non-local and thus complicit in 'contaminating' (or transforming) the places they visit. In Coleman and Crang's (2002) analysis:

> such activity bears with it the ironic seeds of its own destruction, as the very presence of the tourist corrupts the idea of reaching an authentic and totally different culture. … The really authentic unspoiled place is always displaced in space or time – it is spatially located over the next hill, or temporally existed just a generation ago. (p. 3)

The 'authentic' is always just out of reach, a conceptual ideal which can never really be obtained. Further, alternative tourists become 'agents of change' (Westerhausen 2002, p. ix), their presence instigating the development of tourism infrastructure and attracting others to visit, so that eventually, their hidden places may become mass tourism destinations (Kontogeorgopoulos

2009; Law et al. 2007; Coleman & Crang 2002; Meethan 2001). Once this occurs, the alternative tourists find somewhere else to go, driven by 'an often futile attempt to remain one step ahead of the relentless tourism development' (Westerhausen 2002, p. ix), and the cycle repeats.

Clearly, mass tourism and alternative tourism are frequently binarised, with mass tourism perceived as 'bad' and alternative tourism as 'good', as more sustainable, with less negative social and environmental consequences for the host communities and environment (Pons et al. 2009; Kontogeorgopoulos 2003; Westerhausen 2002). Despite what these discourses infer, mass tourism and alternative tourism are not separate phenomena. Not only do they co-exist in contemporary tourism destinations, they also often overlap, intersect and blend together to create hybrid forms. Ecotourism and cultural tourism, for instance, can often exhibit qualities of mass tourism (see Chapter 4). As the demand for these kinds of alternative experiences grows, natural and cultural sites may be staged and commodified to optimise consumption; visitors may expect fun and spectacle *as well as* authenticity and education; and matters of preservation and sustainability may become peripheral concerns.

Tourists, likewise, cannot be strictly categorised as *either* mass *or* alternative, with many wanting experiences relating to both types. An individual may go backpacking alone across Asia for several months on a shoestring budget, but this activity does not preclude him/her from choosing to fly to Ibiza with friends for a week of partying at another point in time. Similarly, a tourist might spend most of his/her vacation on the beach and in theme parks, but may also choose to visit local museums or go for a hike in a secluded forest; while another may want to spend several weeks 'roughing it' in a small village, bookended by stays at five-star hotels at the beginning and end of the trip. This eclecticism is characteristic of the *post*-tourist, who is reflexive, playful and conscious of the contrived nature of tourism, finding pleasure in supposedly inauthentic places and things (Feifer 1985; see also Chapter 4).

These 'types' – post-tourist, mass tourist, alternative tourist and so on – should not be understood as discrete entities or existing in pure form, since a single tourist can exhibit qualities of each of them in different times and spaces. Contemporary tourists are, above all else, hybrid, heterogeneous and flexible in their desires, motives, demands and practices. Tourism destinations can no longer be based only on standardisation and uniformity, but must offer a variety of attractions and experiences to cater for the diverse tastes of visitors. Therefore, even though resorts may be read as mass tourism destinations *par excellence*, they are shaped by trends associated with alternative tourism (see Chapter 2).

Methodology and fieldwork

Taking a cultural studies approach, the research project on which this book is based can be described as *bricolage* – made up of a diverse range of methods, tools and concepts. My applied methods included a mixture of participant observation, photography and semi-structured interviews with resort residents. As a Gold Coast local, my fieldwork in this city and its tourist hub of Surfers Paradise was ongoing. In terms of destinations abroad, I visited each resort from late 2013 to mid-2014, during one of its peak travel periods (December in Thailand,[8] March in Cancún and Miami,[9] July in Ibiza[10]) in order to observe and participate in the tourist presence in its most intensified state.[11] I stayed in Airbnbs and conventional hotels in close proximity to tourist hubs in each destination: Patong Beach in Phuket; Baan Tai Beach on Koh Phangan; the Hotel Zone in Cancún; Miami Beach in Miami; and Playa d'en Bossa in Ibiza. In each place, I visited a combination of cultural heritage sites, local museums, beaches, shopping strips, nightclubs and arts districts, as well as local neighbourhoods that did not have any major tourist attractions.

The observational component of the fieldwork was undertaken by spending time in spaces most heavily used by tourists and locals, recording my impressions in writing, and using photography to capture particular moments. Recognising that all knowledge is situated (Hall 2006 [1990]; Haraway 1991), I aimed to be continually reflexive about how my observations, interpretations, photographic choices and interactions in the field were mediated by my subjective positions and vantage points (Giardina & Newman 2011; Gray 2003; Denzin 1997). In particular, the reader should be aware that the findings throughout this book are shaped by my positionality as a researcher who is a white, heterosexual, able-bodied woman in her mid-twenties, characteristics which undoubtedly influence how I perceive, act and move within spaces, and how others behave towards me. My theoretical interests as a researcher, as well as my experiences as both a local (on the Gold Coast) and a tourist (in other resorts), also shaped the research process and outcomes. Rather than strive for objectivity in such a context, I instead embraced a somewhat autoethnographic approach (see Chang 2008), observing not only the practices of others, but also paying attention to and reflecting upon my own participation, sensations, feelings, memories and embodied experiences. Given that I am a product of the contexts, discourses and structures that I seek to interrogate, my experiences became a key analytic tool in this project (Probyn 1993; Saukko 2003).

However, because I had no first-hand knowledge of the local experience in resorts other than the Gold Coast, and because I could only visit each destination at a specific time of year, the use of anonymous, semi-structured interviews allowed me to gain further insights regarding shared (and disparate) attitudes among locals. I asked questions including: 'Why do you live here?'; 'What do you like and dislike about where you live?'; 'How do you feel about the tourist presence?'; and 'As a local, do you feel the city caters more to locals or to tourists?' Interviewees were recruited through networks among my friends and colleagues, as well as through contacting relevant research centres and departments at universities based in the resorts. As my intention was to produce conceptual – rather than empirical or ethnographic – outcomes, formal sampling techniques were not used. Nonetheless, I ended up with a diverse spread of participants: four women and eight men, ranging in age from 21 to 60, with varied nationalities and ethnic backgrounds (including Australian, British, Colombian, Czech, Filipino, Mexican, Nicaraguan, Spanish and Turkish), and different associations with their localities (including long-time residents, new immigrants, expatriates and transitory tertiary students). These interviews were designed to provide supplementary material, serving to complement the observational and photographic techniques rather than drive the research process.

The *bricolage* of chosen methods were devised to be attuned to the complex, multiple and constantly changing nature of the sites and subjects central to this research. I intended for my methods to be kept flexible and open to negotiation during every step of the process, adapting to the situation in the field and as new theoretical insights developed (Kincheloe, McLaren & Steinberg 2011; Pink 2007). The multimethod approach was not used in an effort to establish a 'complete' picture of the social and spatial phenomena in question (Silverman 2013), but rather to capture some of the key aspects of their spatiality *without* making any totalising claims as to universal experiences or processes. Spaces are assemblages, 'accumulations that don't add up' (Highmore 2005, p. 6), and as such cannot be simplified or comprehensively represented. Soja (2000) compares the problem of representing lived spaces to writing a biography: 'There is too much that lies beneath the surface, unknown and perhaps unknowable, for a complete story to be told' (p. 12). Therefore, taking my cue from Ben Highmore (2005), my objective was 'not to render the city legible, but to render its illegibility legible' (p. 7). The processes and outcomes of my research were deliberately impressionistic, fragmented and partial.

The places, phenomena and observations I discuss throughout this book are taken to be 'examples' in Agamben's (1993) sense. An example 'holds for all cases of the same type, and, at the same time, it is included among these. It is one singularity among others, which, however, stands for each of them and serves for all' (Agamben 1993, p. 10). Thus, an example is '[n]either particular nor universal', always caught between the two (Agamben 1993, p. 10). Examples function as '*generalizable particularities*' (Soja 2000, p. 154, original emphasis) – instances which do not apply to all contexts, but nonetheless provide insight into wider social and cultural processes and forces. 'Resorts' may seem like a universal category, but it is more usefully understood as a term that identifies some commonalities (such as in how these places develop, and how they are imagined, represented and experienced) among singularities, each of which has its own local specificity, nuances and trajectories. That is, each resort is a unique expression of more global processes.

In addition to being a methodological tool, the conceptual moment encountered in Agamben's (1993) work on the example is also one of the key frameworks informing my analysis throughout this book. In the chapters that follow, I aim to disrupt all-too-familiar binaries (like universal/particular) by accounting for the tensions and movements between apparently opposed terms or concepts: macro/micro, global/local, homogeneity/heterogeneity, mobility/fixity, tourist/resident, official/unofficial, real/imagined, authentic/

inauthentic, high culture/popular culture, everyday/exotic. Neither of the terms in each pair exists in pure form, nor can one be privileged over the other. Indeed, the two 'exist only in mixture' (Deleuze & Guattari 2004 [1987], p. 524). Since binarised terms hold significant weight and have long shaped how people think of the world and perceive places like resorts, my intention is not to abandon them altogether, but to approach them with the knowledge that they are relational, manifesting as in-between, liminal or hybrid. Such an approach recognises the conflicts, juxtapositions, heterogeneity and complexity which produce and are produced by lived spaces.

Structure of the book

The conceptual and methodological frameworks outlined above form the basis for the analysis of resort spatiality in the chapters that follow. Chapter 2 provides an overview of the resorts central to this study, organised according to the sequence in which I visited them: the Gold Coast, Thailand, Cancún, Miami and Ibiza. I outline each resort's history and current position in relation to tourism development, its popular imaginaries, how it is represented in official tourism discourses, and some of my initial observations of its lived spaces, focusing on the tourist hubs. The purpose of this chapter is to provide background information on the sites of my research and to begin to analyse some of the factors involved in the spatialisation of resorts. Each resort is examined separately so as to highlight aspects of their local specificity, although similarities between them become increasingly clear as the chapter progresses.

Chapter 3 more explicitly draws together and theorises the similarities that emerged in Chapter 2, as well as exploring key differences. I discuss commonalities in popular imaginaries, representations and dominant narratives of identity, which characterise resorts as escapist, hedonistic, excessive, sexualised, risky, carnivalesque and liminal. I offer examples as to how these elements of conceived space are observable in the built environment and lived spatial practices. I explore these themes through the example of nightlife in resorts, which constitutes a core aspect of tourist activity.

In Chapter 4, I turn to less dominant, emerging tourism narratives, which are increasingly emphasising cultural experiences and attempting to alter existing popular imaginaries of place. This marks a transition from Fordist to post-Fordist styles of tourism, and challenges stereotypes of resorts (and of tourism) as homogenous, depthless, superficial, transient and fake. These issues are explored in relation to culture and capitalism, questions of authenticity, and the interplay between the global and the local.

Chapters 5 and 6 move the focus to the residents of resorts and what exists beyond tourism. To produce a more nuanced conceptualisation of resort spatiality, it is necessary to consider both guests and hosts, tourists and locals. The tourism industry provides the context for local experiences just as localised spaces and cultures provide the basis for tourism. Drawing on insights collected through interviews, I explore the impacts of tourism on resort locals, providing their perspectives and experiences and also drawing on my own. Chapter 5 looks at what locals like and dislike about where they live and how tourism influences their everyday lives and socio-spatial practices. Chapter 6 explores these issues further, examining how tourist-centric places perpetuate inequalities, and how living in such sites affects residents' senses of belonging and community.

Chapter 7, the conclusion, draws together the key arguments made in this book. With reference to the field, I consider the potential implications of my findings for scholars, local governments, urban planners and policy makers. I acknowledge the limitations of this research and at the same time point to how it opens up possibilities for future projects.

What follows in this book is an assemblage of examples, observations, experiences, narratives, concepts, arguments and theories. This book is not about presenting a thorough or exhaustive account of resorts, nor about how to 'manage' or tame their complexity and fluidity, but about how to embrace these characteristics and work with them productively. Indeed, my objective is to produce more nuanced understandings of these particular places, and also of lived spaces more broadly. The resorts that are the focus of this thesis are examples through which to explore the heterogeneous, shifting nature of spatiality, and through which to reimagine the dynamics and effects of mass tourism.

Notes

1 Also known as the 4 S's of tourism: sun, sex, sea and sand (Córdoba Azcárate 2011; Pons et al. 2009; Buhalis 2001; Crick 1989).
2 This does not necessarily imply an inside/outside binary – there are things which are perceived to be 'outside', such as another city across the globe, but there may still be connections to this 'outside' that also make it somewhat part of the 'inside' of the place in question.
3 Soja (1996) similarly refers to these as Firstspace (the perceived), Secondspace (the conceived) and Thirdspace (the lived).
4 The existence of conflicting representations means that people will hold different ideas about what is normal and appropriate in various spaces.
5 This does not mean they are false or inauthentic – indeed, representations and imaginaries capture some of the very real elements of places.
6 In terms of elitist sensibilities which conflate good taste with high culture.
7 Authenticity is highly subjective, fluid and variable, and what authenticity means to one tourist may be very different to another (see Chapter 4).
8 The peak season in Southern Thailand is typically from November to February, when the climate is warm and dry. This is also a popular time to travel because it coincides with Christmas and New Year holiday periods, and school holidays in nearby countries like Australia.
9 This was during Spring Break, a week-long vacation period for North American university students which falls at different times during February and March (see Chapter 3). Celebrating the end of winter, students usually travel to sunny beach destinations like Miami and Cancún.

10 Nightclubs in Ibiza are only open from late May to early October (marked by opening and closing parties) during the European summer.
11 Visiting at quieter times would have yielded somewhat difference observations; however, travelling at two different periods per location was far beyond the fiscal and time constraints of this project.

References

Agamben, G 1993, *The coming community*, trans. M Hardt, University of Minnesota Press, Minneapolis.

Agarwal, S 1997, 'The resort cycle and seaside tourism: an assessment of its applicability and validity', *Tourism Management*, vol. 18, no. 2, pp. 65–73.

Agarwal, S 2002, 'Restructuring seaside tourism: the resort lifecycle', *Annals of Tourism Research*, vol. 29, no. 1, pp. 25–55.

Agarwal, S & Shaw, G 2007 (eds), *Managing coastal tourism resorts: a global perspective*, Channel View Publications, Clevedon.

Aguiló, E, Alegre, J & Sard, M 2005, 'The persistence of the sun and sand tourism model', *Tourism Management*, vol. 26, no. 2, pp. 219–231.

Allen, J 1999, 'Worlds within cities', in D Massey, J Allen & S Pile (eds), *City worlds*, Routledge, London, pp. 53–97.

Andriotis, K 2003, 'Coastal resorts morphology: the Cretan experience', *Tourism Recreation Research*, vol. 28, no. 1, pp. 67–75.

Barrett, JA 1958, 'The seaside resort towns of England and Wales', unpublished doctoral thesis, University of London.

Bennett, T 1983, 'A thousand and one troubles: Blackpool pleasure beach', in T Bennett, L Bland, V Burgin, T Davies, J Donald & S Frith (eds), *Formations of pleasure*, Routledge, London, pp. 138–155.

Bennett, T 1986, 'Hegemony, ideology, pleasure: Blackpool', in T Bennett, C Mercer & J Wollacott (eds), *Popular culture and social relations*, Open University Press, Milton Keynes, pp. 135–154.

Boissevain, J 1996, 'Introduction', in J Boissevain (ed.), *Coping with tourists: European reactions to mass tourism*, Berghahn Books, Providence, pp. 1–26.

Brown, D 1996, 'Genuine fakes', in T Selwyn (ed.), *The tourist image: myths and myth making in tourism*, John Wiley & Sons, Chichester, pp. 33–47.

Buhalis, D 2001, 'The tourism phenomenon: the new tourist and consumer', in S Wahab & C Cooper (eds), *Tourism in the age of globalisation*, Routledge, New York, pp. 69–96.

Butler, RW 1980, 'The concept of a tourist area cycle of evolution: implications for management of resources', *The Canadian Geographer*, vol. 24, no. 1, pp. 5–12.

Butler, RW 2006, 'The concept of a tourist area cycle of evolution', in RW Butler (ed.), *The tourism area life cycle, vol. 1: applications and modifications*, Channel View Publications, Clevedon, pp. 1–12.

Chang, H 2008, *Autoethnography as method*, Left Coast Press, Walnut Creek.

Chhabra, D, Healy, R & Sills, E 2003, 'Staged authenticity and heritage tourism', *Annals of Tourism Research*, vol. 30, no. 3, pp. 702–719.

Cohen, E 1972, 'Toward a sociology of international tourism', *Social Research*, vol. 39, no. 1, pp. 164–182.

Coleman, S & Crang, M 2002, 'Grounded tourists, travelling theory', in S Coleman & M Crang (eds), *Tourism: between place and performance*, Berghahn Books, New York, pp. 1–17.

Córdoba Azcárate, M 2011, '"Thanks God, this is not Cancun!" Alternative tourism imaginaries in Yucatan (Mexico)', *Journal of Tourism and Cultural Change*, vol. 9, no. 3, pp. 183–200.

Crang, M 2014, 'Cultural geographies of tourism', in AA Lew, CM Hall & AM Williams (eds), *The Wiley Blackwell companion to tourism*, Wiley Blackwell, Hoboken, pp. 66–77.

Crick, M 1989, 'Representations of international tourism in the social sciences: sun, sex, sights, savings, and servility', *Annual Review of Anthropology*, vol. 18, pp. 307–344.

Crouch, D, Jackson, R & Thompson, F 2005, 'Introduction: the media and the tourist imagination', in D Crouch, R Jackson & F Thompson (eds), *The media & the tourist imagination: converging cultures*, Routledge, New York, pp. 1–13.

D'Andrea, A 2007, *Global nomads: techno and new age as transnational counter-cultures in Ibiza and Goa*, Routledge, New York.

de Certeau, M 2002 [1984], '*The Practice of Everyday Life*', in G Bridge & S Watson (eds), *The Blackwell city reader*, Blackwell Publishing, Oxford, pp. 383–392.

Deleuze, G & Guattari, F 2004 [1987], *A thousand plateaus: capitalism and schizophrenia*, trans. B Massumi, Continuum, London.

Denzin, NK 1997, *Interpretive ethnography: ethnographic practices for the 21st century*, SAGE Publications, Thousand Oaks.

Desforges, L 2000, 'Traveling the world: identity and travel biography', *Annals of Tourism Research*, vol. 27, no. 4, pp. 926–945.

Edensor, T 2001, 'Performing tourism, staging tourism: (re)producing tourist space and practice', *Tourist Studies*, vol. 1, no. 1, pp. 59–81.

Edensor, T 2010, 'Introduction: thinking about rhythm and space', in T Edensor (ed.), *Geographies of rhythm: nature, place, mobilities and bodies*, Ashgate, Farnham, pp. 1–18.

Falzon, M-A 2016 [2009], 'Introduction: multi-sited ethnography: theory, praxis and locality in contemporary research', in M-A Falzon (ed.), *Multi-sited ethnography: theory, praxis and locality in contemporary research*, Routledge, New York, pp. 1–23.

Feifer, M 1985, *Tourism in history: from imperial Rome to the present*, Stein and Day, New York.

Foucault, M 1991 [1977], *Discipline and punish: the birth of the prison*, trans. A Sheridan, Penguin Group, London.

Fraser, B 2015, *Toward an urban cultural studies: Henri Lefebvre and the humanities*, Palgrave MacMillan, New York.

Garreau, J 1991, *Edge city: life on the new frontier*, Anchor Books, New York.

Getz, D 1993, 'Planning for tourism business districts', *Annals of Tourism Research*, vol. 20, no. 3, pp. 583–600.

Giardina, MD & Newman, JI 2011, 'Cultural studies: performative imperatives and bodily articulations', in NK Denzin & YS Lincoln (eds), *The SAGE handbook of qualitative research*, 4th edn, SAGE Publications, Thousand Oaks, pp. 179–194.

Giddens, A 1991, *Modernity and self-identity: self and society in the late modern age*, Stanford University Press, Stanford.

Gilbert, EW 1949, 'The growth of Brighton', *The Geographical Journal*, vol. 114, no. 1/3, pp. 30–52.

Gladstone, DL 1998, 'Tourism urbanization in the United States', *Urban Affairs Review*, vol. 34, no. 1, pp. 3–27.

Gospodini, A 2006, 'Portraying, classifying and understanding the emerging land-scapes in the post-industrial city', *Cities*, vol. 23, no. 5, pp. 311–330.

Gray, A 2003, *Research practice for cultural studies: ethnographic methods and lived cultures*, SAGE Publications, London.

Griffin, G 1998, 'The good, the bad and the peculiar: cultures and policies of urban planning and development on the Gold Coast', *Urban Policy and Research*, vol. 16, no. 4, pp. 285–292.

Grosz, E 2002 [1992], 'Bodies-cities', in G Bridge & S Watson (eds), *The Blackwell city reader*, Blackwell Publishing, Oxford, pp. 297–303.

Hall, CM 2008, 'Of time and space and other things: laws of tourism and the geo-graphies of contemporary mobilities', in PM Burns & M Novelli (eds), *Tourism and mobilities: local-global connections*, CABI, Wallingford, pp. 15–32.

Hall, P 1997, 'Modelling the post-industrial city', *Futures*, vol. 29, no. 4/5, pp. 311–322.

Hall, S 2006 [1990], 'Cultural identity and diaspora', in B Ashcroft, G Griffiths & H Tiffin (eds), *The post-colonial studies reader*, 2nd edn, Routledge, London, pp. 435–438.

Hannam, K, Sheller, M & Urry, J 2006, 'Editorial: mobilities, immobilities and moorings', *Mobilities*, vol. 1, no. 1, pp. 1–22.

Hannigan, J 1998, *Fantasy city: pleasure and profit in the postmodern metropolis*, Routledge, London.

Haraway, DJ 1991, *Simians, cyborgs, and women: the reinvention of nature*, Routledge, New York.

Hern, A 1967, *The seaside holiday: the history of the English seaside resort*, Cresset Press, London.

Highmore, B 2005, *Cityscapes: cultural readings in the material and symbolic city*, Palgrave Macmillan, New York.

Jeans, DN 1990, 'Beach resort morphology in England and Australia: a review and extension', in P Fabbri (ed.), *Recreational uses of coastal areas*, Kluwer, Dordrecht, pp. 277–285.

Kincheloe, JL, McLaren, P & Steinberg, SR 2011, 'Critical pedagogy and qualitative research: moving to the bricolage', in NK Denzin & YS Lincoln (eds), *The SAGE handbook of qualitative research*, 4th edn, SAGE Publications, Thousand Oaks, pp. 163–177.

Kontogeorgopoulos, N 2003, 'Keeping up with the Joneses: tourists, travellers, and the quest for cultural authenticity in southern Thailand', *Tourist Studies*, vol. 3, no. 2, pp. 171–203.

Kontogeorgopoulos, N 2004, 'Conventional tourism and ecotourism in Phuket, Thai-land: conflicting paradigms or symbiotic partners?', *Journal of Ecotourism*, vol. 3, no. 2, pp. 87–108.

Kontogeorgopoulos, N 2009, 'The temporal relationship between mass tourism and alternative tourism in Southern Thailand', *Tourism Review International*, vol. 13, pp. 1–16.

Lavery, P 1974, 'Resort and recreation', in P Lavery (ed.), *Recreational geography*, Halstead Press, New York, pp. 167–196.

Law, L, Bunnell, T & Ong, C-E 2007, 'The Beach, the gaze and film tourism', *Tourist Studies*, vol. 7, no. 2, pp. 141–164.

Lefebvre, H 1991 [1974], *The production of space*, trans. D Nicholson-Smith, Blackwell Publishers, Oxford.

Lefebvre, H 2004 [1992], *Rhythmanalysis: space, time and everyday life*, trans. S Elden & G Moore, Continuum, London.

Liu, J & Wall, G 2009, 'Resort morphology research: history and future perspectives', *Asia Pacific Journal of Tourism Research*, vol. 14, no. 4, pp. 339–350.

MacCannell, D 1999 [1976], *The tourist: a new theory of the leisure class*, University of California Press, Berkeley.

MacCannell, D 2001, 'Remarks on the commodification of cultures', in VL Smith & M Brent (eds), *Hosts and guests revisited: tourism issues of the 21st century*, Cognizant Communication Corporation, New York, pp. 380–390.

Marcus, GE 1995, 'Ethnography in/of the world system: the emergence of multi-sited ethnography', *Annual Review of Anthropology*, vol. 24, no. 1, pp. 95–117.

Massey, D 1994, *Space, place, and gender*, University of Minnesota Press, Minneapolis.

Massey, D 1998, 'Spatial constructions of youth cultures', in T Skelton & G Valentine (eds), *Cool places: geographies of youth cultures*, Routledge, London, pp. 121–129.

Massey, D 2005, *For space*, SAGE Publications, London.

Massey, D 2007, *World city*, Polity Press, Cambridge.

Massey, D, Allen, J & Pile, S 1999, 'Introduction', in D Massey, J Allen & S Pile (eds), *City worlds*, Routledge, London, pp. 1–2.

Meethan, K 1996, 'Place, image and power: Brighton as a resort', in T Selwyn (ed.), *The tourist image: myths and myth making in tourism*, John Wiley & Sons, Chichester, pp. 179–196.

Meethan, K 2001, *Tourism in global society: place, culture, consumption*, Palgrave, Basingstoke.

Meyer-Arendt, KJ 1990, 'Recreational business districts in Gulf of Mexico seaside resorts', *Journal of Cultural Geography*, vol. 11, no. 1, pp. 39–55.

Meyer-Arendt, KJ, Sambrook, RA & Kermath, BM 1992, 'Seaside resorts in the Dominican Republic: a typology', *Journal of Geography*, vol. 91, no. 5, pp. 219–225.

Mill, RC 2008, *Resorts: management and operation*, 2nd edn, John Wiley & Sons, New York.

Minca, C 2000, '"The Bali syndrome": the explosion and implosion of "exotic" tourist spaces', *Tourism Geographies*, vol. 2, no. 4, pp. 389–403.

Mommaas, H 2004, 'Cultural clusters and the post-industrial city: towards the remapping of urban cultural policy', *Urban Studies*, vol. 41, no. 3, pp. 507–532.

Mullins, P 1991, 'Tourism urbanisation', *International Journal of Urban and Regional Research*, vol. 15, no. 3, pp. 326–342.

Mullins, P 1992, 'Cities for pleasure: the emergence of tourism urbanization in Australia', *Built Environment*, vol. 18, no. 3, pp. 187–198.

Murray, G 2007, 'Constructing paradise: the impacts of big tourism in the Mexican coastal zone', *Coastal Management*, vol. 35, no. 2–3, pp. 339–355.

Pigram, JJ 1977, 'Beach resort morphology', *Habitat International*, vol. 2, no. 5/6, pp. 525–541.

Pink, S 2007, *Doing visual ethnography: images, media and representation in research*, 2nd edn, SAGE Publications, London.

Pons, PO, Crang, M & Travlou, P 2009, 'Introduction: taking Mediterranean tourists seriously', in PO Pons, M Crang & P Travlou (eds), *Cultures of mass tourism: doing the Mediterranean in the age of banal mobilities*, Ashgate, Farnham, pp. 1–20.

Pons, A, Salamanca, OR & Murray, I 2014, 'Tourism capitalism and island urbanization: tourist accommodation diffusion in the Balearics, 1936–2010', *Island Studies Journal*, vol. 9, no. 2, pp. 239–258.

Poon, A 1993, *Tourism, technology and competitive strategies*, CAB International, Wallingford.

Prideaux, B 2004, 'The resort development spectrum: the case of the Gold Coast, Australia', *Tourism Geographies*, vol. 6, no. 1, pp. 26–58.

Prideaux, B 2009, *Resort destinations: evolution, management and development*, Butterwoth-Heinemann, Oxford.

Probyn, E 1993, *Sexing the self: gendered positions in cultural studies*, Routledge, London.

Re Cruz, A 2003, 'Milpa as an ideological weapon: tourism and Maya migration to Cancún', *Ethnohistory*, vol. 50, no. 3, pp. 489–502.

Rojek, C 1993, *Ways of escape: modern transformations in leisure and travel*, Macmillan Press, London.

Rojek, C & Urry, J 1997, 'Transformations of travel and theory', in C Rojek & J Urry (eds), *Touring cultures: transformations of travel and theory*, Routledge, London, pp. 1–19.

Saukko, P 2003, *Doing research in cultural studies: an introduction to classical and new methodological approaches*, SAGE Publications, London.

Scott, N, Gardiner, S & Dedekorkut-Howes, A 2016, 'Holidaying on the Gold Coast', in A Dedekorkut-Howes, C Bosman & A Leach (eds), *Off the plan: the urbanisation of the Gold Coast*, CSIRO Publishing, Clayton South, pp. 31–43.

Shaw, G & Agarwal, S 2007, 'Introduction: the development and management of coastal resorts: a global perspective', in S Agarwal & G Shaw (eds), *Managing coastal tourism resorts: a global perspective*, Channel View Publications, Clevedon, pp. 1–18.

Shaw, G & Williams, AM 1997 (eds), *The rise and fall of British coastal resorts: cultural and economic perspectives*, Mansell, London.

Shaw, G & Williams, AM 2004, *Tourism and tourism spaces*, SAGE Publications, London.

Sheller, M & Urry, J 2004, 'Places to play, places in play', in M Sheller & J Urry (eds), *Tourism mobilities: places to play, places in play*, Routledge, London, pp. 1–10.

Sheller, M & Urry, J 2006, 'The new mobilities paradigm', *Environment and Planning A*, vol. 38, no. 2, pp. 207–226.

Shields, R 1991, *Places on the margin: alternative geographies of modernity*, Routledge, London.

Silverman, D 2013, *Doing qualitative research*, 4th edn, SAGE Publications, London.

Smith, RA 1991, 'Beach resorts: a model of development evolution', *Landscape and Urban Planning*, vol. 21, no. 3, pp. 189–210.

Smith, RA 1992, 'Beach resort evolution: implications for planning', *Annals of Tourism Research*, vol. 19, no. 2, pp. 304–322.

Soja, EW 1996, *Thirdspace: journeys to Los Angeles and other real-and-imagined places*, Blackwell Publishers, Oxford.

Soja, EW 2000, *Postmetropolis: critical studies of cities and regions*, Blackwell Publishers, Oxford.

Stansfield, CA 1969, 'Recreational land use patterns within an American seaside resort', *The Tourist Review*, vol. 24, no. 4, pp. 128–136.

Stansfield, CA & Rickert, JE 1970, 'The recreation business district', *Journal of Leisure Research*, vol. 2, no. 3, pp. 213–225.

Surin, K 2011, 'Force', in CJ Stivale (ed.), *Gilles Deleuze: key concepts*, 2nd edn, Acumen, Durham, pp. 21–32.

Torres, R 2002, 'Cancun's tourism development from a Fordist spectrum of analysis', *Tourist Studies*, vol. 2, no. 1, pp. 87–116.

Tutenges, S 2012, 'Nightlife tourism: a mixed methods study of young tourists at an international nightlife resort', *Tourist Studies*, vol. 12, no. 2, pp. 131–150.

Urry, J 1995, *Consuming places*, Routledge, London.

Urry, J 2000, *Sociology beyond societies: mobilities for the twenty-first century*, Routledge, London.

Urry, J 2002, *The tourist gaze*, 2nd edn, SAGE Publications, London.

Urry, J 2007, *Mobilities*, Polity Press, Cambridge.

Vainikka, V 2013, 'Rethinking mass tourism', *Tourist Studies*, vol. 13, no. 3, pp. 268–286.

Wahab, S & Cooper, C 2001, 'Tourism, globalisation and the competitive advantage of nations', in S Wahab & C Cooper (eds), *Tourism in the age of globalisation*, Routledge, New York, pp. 3–21.

Walvin, J 1978, *Beside the seaside: social history of the popular seaside holiday*, Allen Lane, London.

Webb, D 2005, 'Bakhtin at the seaside: utopia, modernity and the carnivalesque', *Theory, Culture & Society*, vol. 22, no. 3, pp. 121–138.

Westerhausen, K 2002, *Beyond the beach: an ethnography of modern travellers in Asia*, White Lotus Press, Bangkok.

2 Resort cities and regions

Historical perspectives and contemporary developments

Introduction

In this chapter, I provide a brief overview of the resorts I selected for analysis, with a particular emphasis on their tourism industries and associated developments, images and myths. For each resort, I discuss its urban formation; its history and growth in relation to its development as a tourism destination, and some of the economic, cultural and political forces which have contributed to this; the present state of its tourism industry; the dominant popular imaginaries of place (especially those commonly held by tourists and reinforced through news media and popular cultural representations); the images and narratives disseminated by official tourism bodies (sponsored by the city, region or country in which they are located); and some of my initial observations and impressions of the tourist hubs, focusing on flows of tourists in particular spaces and at different times.

Through these overviews, I intend to highlight the centrality of tourism to the development, growth, economy, image and everyday experiences of each resort. By exploring both unofficial and official narratives of identity, I elucidate the tensions that exist between how a place is actually imagined – its reputation, stereotypes and common associations – and how official tourism bodies represent that place. By incorporating some of my own observations and experiences, I point to how these tensions manifest in dynamic relation to the materiality of space – how it is actually *lived*. I begin with an overview of the Gold Coast, Australia, since it is where I live, and is thus the frame of reference I inevitably brought to bear on subsequent places I visited. Each other place is discussed in the order I visited them: Phuket and Koh Phangan, Thailand; Cancún, Mexico; Miami, USA; and lastly, Ibiza, Spain.

Gold Coast, Australia

The Gold Coast, located in the south-east corner of the state of Queensland, is one of Australia's most iconic tourism destinations. Famous for its long stretch of coastline, good surf, lush rainforests (known as 'the green behind the gold') and warm, sub-tropical climate, the city is a popular vacation spot all year round for both regional day-trippers and domestic and international overnight visitors. Beyond its natural attractions, the Gold Coast is known for its numerous family-oriented theme parks and a notorious nightlife scene, being dubbed both the 'theme park capital' (Dedekorkut-Howes & Bosman 2015) and 'nightlife capital' (Surfers Paradise Alliance 2014) of Australia. In the popular imaginary, the Gold Coast has long been marked by tensions between wholesome family fun and more sexualised adult activities.

The tourism industry is a significant asset to the city's local economy. Construction, real estate, tourism, retail and leisure-related industries have been the driving forces of the Gold Coast's development and continue to impel rapid growth in the area (Scott, Gardiner & Dedekorkut-Howes 2016; Dedekorkut-Howes & Bosman 2015; Prideaux 2004). The resident population has grown from roughly 356,000 in 1996 to about 577,000 in 2016, making the Gold Coast the sixth largest city in Australia, surpassing several state capitals (Australian Bureau of Statistics 2017, 2008).

Located on Australia's east coast, bordering the Pacific Ocean, the Gold Coast's sprawling growth has formed a conurbation with Queensland's state capital of Brisbane (about one hour's drive north). With development based on proximity to desirable beaches, the city is dispersed along 57 kilometres of the coast. It is an exopolis in Soja's (1996) terms, lacking a city centre in the traditional sense. There is no clearly defined downtown or CBD,[1] and financial, legal, governmental and cultural institutions are spread throughout the city rather than occupying their own districts (Dedekorkut-Howes & Bosman 2015; Wise 2006; Wise & Breen 2004). Its form can be described as a series of linear strips parallel to the ocean – the beachside high-rise strip at the most easterly edge, the hinterland to the west, and highways, canal estates and suburbia in between (Wise 2006; Wise & Breen 2004). Along the high-rise band, the most intensified hubs for tourism, entertainment and leisure are Surfers Paradise (colloquially known as 'Surfers') and Broadbeach, which together are referred to as the 'Glitter Strip' (see Figure 2.1).

History

Indigenous Australians (primarily the Yugambeh peoples) occupied the area known today as the Gold Coast for many millennia, but the first European settlements did not occur until the 1840s (Dedekorkut-Howes, Bosman & Leach 2016; Jones 1986; McRobbie 1984). Despite the rich diversity of marine and terrestrial resources that sustained the First Peoples, the coastal region was seen by Europeans as undesirable for development due to its isolation and 'useless' dune landscape (Longhurst 1997, 1995). Initial economic activities in the region centred on primary industry, particularly timber and sugar cane but also livestock, maize and arrowroot (Dedekorkut-Howes & Bosman 2015; Blackman 2013). To support these industries and their workers, the towns of Southport and Coolangatta were officially established on the South Coast, as it was then known[2] (Dedekorkut-Howes & Bosman 2015; Prideaux 2004).

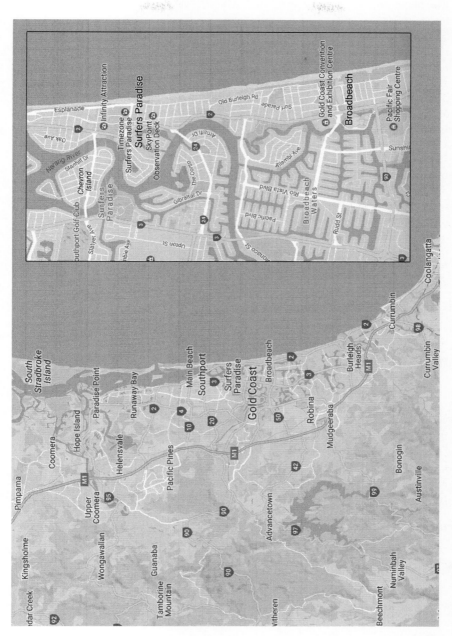

Figure 2.1 Maps of the Gold Coast (Map data ©2017 Google)

By the late 1800s, the timber industry was in decline, but the South Coast was beginning to gain traction as a seaside resort for Brisbane visitors looking for a weekend away (Blackman 2013; Longhurst 1995; Jones 1986). The completion of a railway line from Brisbane to Southport in 1889 (extended southwards to Coolangatta in 1903) made the South Coast considerably easier to access – prior to this, visitors could only come by either stagecoach or coastal steamer (Dedekorkut-Howes et al. 2016; Dedekorkut-Howes & Bosman 2015; Prideaux 2004). Subsequently, Southport was the first suburb to develop as a holiday spot, becoming popular among families for its calm estuary beaches and relaxed atmosphere (Scott et al. 2016; Blackman 2013; Longhurst 1997; McRobbie 1984). Main Beach (close to today's tourist hub of Surfers Paradise) initially attracted only a small number of (mostly young) visitors because of its rougher surf beach and relative inaccessibility (Davidson & Spearritt 2000; McRobbie 1984). However, the construction of bridges and other key infrastructure during the 1920s and 1930s made Main Beach and other parts of the South Coast more accessible (Blackman 2013; Davidson & Spearritt 2000; Longhurst 1997). With these upgrades, and with automobiles quickly becoming the preferred method for travelling to the Coast, the area's tourism industry flourished (Dedekorkut-Howes & Bosman 2015; Prideaux 2004; Longhurst 1997).

While the Coast had relied almost entirely on regional tourism up until that point, the 1930s saw a slight increase in interstate visitors, driven by new rail connections to southern states and the introduction of paid annual leave for many workers (Dedekorkut-Howes & Bosman 2015; Prideaux 2004). Later, during World War II, the area welcomed significant numbers of American servicemen who were temporarily stationed in the Brisbane region and would take leave on the Coast (Prideaux 2004; Davidson & Spearritt 2000; Longhurst 1997, 1995). Regular air services from Coolangatta's airport commenced in 1947, with direct flights between the Coast and Sydney beginning in 1956, attracting even more attention from the national market (Blackman 2013; Prideaux 2004; Davidson & Spearritt 2000). Rapidly increasing car ownership, motel developments and improvements to roads and highways ensured that the regional tourism market remained strong throughout the 1950s (Scott et al. 2016; Dedekorkut-Howes & Bosman 2015; Prideaux 2004; Davidson & Spearritt 2000; Longhurst 1997). The enduring popularity of car ownership meant that the railway from Brisbane became uneconomical and was thus closed by 1964 (Dedekorkut-Howes & Bosman 2015; Blackman 2013; Longhurst 1997).

In 1958, the South Coast officially changed its name to the more glamorous-sounding 'Gold Coast' (Davidson & Spearritt 2000). By this time, the city had established itself as a symbol for Australian beach culture and a major domestic tourism destination, with facilities ranging from restaurants, cabarets and nightclubs to shopping centres and wildlife reserves (Scott et al. 2016; Prideaux 2004; Longhurst 1995). In addition to its ongoing success as a family holiday destination, the media presented the Gold Coast as a place of fantasy, hedonism and escapism, and a fashionable playground for the young and wealthy (Prideaux 2004; Davidson & Spearritt 2000; Longhurst 1997). The spectacular appeal of the Gold Coast, and Surfers Paradise in particular, was further enhanced from the 1960s onwards by the rapid development of high-rise holiday apartments and hotels, supplementing and, in time, largely supplanting, the earlier motels and fibro beach houses (Dedekorkut-Howes & Bosman 2015; Weaver 2011; Wise 2006). As Davidson and Spearritt (2000) observe:

> Surfers Paradise and the Gold Coast took Australia by storm. At last we had a coastal strip and beachside architecture to match the French Riviera, Miami, and Waikiki Beach at Honolulu. Such comparisons were regularly drawn in the promotional literature. (p. 144)

As a consequence of this development boom, however, the Gold Coast quickly gained a reputation for being commercialised, tawdry, gaudy, vulgar and Americanised (McRobbie 1984). This was exacerbated by the city's own marketing techniques, which included launching the Surfers Paradise Meter Maids in 1965 – women in gold bikinis and high heels who were tasked to top up parking meters, provide visitor information and chat to tourists.

Rapid development in the tourism sector continued throughout the 1970s and 1980s, including the establishment of a number of attractions and events that became icons of the Gold Coast experience: large shopping complexes like Pacific Fair; American-style theme parks such as Seaworld, Dreamworld, and Wet'n'Wild; Jupiters Casino (now The Star); and the Billabong Pro surfing contest (Dedekorkut-Howes & Bosman 2015; Blackman 2013; Davidson & Spearritt 2000; Longhurst 1997). The 1980s saw the beginning of direct flights connecting Brisbane to Asia and Europe, and in the later years of the decade, the construction of high-end golf courses, luxury resorts and five-star hotels (Dedekorkut-Howes & Bosman 2015; Prideaux 2004; Jones 1986). The latter changes signified the Gold Coast's emergence as an international mass tourism destination, becoming at that time particularly popular with Japanese visitors (Faulkner & Tideswell 2006; Prideaux 2004).

Throughout the 1990s and 2000s, the Gold Coast continued to expand, with numerous new hotels, restaurants, shopping malls, theme parks and wildlife parks, a new railway line re-connecting it to Brisbane, and a steadily growing resident population (Dedekorkut-Howes & Bosman 2015; Blackman 2013). Intense and ongoing development has meant buildings are quickly knocked down and replaced, then demolished and built again, made (and remade) to be taller and flashier (see Figure 2.2). Thus, the Gold Coast's decades-old reputation for being commercialised and gaudy is continually reinforced by its own displays of spectacle and excess. Despite such negative press and frequent stereotyping in popular discourse, touristic interest in the city has not waned, and the tourism sector remains strong.

Figure 2.2 North facing view from the Q1 SkyPoint Observation Deck, Surfers Paradise

Present context

In the July 2016–June 2017 financial year, the Gold Coast received almost 13 million visitors producing $4.3 billion in expenditure (Tourism and Events Queensland 2017). Of these, 5 million were overnight visitors, with the remainder (7.9 million) being regional day-trippers. Domestic visitors accounted for 79 per cent (3.9 million) of overnight stays, making this market a core part of the city's tourism base. Given Australia's distance from other nations (resulting in long travel times for overseas visitors), it is unsurprising that the Gold Coast receives more conservative numbers of international tourists than the other destinations examined in this book. Comprising about 21 per cent (1,056,000) of total overnight visitors, international tourists come predominantly from China and New Zealand, followed by the UK, Japan, the USA, Taiwan, Singapore, India, Hong Kong and Germany. Despite relatively small numbers, the international market is still very important to the city, especially in terms of tourism expenditure.

Tourist numbers have tended to fluctuate in recent years (see Table 2.1), which may signify stagnation or decline of the destination (Butler 2006). However, the city has been attempting to reinvent its image, distancing itself from the more unfavourable aspects of the popular imaginary – namely, the idea that the Gold Coast, especially Surfers Paradise, is an '[a]gressively superficial' (Rough Guides 2018a) tourist trap (see also Cantillon 2015b). Take, for example, the following descriptions of the city on well-known international travel websites:

Table 2.1 Visitors to the Gold Coast, mid-2011–mid-2017

Year	Visitors	Growth rate
2011–2012	11,139,000	-
2012–2013	11,833,000	+6.2%
2013–2014	11,059,000	–6.5%
2014–2015	11,617,000	+5.0%
2015–2016	13,013,000	+12.0%
2016–2017	12,907,000	–0.8%

Source: Griffith Institute for Tourism (2015) for 2011–2015 figures; Tourism and Events Queensland (2016) for 2015–2016 figure; Tourism and Events Queensland (2017) for 2016–2017 figure.

> Beneath a jagged skyline shaped by dozens of high-rise beachfront apartment blocks, the Gold Coast is Australia's Miami Beach … There's little variation on the beach and nightclub scene … and if you're concerned this will leave you jaded, bored or broke, you're better off avoiding this corner of the state altogether. (Rough Guides 2018a)
>
> The neon lights of the Gold Coast have more in common with the glitz and glamour of Miami or the hedonistic pastimes of Las Vegas than they do Australia. … the most aggressively developed patch in Australia, it's also one of the most popular holiday destinations … (Lonely Planet 2014)

Defining the Gold Coast in terms of resorts like Miami, these descriptions clearly try to capture a sense of place that is set apart from 'normal' Australian lifestyles and urbanism. However, as Lonely Planet (2014) continues on to suggest, 'there's more to the Gold Coast than just the beach', and this is the key message of the city's latest branding strategy.

The previous 'Famous for Fun' campaign – which portrayed the Gold Coast as an exciting playground for all ages – has recently been abandoned in favour of the more understated 'We Are Destination Gold Coast' branding. This shift in marketing coincided with the lead up to the 2018 Commonwealth Games, which the city hosted in April of that year. The event not only bolstered the city's tourist numbers and international visibility, but also instigated the improvement of existing facilities and implementation of new infrastructure. These developments included the construction of sporting venues, a multi-million-dollar renovation of Pacific Fair shopping mall, and the introduction of a light rail rapid transit system that runs through the touristic Glitter Strip.

To complement these changes in the urban landscape, and to further revitalise the city's image, the Gold Coast's official tourism strategies emphasise the destination's diversity. Marketing materials promote the Gold Coast's traditional offerings, including its beaches, theme parks, dining precincts and shopping complexes, but also the region's lesser known natural and cultural attractions.

The official website features a variety of nature-based niche tourism experiences in the city's tranquil hinterland, advertising ecotourism accommodation, rainforest walks, scenic drives, and wineries. Cultural attractions – including museums, galleries and heritage sites – are still only a minor part of tourism promotion, although this sector has been flagged by the city as a targeted area for future growth (see City of Gold Coast 2014).

Despite nightlife's prominence in the imaginary and lived spatiality of Surfers Paradise, it receives only a few brief mentions in official promotional material, doubtless due to a perception that nightlife is associated with 'unsavoury' activities that would undermine the current campaign's 'sophisticated' narratives of place. The Gold Coast's branding strategies aim to position the city as more than a sun, sand and sex beach resort – as a cosmopolitan, vibrant, 'mature, world-class city' (Council of the City of Gold Coast 2018), or a 'real city' (Dedekorkut-Howes et al. 2016, p. 2). The Gold Coast is, thus, selling a lifestyle as well as a destination, promising that all the factors that make the city a great place to vacation also make it a great place to live. This is reflected in the increasing prominence of local lives and insights within official marketing. Under the headings 'Local Love' and 'Inside Stories', the official tourism website offers articles on the best markets, surfing spots, bars and things to do, from the perspective of residents. The website also showcases different neighbourhoods, accompanied by descriptions which cultivate distinct narratives of identity for each area. Those neighbourhoods with the most touristic appeal are paired with short video clips which follow prominent locals (such as famous surfers, athletes and TV presenters) introducing each place and outlining the most notable landmarks, activities and qualities.

Observations

For each other place I overview in this chapter, I offer some of my *initial* observations and experiences, from the perspective of a visitor. What I notice in the field is usually framed by inadvertent comparisons to my own locality, the Gold Coast, since it has a significant influence on my *habitus*, my subjectivity and my embodied experiences. I cannot present initial observations here, however, since I am writing from the perspective of a long-time resident. Thus, below I outline some of my strongest impressions of Surfers Paradise based on my repeated experiences and observations of its rhythms.

During the daytime in Surfers Paradise, families stroll up and down the main streets (see Figure 2.3) – Cavill Avenue, Orchid Avenue and The Esplanade – and hang out on the beach. These streets are lined with restaurants with alfresco dining areas, fast food chains, ice cream stores, souvenir shops, nightclubs and bars. At the corner of Cavill and The Esplanade is the iconic 'Surfers Paradise' sign, where tourists regularly stop to pose for group photos. The people seen here are considerably more ethnically diverse than the official marketing material depicts. There are Westerners in board shorts, bikinis,

Figure 2.3 People walking through Cavill Mall, Surfers Paradise

sunglasses, flip-flops and fanny packs with beach towels slung around their necks, but it is also common to see young families with women in hijabs or men in fezzes, or to hear groups speaking in Mandarin and Japanese. In a pluralistic society like Australia, one cannot assume who among these are international visitors, who are domestic visitors and who are locals.

Conspicuous among the sea of vacationers are young, slender, fake-tanned women in gold bikinis and hot pants – the Meter Maids (see Figure 2.4). Once a key part of the city's marketing strategy, the Meter Maids now seem to most locals to be little more than an embarrassing cliché whose current mundane function is to sell souvenirs and have their photos taken with tourists. My friends and I often remark on how their sexualised presence clashes with the supposed family-friendly image of the Gold Coast, but such oddly paradoxical conjunctions have become emblematic of Surfers Paradise and the Gold Coast more generally.

The early evening is the busiest time in Surfers (see Figure 2.5). Tourists crowd the beachfront markets, which consist of locally-run stalls selling crocheted and bejewelled bikinis, novelty hats, iPhone cases, crystal dolphins and unicorns, and scented candles set in cocktail glasses, as well as regular market fare like jams and pickles, craft work and ceramics. Back on Cavill, large groups form around street performers. Recently, the usual acts include a mime who makes balloon animals for children, a Latin guitarist, a few young men doing tricks on unicycles, and an Indigenous man playing the didgeridoo with a stuffed kookaburra perched on his shoulder.

Figure 2.4 A Meter Maid and a Hare Krishna chat to people in Cavill Mall, Surfers Paradise

Figure 2.5 Crowds at the markets and watching buskers along The Esplanade, Surfers Paradise

Late at night, Surfers Paradise becomes the domain of young people going to bars and nightclubs. Until the early hours of the morning, intoxicated club-goers can be observed stumbling between venues, laughing with friends, making out, getting into fights (both verbal and physical), crying, vomiting in gutters, and eating kebabs and pizza slices from all-hours take away shops, littering the streets with food scraps and wrappers as they go (see also Cantillon 2015a). Police on foot and horseback and community services like the Chill Out Zone van (offering water, first aid and other assistance) work to regulate these disorderly rhythms. Quite frequently, families with young children can still be seen walking around Surfers at this time of night, signalling a sharp discontinuity between how the area is marketed, and how it is consumed and lived.

Late at night is also the time when more locals are consuming Surfers as entertainment. Frequently, tourists assume that our presence in the tourist hub's leisure spaces means that we must be visitors as well. While many young Gold Coast residents can easily stay away from Surfers during the day – when we work, go to university or school, go shopping, go to quieter beaches, and so on – our only options in terms of clubbing venues are in the tourist hubs. Thus, for many residents, Surfers is inextricably linked to the transgressive, sexualised, seedy, drug- and alcohol-fuelled socio-spatial practices of the nightlife scene. Despite the city's attempts to downplay this narrative, the lived experience of Surfers highlights that nightlife is still very much a core part of its spatiality.

Apart from nightlife venues, there are many other forms of leisure practices available to locals beyond the tourist hubs. Dispersed across the city are restaurants, cinemas, parks, arts and cultural festivals, surf clubs and local taverns offering entertainment options during the daytime and at night. Such spaces and activities are central to everyday local rhythms, highlighting the extent to which the Gold Coast encompasses more elements of 'normal' Australian life than might be initially expected or inferred through popular cultural representations.

As a tourist resort, the Gold Coast is marked by multiplicities and contradictions. It shares many of the characteristics associated with resorts of its kind – most obviously, an emphasis on sun, sand, sex and enthusiastic consumption. Consequently, it has acquired a widely held set of stereotyped associations also shared by such resorts, prompting the city to shift its tourism marketing strategies in recent years to emphasise that it is much more than just a beach resort. However, despite the Gold Coast's reputation for over-the-top development, tacky commercialisation and a decidedly sleazy underbelly, the city nonetheless continues to attract domestic and international visitors drawn by its natural attractions, excellent facilities and opportunities for fun and relaxation. The tensions between the city's often conflicting representations and imaginaries are a product of the complexity, richness and heterogeneity of its material and symbolic affordances, and of how they are embodied and lived out by millions of different visitors and locals. These effects and their consequent affects belie the over-simplifications of both official tourism narratives and stereotypes entrenched in national media and popular discourse.

Phuket and Koh Phangan, Thailand

Thailand's appeal as a tourism destination[3] lies predominantly in its natural assets – the beaches, lush jungles, limestone karsts and tropical weather – and in its culture – the Thai people, cuisine and historic sites such as temples. This particular mix of natural and cultural attractions contributes significantly to a Western popular imaginary of Thailand as being an 'exotic' getaway and a 'paradise'. Thailand's tourism industry has successfully capitalised on these real and imaginary attributes, marketing each destination as offering a variety of tourism styles, including ecotourism, adventure tourism, cultural tourism, medical tourism, and, of course, sun, sand and sex mass tourism.

Growing up in Australia, I had often heard people say they were 'going to Thailand', referring to the nation as opposed to a specific island or city. The Australian popular imaginary seemed to conceptualise Thailand as somewhat uniform or cohesive, despite the fact that places like Bangkok, Pattaya and Chiang Mai are each incredibly different from one another. I visited numerous Thai beach destinations, two of which, Phuket and Koh Phangan, emerged as particularly interesting in light of my interest in resorts. While each is unique, these islands share commonalities that are representative of a particular kind of tourism that marks Southern Thailand as a resort region. Below, I discuss tourism in Thailand more broadly as well as outlining the particular characteristics and histories of Phuket and Koh Phangan.

Phuket is Thailand's largest island (roughly 540 square kilometres), situated in the country's southwest in the Andaman Sea (see Figure 2.6). While Phuket is home to a mere 378,000[4] residents, it attracts more than 13 million[5] visitors per year (Department of Tourism 2016; Department of Provincial Administration 2015b). In popular imaginaries, Phuket is most readily associated with packaged holidays, crowded beaches, luxury hotels, bargain shopping, strong drinks and a seedy nightlife. Koh Phangan, on the other hand, has had a long association with marginality, hedonism and illicit drugs, making it a particularly popular destination for young Western tourists. A small island (125 square kilometres) located in the Gulf of Thailand in the country's southeast (see Figure 2.7), Koh Phangan is also known for its coral reefs, marine life and beaches, many of which are still relatively undeveloped. With a population of about 7,258[6] and 903,255[7] visitors per year, residents are often far outnumbered by tourists (Department of Tourism 2016; Department of Provincial Administration 2015a).

History

Prior to the development of tourism, many areas in Southern Thailand had agriculture-based industries producing tin, rice, rubber and coconuts, with

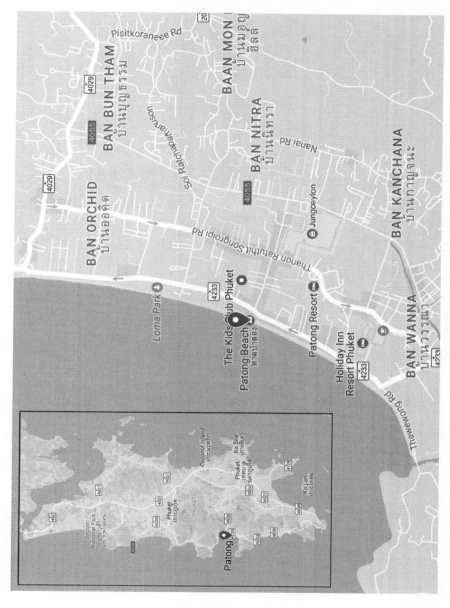

Figure 2.6 Map of Phuket and Patong Beach (Map data ©2017 Google)

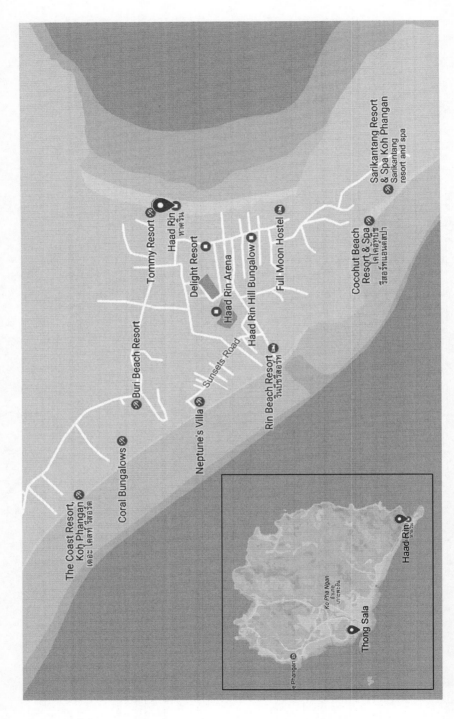

Figure 2.7 Map of Koh Phangan and Haad Rin (Map data ©2017 Google)

small fishing communities scattered across the coastline (Cohen 1982, 2008; Gurtner 2007; Kontogeorgopoulos 2004a). International tourism in Thailand began to flourish in 1960, following the establishment of the nation's flagship carrier, Thai Airways International, and the Tourist Organization of Thailand (now known as the Tourism Authority of Thailand [TAT]) (Tourism Authority of Thailand 2015; McDowall & Wang 2009; Cohen 2008). That year, Thailand attracted 81,000 international visitors (Tourism Authority of Thailand 2015). Although the development of tourism in Thailand has been largely funded by private investments and enterprises, the Thai government has played an instrumental role in supporting the growth of the industry through policy (Cohen 2008). Beginning in the late 1970s with the Fourth Economic and Social Development Plan (1977–81), tourism featured more prominently in the nation's strategies for economic growth as a means to attract foreign currency, generate foreign exchange and provide employment (Cohen 2008; Kontogeorgopoulos 1999; Peleggi 1996). During these early years, visitors to Thailand were primarily international 'elites' visiting Bangkok, and domestic tourists and backpackers travelling through less-established areas in the north and south, including Phuket (Cohen 2008; Kontogeorgopoulos 2009, 2004a, 2003).

The nation's first official tourism campaign was launched in 1980, and in the same year the country hosted two million international visitors (Tourism Authority of Thailand 2015). By the next year, the tourism industry had surpassed rice as Thailand's biggest source of foreign exchange and its top export, marking a shift away from an agriculture-based economy (McDowall & Wang 2009; Gibbons & Fish 1988). Phuket's tourism industry, in particular, thrived during this period, supported by efforts by the TAT as well as the construction of an international airport in 1979 (Kontogeorgopoulos 2009, 2004b; Cohen 1982). The resort (especially around Patong Beach) grew rapidly from that point onwards, quickly establishing itself as one of the most popular beachside mass tourism destinations in Asia. Due to decades of relentless, unregulated and unsustainable growth, Phuket is now frequently criticised for turning into a tacky, overdeveloped mass tourism destination (Kontogeorgopoulos 2009, 2003). Nonetheless, tourism on the island continues to expand, and is becoming increasingly more expensive and upmarket.

Koh Phangan, by contrast, developed slightly later. In the early-to-mid 1980s, it attracted day-trippers from nearby Koh Samui (a larger, more developed, more easily accessible island) seeking quiet, relaxed experiences in an 'authentic', 'untouched' paradise[8] (Malam 2008; Westerhausen 2002). Adding to the island's appeal was the fact that marijuana was cheap and widely available, and the lack of a police presence meant visitors could do drugs freely (Malam 2008; Westerhausen 2002). Tourism development centred on the peninsular beach of Haad Rin and was spearheaded by local landholders who constructed tourist facilities to cater to the increasing numbers of visitors (Malam 2004; Westerhausen 2002). The major catalyst for tourism development on Koh Phangan, however, was the inception of the Full Moon Parties, which coincided with the rise of rave and party drug cultures. The first

Full Moon Party was held in 1988, a private beach party hosted by a local with around 50 attendees (Malam 2004, 2008). Party-goers have inundated the island ever since, and today Full Moon Parties host up to 30,000 people during peak times.

In the span of a couple of decades, Koh Phangan has evolved from an alternative, 'marginal paradise' (Malam 2008, p. 336) to a mainstream mass tourism destination. In addition to the monthly Full Moon Parties, there are now Black Moon Parties (monthly), Half Moon Parties (fortnightly) and a variety of other events to provide visitors with the Full Moon experience at any time. Although Haad Rin has a high volume of visitors, much of the island remains relatively undeveloped for tourism. Over 70 per cent of the island consists of mountainous tropical jungles, much of the interior has very limited road access, and small fishing and farming communities continue to exist near the quieter beaches (Malam 2008; Westerhausen 2002). The island is still not as easily accessible as many other similar destinations, as it can only be reached via ferry or speedboat, although a small airport has been slowly under construction for several years.

Present context

The tourism industry continues to be vital to Thailand's economic and social development. In 2017, tourism's total contribution to the GDP was 21.2 per cent and total contribution to employment was 15.5 per cent, with these numbers increasing each year (World Travel & Tourism Council 2018). As one of the most popular destinations in the world, international arrivals and visitor expenditure are still increasing, with a record-high 35 million international visitors in 2017 (see Table 2.2; Ministry of Tourism and Sports 2018). This is a substantial number considering the country's population is just over 68 million (The World Bank 2017). The country's tourism industry has a history of recovering well after political and economic crises and natural disasters – even after the 2004 Indian Ocean tsunami, which devastated several of Southern Thailand's popular beaches, tourism arrivals returned to normal levels relatively quickly in the years

Table 2.2 International visitors to Thailand, 2012–2017

Year	Visitors	Growth rate
2012	22,353,903	-
2013	26,546,725	+18.7%
2014	24,779,968	–6.6%
2015	29,881,091	+20.6%
2016	32,588,303	+9.1%
2017	35,381,210	+8.6%

Source: Department of Tourism 2017, Ministry of Tourism and Sports 2018.

that followed (Kontogeorgopoulos 2009; Cohen 2008). Tourism in Thailand is relatively seasonal, with the greatest number of visitors coming from November to February, when the weather is warm and dry. Despite ongoing efforts to appeal to Western visitors (who are responsible for greater expenditure and longer stays), over half of Thailand's international tourists are from nearby Asian countries – particularly China, Malaysia, South Korea, Laos, Japan and India – with the most significant Western markets being Russia, the USA, the UK, Germany and Australia (Ministry of Tourism and Sports 2018).

Unlike the other destinations I visited for this project, I already had quite a detailed imaginary of Thailand before I went there. Based on travel stories from friends, popular cultural representations and sensationalised current affairs programs on Australian television, I had developed specific expectations about what typically goes on during a Thailand holiday: tanning at the beach, drinking from coconuts, riding elephants, visiting Buddhist temples, venturing into one of Patong's infamous ping pong shows, eating from street food carts, getting Thai massages (potentially with a 'happy ending'[9]), using tuk tuks for transport, trying mushroom shakes at the Full Moon Party, bargaining with shopkeepers over the price of designer knock-offs. The following descriptions of Thailand further reinforce these elements of the popular imaginary:

> Thailand is a wondrous kingdom, featuring Buddhist temples, exotic wildlife, and spectacular islands. Along with a fascinating history and a unique culture that includes delectable Thai food and massage, Thailand features a modern capital city, a pastoral countryside, and friendly people who epitomize Thailand's 'land of smiles' reputation. (Tourism Authority of Thailand 2018)
>
> Friendly and fun-loving, exotic and tropical, cultured and historic, Thailand radiates a golden hue from its glittering temples and tropical beaches to the ever-comforting Thai smile. (Lonely Planet 2018)
>
> … despite [its] vast influx of visitors, Thailand's cultural integrity remains largely undamaged – a country that adroitly avoided colonization has been able to absorb Western influences while maintaining its own rich heritage. (Rough Guides 2018c)

A common narrative emerges out of these representations: Thailand is authentic, traditional and exotic, yet still welcoming, safe and familiar, with an abundance of cultural and natural attractions to appeal to any visitor. For the Western tourist in particular, Thailand's exoticism and Otherness is what sets it apart from Western beach destinations. Cultural activities like visiting historical sites, going to Muay Thai boxing matches or eating local delicacies are standard parts of the tourist itinerary in Thailand, not just for those seeking 'authentic', alternative travel experiences.

The country's current tourism campaign, 'Amazing Thailand', plays on this Western desire for a cultural experience, with its slogan inviting visitors to

'Discover Thainess'. Thai culture is commodified for touristic consumption, and the visitor is encouraged to observe, or temporarily partake in, staged versions of Thai traditions and ways of life. A key aspect of this strategy is assuring visitors that the hosts embrace their presence – as can be seen in the quotes above, Thailand's people are often described as friendly and hospitable. Thus, visitors are promised opportunities to casually interject themselves into the everyday lives of the Other without fear of hostility. This experience is part of a larger touristic imperative (particularly for Westerners) to feel as though they are experiencing something different to home without compromising on the comforts to which they are accustomed (see Chapter 4).

Considering these touristic desires, it is unsurprising that the TAT foregrounds cultural tourism in official narratives. Since 2007, the TAT has shifted its tactics to target higher quality tourists – those who spend more money, stay longer and are more environmentally aware – rather than simply aiming to attract large numbers of tourists (Tourism Authority of Thailand 2015; McDowall & Wang 2009). To accomplish this, the TAT has focused on diversifying the tourism industry by promoting sustainable development and niche tourism experiences. For example, Thailand's official tourism website foregrounds Phuket's beaches, water activities and shopping tours, but also its historic architecture, museums and Chinese cultural influences. Koh Phangan, on the other hand, is noted as home to the Full Moon Parties, but also to beautiful coral reefs, waterfalls, mountains, forests, farms and temples.

Such natural and cultural attractions provide Thailand with a competitive edge over other mass tourism destinations internationally, while also working to mitigate some of the reputational consequences of conventional mass tourism development. Peleggi (1996) suggests that one reason for the TAT's focus on cultural and heritage tourism over the past few decades is that it may downplay some of the less desirable elements of Thai tourism, such as associations with illicit drugs, sex tours and prostitution. Likewise, increasing emphasis on developing nature-based and ecotourism initiatives (which have long been present in Thailand) may help to ease concerns surrounding the environmental ramifications of mass tourism (McDowall & Wang 2009; Kontogeorgopoulos 1999).

Initial impressions

Phuket was the first stop of my fieldwork. I stayed in Patong Beach, the most intensified area for tourism development on the island. This trip also happened to be my first time travelling overseas, so my initial impressions were largely informed by how different Thailand seemed to Australia, and how my lived experiences deviated from my expectations and imaginaries. Walking along the main road (Thanon Ratuthit Songroipi Road) one block from the beach, I noticed the haziness and pungent smells in the air – a mix of open drains, garbage accumulating on sidewalks, and smoke rising from street food carts – as well as the mountainous backdrop, run-down buildings

Figure 2.8 Buildings in Patong Beach

and the imposing bundles of power lines above (see Figure 2.8). The following excerpt from my field journal captures more of these observations.

> Every few metres, someone (usually a man) to the side of the pathway calls to me: 'taxi?', 'good morning', 'hello', etc. There are women sitting outside of massage parlours with their price lists, but they don't talk to me. Along the way I see several currency exchange services and tourist booths advertising tours, which signals the degree to which this place caters to visitors. In between these kinds of sights, however, I also see shrines to the king – an expression of local culture.
>
> I can tell when I get to Bangla Road [one of the most famous tourist strips in the area] because there's a huge 'Patong Beach' sign hanging above the road, much like the Surfers Paradise signs on either end of Cavill Avenue. I guess this indicates that the place is iconic enough to warrant a novelty sign. ... Running along either side of the road are souvenir shops, bars (filled with people even in the daytime), and all the Western staples: McDonald's, Starbucks and KFC.
>
> When I get to the end of Bangla Road where it meets the beach, I can hardly see any ocean. My view is obscured by hundreds of uniform, brightly coloured beach umbrellas and sun beds, packed in tightly, blocking access to the beach [see Figure 2.9]. ... I return to the road running parallel to the beach (Thaweewong Road). One side of the

Figure 2.9 Umbrellas on Patong Beach

footpath, at the edge of the sand, is lined with stalls offering massages, manicures and pedicures, body scrubs, henna, cocktails, fruit and fruit juices, and Western snacks like fries, sandwiches and hot dogs. The opposite side of the footpath, at the edge of the road, is lined with parked motorbikes and men offering taxi and tuk tuk rides. Across the road are stores filled with cheap handbags, shoes, shirts, sunglasses and other designer knock-offs. (Field journal, 7 December 2013)

At night, Bangla Road was closed to traffic and filled with people. Although I was expecting groups of young, drunk people, there were many couples and families present who, like me, were there to observe the spectacle of it all, not necessarily to go to the bars or shops. We strolled up and down the road, occasionally stopping to watch and take photos of buskers, vendors demonstrating cheap light-up toys, Thai women dancing provocatively in the infamous go-go bars, and strippers who could be seen up above, dancing in the second-floor windows of adult entertainment establishments. Scattered through the crowd were scantily-clad white women holding signs promoting a 'Russian strip show', as well as Thai people advertising ping pong shows. Bangla Road's adjoining alleyways were lined with bars and clubs, their promoters shouting offers for cheap drinks and no cover charge, and their intoxicated patrons sexually harassing women walking by – 'How much?', 'Puta!', 'Can I come with you? I want you' and so on. Despite what the characteristics of many of the tourists might indicate, much like Surfers Paradise, Patong's main drag is clearly a sexualised space.

While Koh Phangan shared some of these characteristics, it had its own distinct atmosphere. The ferry from Koh Samui to Koh Phangan was filled with dishevelled (mostly white) young people with accents from around the world, some of whom were already smoking pot and drinking beer. When I arrived at the pier in Haad Rin, the narrow streets were backed up with taxis and hotel transfers awaiting our ferry's arrival. The 10-minute car ride to my hotel – a winding, rolling, scenic drive through the jungle – confirmed that the congestion was largely restricted to Haad Rin. Despite feeling more secluded, the hotel nonetheless had the same atmosphere as the ferry and the town, with loud, intoxicated groups of young people walking the grounds and hanging out by the pool.

Knowing that Haad Rin would be entirely different during the Full Moon Party, I spent some time there before the festivities began. Haad Rin is quiet during the day, apart from the times immediately preceding and following ferry arrivals and departures. The town is tiny and entirely walkable, made up of small, low-rise buildings and a few unpaved roads. Although this is not the kind of sanitised, polished built environment one would usually expect of a resort, the significance of tourism was still visible in other ways:

> Everything here appears to be devoted to the Full Moon Parties – walking around for a few minutes, I've seen empty booze stands, toilet signs (with a 20-baht entry fee), the 'Tourist Police' office, and Full Moon Party signage indicating rules and safety tips [see Figure 2.10]. There's also the usual touristy shops selling brightly coloured shirts, many of which are Full Moon Party-themed. ... I also see medical clinics (some designated as 'Western'), restaurants (like Planet Hollyfood – a play on the Planet Hollywood chain), laundromats, convenience stores, pharmacies, hostels, ATMs – all the things tourists need.
>
> On the beach itself, where the parties are held, there are no sunbeds and umbrellas like you'd see in Patong, but there are a few people lying on the sand. The beach is filthy, strewn with garbage like straws, drink cups, lost shoes and broken bottles constantly shifting with the rhythmic swash of the ocean [see Figure 2.11]. Tables, chairs and alcohol stands are piled up at the edge of the beach, ready to be set up for tonight. (Field journal, 17 December 2013)

Later that night, Haad Rin was completely transformed by the disorderly, energetic night-time rhythms of the Full Moon Party. The streets were lined with stalls selling pizza, hot dogs and burgers, alcoholic bucket drinks (see Figure 2.12) and themed merchandise. On the beach, a mass of intoxicated young people danced under the full moon to electronic music being blasted by nearby bars. The party continued well into the early hours of the morning, after which revellers slowly began to leave, piling into tuk tuks to head back to their hotels.

Figure 2.10 Empty food and drink stands in Haad Rin

Phuket, Koh Phangan and the Gold Coast clearly share some key similarities. They are all beach destinations associated with sexualised, drug- and alcohol-fuelled adult fun, whether in nightclubs, strip clubs, bars or at parties. In Phuket and on the Gold Coast, this contrasts strongly with the simultaneous presence of families. On Koh Phangan, on the other hand, tourism is almost entirely geared

Figure 2.11 Rubbish, tables and chairs along Sunrise Beach, Haad Rin

Figure 2.12 Stands selling alcoholic bucket drinks at the Full Moon Party

towards young adult party-goers. Despite Phuket's established reputation for being overdeveloped, it appears that Koh Phangan's infrastructure is more obviously struggling with its large influx of visitors, as indicated by major problems with traffic, rubbish and accessibility. Such issues could potentially lead Koh Phangan into periods of stagnation or decline (see Butler 2006). Like the Gold Coast, Thailand's official tourism discourses have attempted to downplay the transgressive, hedonistic aspects in favour of highlighting the diverse range of activities that can be enjoyed beyond the beach and nightlife districts. These alternatives often work to capitalise on Western popular imaginaries, which characterise the region as an exotic, escapist paradise, and as culturally rich and unique.

Cancún, Mexico

It is clear why Cancún is one of the world's most iconic destinations – the vivid turquoise waters and white sand surrounding the city are a true spectacle. Located in the state of Quintana Roo in south-east Mexico, Cancún is situated on the Yucatán Peninsula, bordering the Caribbean Sea. Cancún's development is based around its natural beauty, with hotels and mansions positioned along the 25-kilometre beachfront strip, the Hotel Zone, or Zona Hotelera (see Figure 2.13). Sitting behind this, bordering the Nichupté Lagoon, are restaurants, shopping complexes, nightclubs and cheaper accommodation. Connected to the Hotel Zone by a single main road running along a narrow isthmus, and set back away from the beach, is downtown

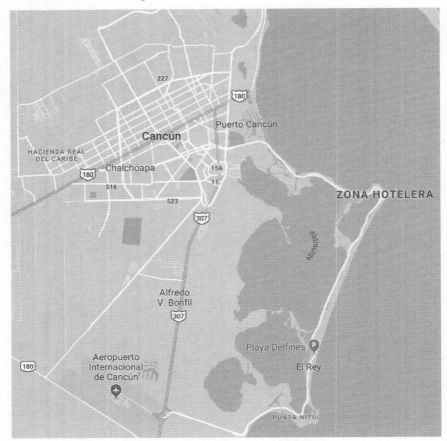

Figure 2.13 Map of Cancún (Map data ©2018 Google, INEGI)

Cancún, predominantly occupied by local businesses and services, shops, hospitals, schools and housing for the city's estimated 806,000 residents (Consejo Nacional de Población 2018).

In the popular imaginary, Cancún is to North America what Thailand's beach resorts are to Australia – perceived as an exotic, pristine, tropical paradise combining beautiful beaches with cultural experiences and heritage attractions (Castellanos 2010a; Pi-Sunyer, Thomas & Daltabuit 2001). Simultaneously, however, it is also associated with the behaviours and consumption practices common among American mass tourists and young party tourists, including Spring Breakers. These associations have been firmly entrenched through popular cultural representations of the resort, such as in the documentary *The Real Cancun* (2003), the reality television series *The Real World: Cancun* (2009), and season three of the UK reality television show *Geordie Shore* (2011–present). At the same time as being imagined as a tropical paradise and a hedonistic party destination, Cancún is also perceived as having a 'dark side' marked by an illicit drug trade and gang violence.

History

In the 1960s, the Mexican federal government, along with its central bank,[10] determined that tourism would be one of the key strategies to remedy the country's growing economic problems and increasing debt (Wilson 2008; Torres & Momsen 2006; Re Cruz 1996). They initiated a search for the ideal location to develop a master-planned resort, flying over 35 potentially suitable sites before choosing Cancún (Fondo Nacional de Fomento al Turismo 2015; Mugerauer 2004; Torres 2002; Hiernaux-Nicolas 1999). It had all the desirable elements of a sun, sand and sea tourist destination: a warm climate, attractive beaches, coral reefs, and a prime position that allowed developers to capitalise on already well-established imaginaries and myths surrounding Caribbean tourism (Brown 2013; Agarwal & Shaw 2007; Momsen 2005). Further, it was easily accessible for North Americans as well as being close to several Maya archaeological sites that would appeal to cultural tourists from many countries (Castellanos 2010a, 2010b; Torres & Momsen 2006; Momsen 2005; Mugerauer 2004).

Cancún also had the perceived benefit of being sparsely populated and largely untouched by modern development (Castellanos 2010b; Clancy 2001). At the time, Cancún was an isolated barrier island with only several hundred inhabitants occupying the surrounding areas, mostly indigenous Maya people undertaking subsistence agriculture (Torres & Momsen 2006; Mugerauer 2004; Clancy 2001). The government's rationale for developing Cancún suggested that it would stimulate the regional economy, provide employment opportunities (in the form of cheap labour in construction and hospitality roles) for the surrounding communities, modernise the area by improving infrastructure, and encourage migration to the peripheral regions of Mexico (Castellanos 2010a, 2010b; Agarwal & Shaw 2007; Torres & Momsen 2006; Mugerauer 2004).

Beginning in the early 1970s, the Bank of Mexico and the Trust Fund for Tourism Infrastructure (INFRATUR) oversaw the construction of Cancún's tourist facilities, hotels and other infrastructure, financed predominantly by federal funds and loans from the Inter-American Development Bank and the World Bank (Castellanos 2010a; Wilson 2008; Murray 2007; Hiernaux-Nicolas 1999; Re Cruz 1996, 2003). A downtown area was constructed specifically to support the Hotel Zone, cater to the influx of new workers, and intentionally segregate residents and tourists (Murray 2007; Torres & Momsen 2006; Clancy 2001). The first hotels in Cancún opened in 1974, and in the following year 100,000 tourists visited

(Fondo Nacional de Fomento al Turismo 2015; Castellanos 2010a; Evans 2005; Clancy 2001). Although originally intended to be an upmarket resort with five-star hotels appealing to wealthy visitors, in the 1980s Cancún started to cater more to the packaged mass tourism market (Castellanos 2010a; Torres & Momsen 2006; Torres 2002). Not only did this see an increase in tourist numbers, but in the resident population as well, which expanded from several hundred people in the mid-1970s to several hundred thousand by the mid-1990s. Since then, the destination has continued to experience steady growth in terms of its population, amenities, infrastructure and tourist arrivals (see Table 2.3). Of course, the resort has also experienced temporary lulls over the years, particularly after Hurricane Gilbert in 1988 and Hurricane Wilma in 2005, both of which caused substantial environmental and structural damage; and after the 9/11 terror attacks in 2001, which caused a short-term decrease in US visitors (Agarwal & Shaw 2007).

Present context

Today, Cancún is the biggest resort in Mexico, and one of the most famous tourism destinations in the world (Agarwal & Shaw 2007; Evans 2005; Torres 2002). Development has expanded far beyond Cancún to other areas in the Yucatán, such as the collection of beaches and sites that comprise the 'Riviera Maya' district to its south (Brown 2013). In Cancún itself, the tourist presence has begun to extend beyond the Hotel Zone and into downtown. Despite being planned as an exclusive resort, Cancún is now strongly established as a site for mass tourism, packaged holidays, middle-class guests and family-oriented activities. Shopping complexes, restaurants, outdoor activities and affordable accommodation like hostels continue to be developed around the lagoon and downtown to meet the needs of these visitors (Torres & Momsen 2006; Mugerauer 2004).

Table 2.3 Visitors to Cancún, 2011–2016

Year	Visitors	Growth rate
2011	3,115,177	-
2012	3,642,449	+16.9%
2013	4,093,942	+12.4%
2014	4,387,798	+7.2%
2015	4,622,286	+6.2%
2016	4,761,482	+3.0%

Source: Secretaría de Turismo del Estado de Quintana Roo (2016).

Cancún caters especially to American tourists, who have been the resort's most significant market for decades – in 2010, of Cancún's roughly 3 million visitors, 2.1 million were foreign hotel guests, with 78.9 per cent of them coming from the USA (Caribbean Tourism Organization 2015). In addition to families, Cancún appeals to young American party tourists, having become an iconic destination for bachelor and bachelorette parties, birthdays and Spring Break, forms of travel that are strongly associated with leisurely beach activities by day and bar-hopping and clubbing by night. The Spring Break market in particular is a point of contention among businesses, residents and other tourists alike. Spring Breakers may fill hotel rooms and boost spending, but they are also notorious for being noisy, rowdy and disrespectful of property and attractions (Torres & Momsen 2006; see also Chapter 3).

To mitigate the perceived negative effects associated with this segment of the mass tourism market, the official tourism discourses of Cancún have shifted over recent years. Torres and Momsen (2006) observe that 'Cancún has been radically transformed over the past fifteen years from a strictly "sun and sand" tourism bubble into a postindustrial, urban tourism space offering a "kaleidoscope" of activities' (p. 60). The current official tourism narratives of Cancún emphasise the diversity of its attractions, highlighting alternative tourism experiences while also promoting the variety which exists within mainstream tourism practices. Take, for example, the following excerpts from the official tourism websites for Cancún and Mexico:

> Cancun is known all over the world for its spectacular beaches, unique beauty, breathtaking turquoise waters, and colorful culture … Cancun is a multifaceted destination that combines the very best in luxury, nature, Mayan culture, glamour and world-class amenities with seductive adventure offerings and an up-and-coming gastronomy scene. (Cancún Convention & Visitors Bureau 2015)
>
> Cancun delivers to travelers the best of many worlds: the Caribbean and Mexico; modern and ancient; action packed and laid back. Cancun is unequaled in its ability to offer cultural treasures, natural beauty, infinite activities and North American-style conveniences. (Mexico Tourism Board 2012)

These official narratives aim to position the resort as having something for everyone, appealing to a range of burgeoning niche tourism interests. At the same time, however, they play on already well-entrenched place-images and myths, actively reinforcing existing popular imaginaries and assuring Western tourists that the destination provides all the sights and comforts they have come to expect.

The official Cancún visitors' website promotes typical mainstream attractions and activities such as snorkelling, scuba diving, fishing, golfing, shopping, day trips to surrounding islands, day spas, restaurants, cruises and nightclubs. Some of the most frequently promoted cultural attractions are the numerous Maya archaeological sites present in the Yucatán, including Chichén Itzá, Tulum, Cobá and Ek' Balam, which provide a sense of exoticism and 'authenticity' to the tourism imaginary. Two nearby archaeological sites – Xcaret and Xel-Há – have also been integrated into eco-parks[11] (theme parks with an ecotourism slant). This is part of a wider trend to tap into the ecotourism market (Agarwal & Shaw 2007), as can be seen with promotion of sustainable or 'green' hotels and attractions such as cenotes, jungle tours and an underwater museum. Much like what is occurring in Phuket, this often manifests as soft ecotourism (Kontogeorgopoulos 2009). That is, the eco-parks incorporate elements of nature and ecotourism into a mass tourism product, and in doing so, have threatened the integrity and sustainability of the Maya ruins and surrounding environment (Agarwal & Shaw 2007).

Initial impressions

I visited Cancún in the spring of 2014. During my stay, I met groups of Americans celebrating birthdays, family reunions and bachelor parties; travellers escaping the 2014 North American 'polar vortex' cold wave who were overjoyed to be able to wear shorts and lie out by the pool; and young university students on Spring Break vacations, taking pleasure in the temporary relief from studying, snow and sub-zero temperatures. For many tourists, the warm climates of resorts provide a major point of difference from their own localities.

I stayed at a four-star, all-inclusive hotel (accommodation at which all food and beverages are included in the room rate) in the heart of the Hotel Zone, near a cluster of nightclubs, fast food restaurants and retail stores. The all-inclusive model, though very common in a destination like Cancún, is marked by extravagance and excess. My hotel's wristband granted me access to six restaurants, two pools, a private beach, a day spa, a hot tub, a gym, a sauna, a souvenir shop, a bar, a nightclub in the adjoining hotel, 24-hour room service, a free mini bar, and a variety of activities and water sports.

During the day, guests would feast at the buffet, order cocktails by the beach, work on their tans (and sunburns), or join in on the games run by the poolside DJ. The following excerpt from my field journal illustrates a typical scene:

> I'm lying on a sunbed on the short, crowded stretch of beach that belongs to my hotel [see Figure 2.14]. I'm recovering from a throat infection and a trip to the hospital in downtown yesterday ... [but] there's no point staying in bed here – the poolside DJ blasts dance music all day and evening, and closing my room's windows hardly

Figure 2.14 Hotel beach in Cancún

works to block it out. I guess that's just a part of the atmosphere here – always a party.

I'm surrounded by young adults, older couples and a few young families in their bathing suits, ordering drink after drink and occasionally dipping into the ocean to cool off. The bright blue water ahead of me is occupied by some swimmers and a few yachts, speedboats, cruise ships, and the Captain Hook party boat (whose accompanying loud music and MC-ing are another regular feature in the soundscape) in the distance. I'm watching a middle-aged couple – the woman in a thong bikini, the man in a Speedo – making out and groping at the water's edge.

I'm reminded of Thailand and its beach vendors when a Mexican man walks past with a Coca-Cola branded box full of food on his head. Next, another Mexican man trying to sell silver chains to us, and shortly after, another selling sarongs and beach totes. (Field journal, 6 March 2014)

Unlike the other sites of my fieldwork, my observations in Cancún were very much focused on my hotel. The all-inclusive concept implies that guests will have everything they need available and pre-paid for at their accommodation, with no unexpected extra expenses or inconveniences. The hotels become their own little worlds, with (almost) every service, comfort and experience guests may desire during their stay. Many visitors to Cancún come *for* the hotel, the picturesque views and the warm weather. Unfortunately, this means that they are less likely to spend money in surrounding local businesses. Indeed, about 85 per cent of tourists in the Hotel Zone do not venture beyond their hotel to explore, eat or shop (Córdoba Azcárate, Baptista & Domínguez Rubio 2014).

The Hotel Zone is dispersed across a long distance, making it not at all walkable, and fairly narrow, featuring little more than a mundane main road

Figure 2.15 Daytime in the Hotel Zone, Cancún

and a series of hotel entrances and the odd plaza or restaurant by the lagoon. The layout of the Hotel Zone is not conducive to the kind of exploring one would attempt in, for example, a city like New York or Paris, or even Miami, where points of interests like shops, bars, cafes and other attractions are densely packed into a small area and are easy to stumble upon. To visit places other than your hotel, you have to have a specific intention to do so, and make the effort to organise travelling there, whether by public bus, taxi or private transfer. As a result, it is easy to stick to the portion of the Hotel Zone which is in direct proximity to one's hotel. During the day, the area closest to my hotel was fairly empty, with only a few tourists hanging around outside the Forum by the Sea shopping mall, and a few others in local bars and the Hooters restaurant (see Figure 2.15).

Late at night and into the early hours of the morning, the rhythms of this area changed dramatically. It became packed with tourists – adults of all ages – drinking and dancing at bars and clubs, or watching the spectacle from the streets. Just as in Thailand, several bars and clubs were not enclosed venues (such as La Vaquita, Congo Bar and Mandala), inviting the gaze of passers-by. Crowds of people stood outside or across the street, watching the hired female dancers and patrons dancing sexually on podiums (see Figure 2.16).

If visitors do intend to travel beyond the Hotel Zone, Cancún's downtown is accessible by taxis or public buses (mainly occupied by hotel workers and a few tourists). In downtown, many of the main roads are named after Maya archaeological sites popular among tourists, with avenues called Chichén Itzá,

Figure 2.16 Crowds outside bars and nightclubs in the Hotel Zone, Cancún

Bonampak, Tulum, Uxmal, Xel-Há and Xcaret. This highlights not only how new the city is, but how it was purpose-built to be devoted to tourism. While there were numerous shops, restaurants and a few cheaper hotels around this area, it had a more local feel, with substantially fewer English-speaking workers in stores and other establishments. People on the streets were predominantly Mexican, and I felt out of place – not only because I was a white tourist, but because I was taking photos of seemingly unremarkable sights. The roads and buildings appeared run-down, and it was clear that less attention had been paid to the upkeep of these areas than the Hotel Zone, which, nevertheless, has itself several derelict former hotels, shops and restaurants (see Figure 2.17).

Cancún shares commonalities with the Gold Coast, Phuket and Koh Phangan in that it is a sun, sand and sex destination that is trying to diversify its tourism offerings and markets. In particular, like the Southern Thailand resorts, Cancún is capitalising on its image as an exotic paradise by promoting cultural tourism and ecotourism experiences. Cancún is different to the other destinations discussed in this book, however, in that it is a master-planned, purpose-built resort. The careful planning of the city included a rationale emphasising the benefits of its development for the local people, the regional economy and the nation. While Cancún provides a good example of successful *planning* (especially compared to a resort like Koh Phangan), the ongoing *management* of its development has not necessarily been as effective[12] (see also Chapter 6). I have mentioned, for example, the abandoned, deteriorating buildings present in the tourist hub. This speaks to the all-inclusive, hotel-centric nature of a typical Cancún holiday (which limits the opportunities for tourists to encounter anything unsightly), but it also highlights the extent to which I am accustomed

Figure 2.17 Shopfronts in downtown Cancún

to such sites being swiftly knocked down and rebuilt as a part of my own locality's tourism management strategy: to constantly renew itself.

Miami, USA

For almost a century, Miami has been one of the world's most famous resort destinations. In popular imaginaries, the city is most commonly associated with year-round warm weather, sandy beaches, Art Deco architecture, Latin American culture, exclusive nightclubs, flashy cars, beautiful people and illicit activities. My own expectations of Miami were largely shaped by representations of it in film and television, as well as the frequent comparisons made between it and the Gold Coast by tourism bodies, club promoters, news media and scholars alike. Of all the resorts examined in this book, Miami is the most mature destination, having reinvented itself multiple times over the last century amid intermittent periods of decline.

Miami is located on the southeast tip of Florida, overlooking Biscayne Bay and the Atlantic Ocean (see Figure 2.18). Given its position geographically, Miami was once a peripheral place, relatively isolated from the rest of mainland USA. Today, the Miami region is one of the largest and most developed urban areas in the country, and functions as a central node connecting the north and south of the Americas (Nijman 2011). Due to its sprawling development, Miami is decentred and lacks defined borders. 'Miami' technically refers to the CBD (Downtown Miami) and surrounding areas which comprise the City of Miami, but 'Miami' is used colloquially to encompass a number of other cities and neighbourhoods in the county, such as

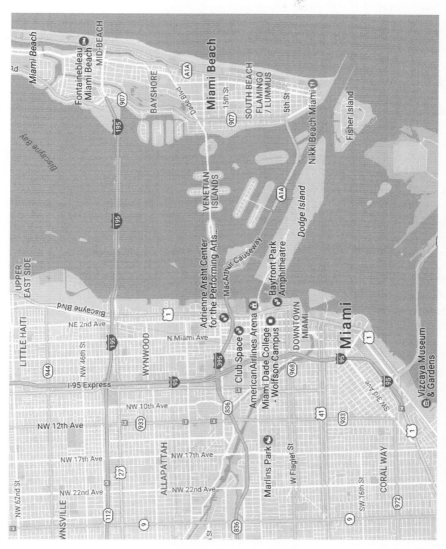

Figure 2.18 Map of Downtown Miami and Miami Beach (Map data ©2017 Google)

Miami Beach, Coral Gables and Kendall. This region (known officially as Miami-Dade County or Greater Miami, and sometimes unofficially as 'the Gold Coast') extends from Aventura in the north to southwards of Homestead. The county has a resident population of over 2.7 million, of which only 91,917 live in the tourist hub of Miami Beach (United States Census Bureau 2018).[13]

History

Unlike Thailand and Cancún, Miami's development as a resort is attributed to the initiatives of certain 'pioneers' rather than the government. Although Southern Florida had long been inhabited by Native Americans, the area was largely untouched by Western development until the late 1800s (Lavender 2002). At this time, the area was difficult to access and somewhat uninviting. Miami Beach, for example, was still a sandbar disconnected from the mainland, made up of mangrove swamps and occupied by rattlesnakes, crocodiles, rats, wildcats and mosquitos (Nijman 2011; Lavender 2002; Bush 1999).

Downtown Miami's development in the late 1800s was pioneered by key figures including Julia Tuttle, a Cleveland woman who inherited large expanses of land north of the Miami River, and Henry M Flagler, a multimillionaire business tycoon (Nijman 2011; Revels 2011; Buchanan 1978). Tuttle was eager to develop the area into a resort, offering Flagler some of her land as an incentive for him to extend his railway southwards from West Palm Beach (its planned termination point) to Miami (Nijman 2011; Revels 2011; Alonso 2007; George 1981). Flagler obliged, constructing the railway and eventually funding other vital infrastructure in the area. In 1896, the first train pulled into Miami, and the city's population and economy grew considerably from that point onwards (Nijman 2011; Alonso 2007; Bachin 2006; George 1981; Buchanan 1978).

During the early 1900s, the nearby barrier island of Miami Beach started being developed as well, through the efforts of landholders including John Collins, Carl Fisher and the Lummus Brothers. A bridge connecting Miami Beach to the mainland was completed in 1913, and over the next several years, Collins and Fisher initiated projects to clear mangroves, construct roads, dredge Biscayne Bay, and increase Miami Beach's total area using landfill (Nijman 2011; Bachin 2006; Lavender 2002). Fisher, in particular, was instrumental in establishing the island's tourism industry, contributing large sums of money to develop Miami Beach 'as a winter-sports playground for the wealthy' (Lavender 2002, p. 15).

The Miami area grew rapidly during the early 1920s, with a real estate boom attracting outside investment and an increasing resident population (Jarvis 2011; Nijman 2011). Miami Beach alone expanded from a population of 644 in 1920 to an estimated 6,500 in 1930 (Nijman 2011). City boosters cultivated powerful myths about Miami to appeal to tourists – promotional material portrayed the region as an exclusive tropical paradise with spectacular beaches, palm trees and exotic Mediterranean Revival architecture, as well as golf courses, casinos, luxury hotels, yacht clubs and star-studded parties (Nijman

2011; Revels 2011; Alonso 2007; Bush 1999). Celebrities and other elites from the northern states flocked to Miami Beach, especially during winter, when residents were significantly outnumbered by visitors (Nijman 2011). Despite its upmarket, glamorous associations, Miami also garnered a reputation for being 'depraved', immoral and transgressive (Revels 2011). Illegal gambling rooms were common throughout Miami, and Prohibition laws were scarcely enforced for fear that it would harm tourism (Revels 2011). Organised crime began to flourish due to alcohol smuggling, the establishment of moonshine distilleries, and the presence of infamous gangsters, like Al Capone, who owned vacation homes in the area (Nijman 2011; Revels 2011).

By the second half of the 1920s, there was a downturn in tourism. In addition to the onset of the Great Depression in 1929, Miami also suffered from the end of its real estate boom in 1925 and a devastating hurricane that hit in 1926 (Revels 2011; Bachin 2006; Lavender 2002). Following the hurricane, which destroyed many homes and tourist facilities, the South Beach area was rebuilt in the Art Deco style for which it is now famous (Nijman 2011; Revels 2011; Alonso 2007). Although Miami entered an economic depression sooner than the rest of the country, it also recovered more quickly, with tourism and population growth picking up again in the 1930s (Nijman 2011; Lavender 2002). Revels (2011) posits that this may be attributed to tourism's relative durability compared to traditional industries, especially considering Miami's capacity to appeal to fantasies of escapism during times of hardship.

Tourism experienced another brief lull in the early 1940s during World War II, with over 85 per cent of Miami Beach hotels being temporarily taken over for military use (Revels 2011; Alonso 2007). During the 1950s, South Beach and its Art Deco district started to decay as tourists moved further north in Miami Beach, where several new major luxury hotels were being constructed (Alonso 2007). Although these establishments catered to the celebrities and wealthy elites for which Miami was famous, their success was hampered by the increasing arrival of more middle-class mass tourists and college-aged Spring Breakers (Desrosiers-Lauzon 2011; Nijman 2011; Revels 2011).

Tourism in Miami was stagnant in the 1960s and declined throughout the 1970s (Nijman 2011; Dombrink & Thompson 1990). More affordable and extensive air travel networks meant Miami's usual visitors could now also reach farther off, more exotic destinations with greater ease than ever before (Alonso 2007; Bush 1999; Dombrink & Thompson 1990). Further, the opening of Disney World in 1972 drew tourists' attention away from southern Florida to central Florida (Gross 1997; Dombrink & Thompson 1990). At the same time that tourists were heading elsewhere, Miami's facilities were becoming dated, and several hotels went bankrupt while several more were demolished (Desrosiers-Lauzon 2011; Dombrink & Thompson 1990). Miami Beach's residents and visitors were ageing as well – in 1970, the median age of residents was over 65 (Desrosiers-Lauzon 2011; Gross 1997); by 1975, 64 per cent of vacationers were over 50 (Dombrink & Thompson 1990). A far cry from its former image as a glamorous destination for the nation's elite, Miami Beach became known as 'God's waiting room', populated by poor Jewish[14] retirees and Cuban immigrants who lived in dilapidated South Beach hotels that had been converted into apartments (Desrosiers-Lauzon 2011; Nijman 2011; Alonso 2007; Gross 1997).

By the early 1980s, Miami's reputation had worsened. It reportedly had the highest crime rate and murder rate in the nation, and the news media branded it America's drug capital (Desrosiers-Lauzon 2011; Nijman 2011; Alonso 2007).[15] Additionally, there was significant news coverage of Miami's racial tensions amid the 1980 Liberty City riots and the arrival of many Haitian refugees throughout the decade (Nijman 2011; Revels 2011; Alonso 2007). Alonso (2007) reflects on the contradictions this produced in the city's popular imaginary:

> Images of sunny beaches were eclipsed by images of Cuban refugees living in a tent city under Interstate highway 95, Haitian refugees arriving ashore in homemade rafts, Liberty City smouldering during the riots, and drug shootouts on the streets of Miami. (p. 173)

In the mid-1980s, however, the tide was turning once again. The recovery of Miami's tourism industry is often attributed in part to the internationally popular television series *Miami Vice* (1984–1989). Despite its focus on crime, drugs and corruption, the series' shots of the Art Deco district, mansions, beaches and high-rises made Miami seem cool and sexy again (Nijman 2011; Alonso 2007; Bush 1999; Gross 1997). Much of this Art Deco architecture was now listed on the National Register of Historic Places thanks to a successful 1979 campaign by the Miami Design Preservation League (Desrosiers-Lauzon 2011; Bachin 2006; Gross 1997). Local tourism boosters, including the Greater Miami Convention and Visitors Bureau, strategically focused on promoting the Art Deco district in an attempt to rejuvenate Miami's image (Alonso 2007).

Towards the end of the 1980s and into the 1990s, South Beach's gentrification was well under way, and the poor and elderly residents of previous years were being displaced (Desrosiers-Lauzon 2011; Gross 1997). The area became trendy, with affluent families, artists and a significant LGBT community moving in (Desrosiers-Lauzon 2011; Gross 1997). The 1990s saw Miami Beach regain its glitzy image and celebrity clientele, as well as evolving into a premier LGBT destination (Kanai & Kenttamaa-Squires 2015; Revels 2011; Gross 1997).

Present context

In contemporary imaginaries, Miami still carries associations from the past – as a winter playground, as a retiree's paradise, as a drug and crime capital, as a glamorous holiday destination – but it has evolved as well. Over recent decades, Miami has developed from being a quintessential resort town into a burgeoning global city, with its downtown becoming a major centre for international trade and banking. Although its economy has been increasingly diversifying, tourism remains one of Miami's most important industries. Miami's tourist arrivals continue to grow, albeit not as rapidly as emerging resort destinations. In 2016, Miami received a record high 15.7 million overnight visitors contributing $25.5 billion in expenditure (see Table 2.4; Greater Miami Convention & Visitors Bureau 2017). Of these visitors, roughly half are international and half are domestic. Most international visitors are from Latin America (68 per cent), with Europe and Canada being smaller, but still important, markets. Overall, the top international markets are Canada, Colombia, Brazil and Argentina. A far cry from the elderly tourist base of the 1970s, Miami now attracts mostly young people – only 13.6 per cent of vacationers in 2015 were over the age of 55. Visitor numbers are fairly consistent throughout the year, peaking in December, January and March.

One of the city's current tourism campaigns – marked by the tagline 'It's So Miami' – aims to accentuate Miami's variety and diversity by showcasing the region's iconic elements as well as lesser-known aspects of its lived spatiality, like its cultural life and natural attractions. The campaign's posters depict beaches, palm trees, cocktails, shopping, parties, Art Deco and high-rises, but also art galleries, the Everglades, and cultural arts such as performances by orchestras and ballets. One such image features an expensive sports car (a McLaren MP4–12C) parked outside a shop selling 50 cent Cuban coffees, with patrons including an elderly Hispanic man, a woman in exercise gear, and a few young men in corporate attire. The use of juxtaposition clearly sets out to capture Miami's diversity, while also inadvertently pointing to its inequalities (see also Chapter 6).

The theme of this campaign carries throughout Miami's other promotional efforts. The city's official tourism website presents the destination in the expected, traditional ways to appeal to mass tourists, while also emphasising alternative attractions. Miami is described as offering exclusive nightlife, shopping, restaurants, 'picturesque' weather, unique architecture, water activities (sailing, snorkelling, fishing), golf courses and casinos (Greater Miami Convention & Visitors Bureau 2018, 2017). Despite the success of these

Table 2.4 Overnight visitors to Miami, 2011–2016

Year	Visitors	Growth rate
2011	13,444,200	-
2012	13,908,600	+3.4%
2013	14,218,900	+2.2%
2014	14,536,200	+2.2%
2015	15,496,300	+6.6%
2016	15,724,300	+1.5%

Source: Greater Miami Convention & Visitors Bureau (2017).

familiar facets of Miami's tourism industry, promotional material from both unofficial and official tourism organisations highlights what else the region has to offer:

> M[iami] is intoxicatingly beautiful, with palm trees swaying in the breeze and South Beach's famous Art Deco buildings glowing in the warm sunlight. Even so, it's the people … that make it so noteworthy. … Miami has a range of districts that mirror its variegated cultural, economic and social divisions. (Rough Guides 2018b)
>
> there's less-conventional beauty: a poetry slam in a converted warehouse, or a Venezuelan singing Metallica en español in a Coral Gables karaoke bar, or the passing shalom/buenas días traded between Orthodox Jews and Cuban exiles. Miami is so many things. All glamorous, in every sense of the word. (Lonely Planet 2015b)
>
> the Miami area offers multiple enticements for everyone: The trendy nightlife of South Beach, bejeweled by the eye candy of the Art Deco district. The bustle of Calle Ocho and the highly caffeinated energy of Little Havana. The plush hotels of Miami Beach and the historic hideaways of Coral Gables. (Visit Florida 2018)

The Greater Miami Convention & Visitors Bureau (2018) aims to capitalise on the region's size and heterogeneity by positioning it as 'a paradise of interconnected oceanfront cities, urban hubs, charming villages and tropical parks'. Beyond Miami Beach (which attracts 55 per cent of overnight visitors [Greater Miami Convention & Visitors Bureau 2017]), tourists can also choose to explore numerous other neighbourhoods like Coconut Grove, Coral Gables, the Design District, Little Haiti, Little Havana, Overtown and Wynwood, which are sold to the consumer as providing unique historical, cultural and natural attractions.

As is clear in the descriptions above, the local people are one of Miami's main selling points. In stark contrast to the rest of Florida,[16] more than half of the population of Miami-Dade County are foreign-born, with significant numbers of Cubans, Haitians, Colombians, Jamaicans, Nicaraguans and Venezuelans (United States Census Bureau 2018; Nijman 2011; Portes & Stepick 1993). Hispanic and Latino peoples account for more than 67 per cent of the county, with another 18.5 per cent being black and only 13.8 per cent being non-Hispanic white (United States Census Bureau 2018).[17] This, along with its geographic centrality in the Americas, has earned Miami the title of 'capital of Latin America' in the media (Rose 2015; Alonso 2007).

As well as its Hispanic and Caribbean cultures, Miami also promotes its Native American, African American and Jewish heritage. These different cultural groups have formed particular enclaves in the region, giving tourists the option to 'experience' each culture and its history by visiting these places. For example, Overtown (previously Colored Town) is the formerly segregated neighbourhood next to Downtown Miami, established in the Jim Crow era to house black workers. Today, it is advertised as 'Historic Overtown', with tourist attractions including murals, the Lyric Theatre and soul food restaurants. Further emphasising the region's local cultures, the official tourism website features a series of 'insider's guides' (much like the 'inside stories' on the Gold Coast's tourism website) to Miami's neighbourhoods in the form of short videos narrated by residents. Locals are also identified as a key target market, since their patronage is vital to sustaining tourism services and attractions during seasonal lows. The website reminds residents that 'you live where they vacation' – in a 'paradise', a 'playground' – and encourages them to break out of their routines in order to experience Miami like a tourist (Greater Miami Convention & Visitors Bureau 2018).

Initial impressions

Arriving in Miami, I marvelled at its similarities to the Gold Coast – a long strip of high-rises on the oceanfront, and expanses of sparkling blue water surrounded by palm trees and mansions. I stayed in an Airbnb apartment off Washington Avenue, one of the main strips running parallel to the beach, the other two being Collins Avenue and Ocean Drive. Washington and Collins Avenues were lined with palm trees, retail outlets, restaurants, convenience stores, bars and a few hotels on either side. Ocean Drive (which I described to people back home as 'the Cavill Avenue of Miami') had low- to mid-rise Art Deco facades housing hotels, bars and restaurants on one side, with the neatly landscaped Lummus Park on the other, and the beach beyond that. Due to its historic architecture, most of the portion of South Beach where I stayed has been protected from the rampant, large-scale development characteristic of most contemporary resorts.

As with Cancún, I was in Miami during Spring Break. South Beach, and Ocean Drive in particular, had a distinct party vibe, filled with rowdy young adults in beachwear. There were a few older couples and groups, and very few families with small children. The following excerpt from my field journal captures some of the rhythms one late afternoon to early evening when I was out in South Beach:

> I'm at the corner of Washington Avenue and 13th Street, and four girls in bikinis just walked past me holding huge, colourful plastic cups filled with what I can reasonably assume is alcohol. One girl laughs 'I can't believe how drunk I am right now', her friends run across the road and another shouts 'I hope we don't get arrested!' …
>
> Ocean Drive is teeming with people [see Figure 2.19]. The sun is setting, but most are still in beachwear, board shorts, swimsuits, sarongs. People are dancing and drinking on their balconies, watching the street below. Dance music is blaring from the different bars, filling the streets, and every few minutes a car drives by blasting a rap song, throwing its own tune into the mix. They drive past *very* slowly, of course, because the

Figure 2.19 Crowds on Ocean Drive, South Beach

street is ridiculously congested with fancy cars – convertibles, SUVs, Lamborghinis, Jaguars, Aston Martins, Ferraris and Porsches – all with their windows down playing hip hop or rap. ... I can't imagine it's an efficient route to take [see Figure 2.20]. But by the looks of the cars, I feel like half of these people are just driving here to be seen in them.

From the footpath along Ocean Drive, I cut across the grass to see what's going on at the paved boardwalk in Lummus Park. ... People are walking and jogging along, riding their bikes, others are standing in groups chatting. Where the sand starts I see people playing volleyball. Further down the beach, I stop to join a crowd of spectators – we're watching athletic, attractive, half-naked people performing chin-ups and other displays of athleticism. A few of them start to do gymnastic tricks and pole dance moves, which garners more attention and praise from the crowd [see Figure 2.21]. Normally I'd feel weird stopping here to watch and take photos, but everyone else is doing it – these informal performers are creating a spectacle for us to enjoy, and the voyeuristic aspect seems to be normalised and invited. (Field journal, 15 March 2014)

The early evening period, as described above, was the busiest time of day around Ocean Drive. In the morning it was considerably quieter, with people out jogging, on bicycles, Segways or roller skates, or going to breakfast (see Figure 2.22). From noon onwards, the number of people increased before peaking in the evening. Once it was dark, the strip became progressively

Figure 2.20 Traffic along Ocean Drive, South Beach

Figure 2.21 Athletic men at Lummus Park, South Beach

Figure 2.22 Daytime in Lummus Park, South Beach

quieter along the pathways, although the bars and restaurants remained consistently full. Late at night, activity was most intensified around nightclubs, which are scattered in clusters of two or three across Miami Beach and into Downtown Miami.

Away from Ocean Drive, Miami Beach felt surprisingly laid back, with quiet streets, mid-rise apartment blocks (many in Art Deco or MiMo style), grocery stores, parks, shopping strips like Lincoln Road, dining precincts such as Española Way (styled in Spanish colonial architecture), and a beautiful historic City Hall, now used to house organisations like the Miami Beach Cinematheque, the LGBT Visitor Center and the Miami-Dade Gay & Lesbian Chamber of Commerce. Although I was expecting Miami to be a lot like the Gold Coast – and, indeed, it did remind me a lot of home – exploring these lived spaces revealed to me many of the particularities and idiosyncrasies that make Miami unique.

As the most mature (and perhaps the most famous) destination in this study, it is no surprise that traces of Miami can be found in other resorts. These traces are most obvious on the Gold Coast, a place that has long defined its identity in terms of comparisons to Miami. My expectations of Miami, informed by popular imaginaries, popular cultural representations and their associated narratives, were at times reaffirmed but at other times unsettled through my *in situ* experiences of the city. I took pleasure in encountering things that were common back home, but that I have rarely seen in more 'normal', conventional cities – palm trees lining the streets, waterfront mansions on artificial islands, and an intense focus on voyeurism regarding bodies: on the beach, on hotel balconies and in luxury cars. However, I was also taken by Miami's distinctive elements – the preservation of its Art Deco buildings, the influence of Latin and LGBT cultures, and the thriving arts scene. Like the Gold Coast, Miami is in the process of evolving from a resort destination to a diverse, vibrant urban milieu.

Ibiza, Spain

Blessed with a striking rocky coastline, scenic beaches and a warm climate, Ibiza is one of Europe's most popular summertime vacation spots. Its claim to fame, however, is its reputation as the clubbing capital of the world. Ibiza is known as a youthful destination which caters less to tourists focused on relaxation or family holidays, and more to those seeking partying, drugs, sex and indulgence in sensuous pleasures. Ibiza is also an important and unique site for built heritage, although this is often absent from popular imaginaries, overshadowed by more dominant narratives.

Ibiza is an island in the western Mediterranean, located just off the east coast of mainland Spain. It is the third largest island in the Balearic Islands archipelago, one of Spain's autonomous communities. At 572 square kilometres, Ibiza is roughly the same size as Phuket Province, but has a population of only 143,856[18] (Institut d'Estadística de les Illes Balears 2017). Tourism has been the most significant driving force in the development and economic growth of the Balearic Islands. Ibiza, in particular, has reaped substantial economic benefits from tourism, boasting one of Spain's highest income rates per capita (Briggs 2013; D'Andrea 2007, 2006).

Urban development in Ibiza has been primarily focused along the coastline, with several smaller towns scattered inland. Tourism development is most concentrated in the following areas: Eivissa[19] (Ibiza in Spanish, also commonly referred to as Ibiza Town), the largest city and historic old town; Sant Antoni de Portmany (San Antonio), the most mature and most iconic tourist hub on the island, known for its popularity among young British tourists; the airport and surrounding beaches (such as Platja d'en Bossa/Playa d'en Bossa) in the Sant Josep de sa Talaia municipality; and to a lesser extent, Santa Eulària des Riu (see Figure 2.23). Other areas of the island have some tourism infrastructure but are less popular destinations for visitors to stay in. The village of Sant Rafel de sa Creu (San Rafeal), for example, is home to two of the island's biggest nightclubs, Amnesia and Privilege, but offers little in the way of accommodation options.[20] It is clear that the term 'Ibiza' is used among tourists as a catch-all term that may refer to any number of these different areas, much as 'Thailand' tends to stand for a collection of resorts in popular discourse.

History

Tourism infrastructure and facilities started to develop in the Balearic Islands during the 1920s to mid-1930s. These efforts were supported by pro-tourism

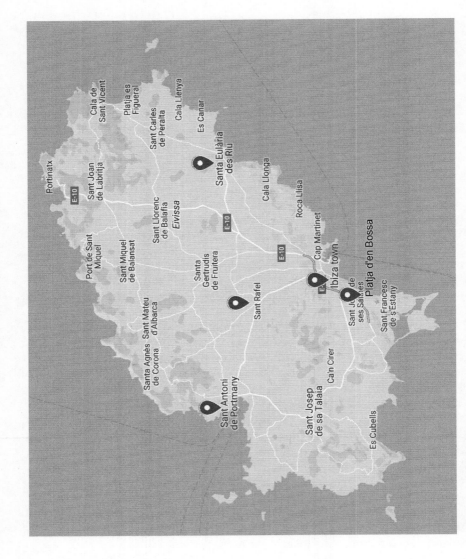

Figure 2.23 **Map of Ibiza (Map data ©2017 Google)**

regional government policies and capital from investors within the Balearics and from Northern Europe who were interested in cashing in on the success of other nearby Mediterranean resorts, specifically those along the French Riviera (Pons, Salamanca & Murray 2014; Bardolet & Sheldon 2008). Although development was predominantly focused on the Balearics' largest island, Mallorca (Majorca), Ibiza benefited as well (Pons et al. 2014). From the 1930s to the 1950s, Ibiza consistently attracted small numbers of visitors, primarily middle-class Europeans, and some cultural and artistic figures – Walter Benjamin now being one of the most famous examples (Pons et al. 2014; Briggs 2013; Polo & Valle 2008).

Briggs (2013) notes that many of these early visitors were, like Benjamin, long stay visitors rather than short-term tourists, with Germans, Italians and other Spaniards seeking temporary escape from the fascist political regimes in their own countries. Similarly, from the late 1950s into the 1960s and early 1970s, Ibiza became popular among bohemians, beatniks and hippies. This contributed to imaginaries and myths of the island as an escapist paradise, with the hippie associations bringing an increasing emphasis on expressions of hedonism, sexuality and liberation (Briggs 2013; D'Andrea 2007). With the full advent of mass tourism, however, Ibiza quickly transformed from a quiet, alternative retreat into an international destination for packaged holidays (Pons et al. 2014; Briggs 2013; Bennett 2004; Diken & Laustsen 2004). As a result, seaside resort towns throughout Ibiza grew rapidly over the following decades.

One of the most important aspects of Ibiza's evolution as a tourism destination has been the popularity of its nightlife since the 1980s. The rise of club culture in Ibiza was fuelled by the burgeoning electronic dance music scene and its links to the use of the party drug ecstasy (Sandvoss 2014; Wilson 2006). DJs in Ibiza at this time mixed electronic dance music styles originating elsewhere – house music from Chicago and New York City and techno from Detroit, along with reggae, rock and Euro pop influences – to create a distinct style known as 'Balearic Beat' (Goulding & Shankar 2011; D'Andrea 2007; Wilson 2006; Bennett 2001, 2004). This style was exported to the UK by DJs and British youth (one of Ibiza's largest tourist markets), playing a pivotal role in the emergence of acid house music and rave culture in the late 1980s (Wilson 2006).

Subsequently, Ibiza earned a certain cachet derived from its historical importance in the development of dance music, and it is now often considered one of the birth places of rave and the 'spiritual home' (Sandvoss 2014, p. 116) of electronic dance music (Goulding & Shankar 2011; Wilson 2006; Bennett 2004). Ibiza became and remains a main node in the international clubbing circuit and a highly influential site of innovation for contemporary dance music. Over the years, however, Ibiza's clubbing milieu has transformed from alternative and countercultural to commercialised and mainstream (D'Andrea 2007; Wilson 2006; Bennett 1999). As D'Andrea (2006) argues, '[c]apitalist interests have largely undermined nightclubs' organic connections with hippie, gay and bohemian countercultures, integrating such venues into the island's tourism industry and its logic of predatory profiteering' (p. 62). While the mainstream popularity of Ibiza's nightlife provided a major boost to the island's economy, the associated behaviours – binge drinking, illicit drug use, increased incidences of violence and disorderly conduct – tarnished the island's image.

Issues with Ibiza's tourism industry were not restricted to its club culture. During the 1990s, it became apparent to Ibiza officials and residents that the island's tourism model was having damaging effects that threatened the long-term sustainability of the industry and the environment. Serra Cantallops (2004) observes that this model had become 'based on volume, price competition, standardisation of the holiday experience ... mainly focused on sun, sand and sea' (p. 41). Until this point, tourism development in Ibiza had been largely unregulated and poorly planned, leading to problems with overcrowding, extreme pressure on natural resources, high levels of waste production and water consumption, and the deterioration of beaches and rocky coastal areas (Briggs 2013; Aguiló, Alegre & Sard 2005; Serra Cantallops 2004). These issues were compounded by Ibiza's underdeveloped public infrastructure and tourist facilities that were quickly becoming obsolete (Aguiló et al. 2005). Tourism had also become progressively more seasonal: tour operators focused their business on the lucrative summer months, resulting in excessive demands on resources during those times, followed by periods of seasonal unemployment (Briggs 2013; D'Andrea 2007).

In response to this situation, Ibiza's local government set out to dismantle assumptions that the island offered little more than sun, sand and sex (Jarvie & Lusher 2001), and to transform its tourism model into one that favoured quality over quantity. That is, rather than attempting to attract as many tourists as possible, the aim was to attract the *right kind* of tourists – those who spent more money, stayed longer, were more environmentally-conscious, and interested in a range of activities and attractions beyond only beaches and nightlife. Regulations were passed during the 1990s to limit urban growth and carrying capacity by restricting the construction of additional hotel beds (Pons et al. 2014; Bardolet & Sheldon 2008; Serra Cantallops 2004). Measures to increase competitiveness were also introduced, such as encouraging the modernisation of existing tourism accommodation and facilities and requiring all new hotels to be at least a four-star rating (Serra Cantallops 2004). To mitigate seasonal demand and alleviate overcrowding in specific tourist hubs, strategies have been undertaken to diversify the industry by, for example, increased promotion of convention/conference tourism, ecotourism, rural tourism and cultural and heritage tourism (Anderson 2009; Bardolet & Sheldon 2008; Serra Cantallops 2004; Jarvie & Lusher 2001).

In 2001, the government of the Balearics introduced a tourism tax, the Ecotax, aimed at generating funds[21] to gradually change the dominant model for tourism in order to make the industry more sustainable; support host communities and improve their quality of life; protect against further environmental damage; and preserve cultural heritage (Serra Cantallops 2004). The policy was welcomed by residents, but strongly opposed by the tourism industry, particularly the large hotel companies and tour operators who lobbied against it (Serra Cantallops 2004). Consequently, the Ecotax was short-lived – it was enforced from 2002, but abolished in 2003 following the election of a new regional government (Serra Cantallops 2004). A similar tax, the Sustainable Tourism Tax, was re-introduced in 2016, again with negative media coverage and opposition from the tourism industry (see Calder 2016; Salmon 2016; Sobot 2016). In 2018, it was announced that the tax would be doubled for tourists visiting Ibiza during peak season (Sobot 2018).

Present context

Despite these measures, tourism in Ibiza has not yet experienced significant changes. It is still a global clubbing mecca closely associated with dance music, partying, drugs, sex, sun and sand. As a consequence, tourism continues to be very seasonal (significantly more so than any of the other destinations discussed in this book) due to the importance of a warm, sunny climate for beach activities, and because nightclubs are only open during the summer (marked by 'opening parties' from late May to mid-June and 'closing parties' from mid-September to early October). May to September are the most popular months (especially for international tourists from Britain, Italy, Germany and France), with 82 per cent of the total annual visitors staying during this time[22] (Institut d'Estadística de les Illes Balears 2018). In winter months, the majority of tourists are Spanish (domestic). Visitor numbers are still increasing, with Ibiza receiving more than 3.2 million visitors in 2017 (see Table 2.5).

Ibiza's reputation as a hedonistic clubbing capital, and sun and sand destination, persists because of how it is continuously represented by popular media and lived by the tourists who visit it. The associated imaginaries of Ibiza are shaped and reinforced by international news media, current affairs programs, documentaries, films like *Kevin & Perry Go Large* (2000), *It's All Gone Pete Tong* (2004) and *Ibiza* (2018), dance music compilations and song lyrics,[23] travel

Table 2.5 Visitors to Ibiza, 2012–2017

Year	Visitors	Growth rate
2012	2,334,692	-
2013	2,447,575	+4.8%
2014	2,733,558	+11.8%
2015	2,779,796	+1.7%
2016	3,061,896	+10.1%
2017	3,236,268	+5.7%

Source: Institut d'Estadística de les Illes Balears (2018, 2016).

websites and publications, and the stories and myths circulated online and in person by those who have visited the island. In the case of Ibiza, these unofficial narratives significantly override the official tourism narratives produced by the local government, which position the destination differently.

Ibiza's official tourism website features images advertising Dalt Vila (the historic old town of Ibiza), cycling tracks, local cuisine, traditional cultural practices, family activities, environmental sustainability, and a 'cosmopolitan' nightlife and music scene (Consell d'Eivissa 2018). Although the website promotes a range of attractions and activities such as adventure sports, hiking, horse riding, kayaking, food and wine, travels through the country-side, scenic views and beaches, there is a strong focus on Ibiza's cultural heritage and historical structures. Since 1999, Ibiza has been a part of UNESCO's World Heritage List due to its highly valued cultural and natural assets, including several archaeological sites, Renaissance era military architecture found in Ibiza Town (see Figure 2.24), and unique marine ecosystems (UNESCO World Heritage Centre 2015). The official tourism website describes the island as 'authentic and natural', a 'melting pot of peoples and cultures' with a 'rich catalogue of architectural and cultural heritage sites [that] will pull in anyone keen on an enthralling history lesson', and provides lists of heritage sites and museums to visit (Consell d'Eivissa 2018).

The local council promotes these attractions and activities to highlight that Ibiza is about more than its most common associations. Online travel websites also mention alternatives, but it is nightlife that is nonetheless foregrounded:

Figure 2.24 Dalt Vila, Ibiza Town

The all-night raver, the boho-cool hippie chick, the sexiest babe on the beach – Ibiza is all this and more to those who have a soft spot for the party-loving sister of the Balearics. ... But there's more to this sun-kissed, beach-bejewelled, pine-clad island than meets the bleary eye. (Lonely Planet 2015a)

Ibiza ... is definitely one of Europe's favourite nightlife playgrounds. Ibiza boasts more than 100 miles of coastline with some 50 beaches, plus plenty of restaurants, bars, and water sports – and clubs, of course. Fit in a little culture and visit Ibiza's UNESCO-designated old town. (TripAdvisor 2018)

Despite nightlife's popularity, and its overwhelming presence in the lived spaces of the tourist hubs, its significance is downplayed in official promotional material. Even on its page on nightlife, the official tourism website makes sure to reinforce its natural and cultural offerings: 'Ibiza is a little island where fiesta, glamorous beaches and the latest musical trends fuse with tranquility, the outdoors and a cultural and natural heritage linked to many centuries of tradition' (Consell d'Eivissa 2018). Considering the previous discussion of Ibiza's tourism model, it is clear that the growing emphasis on natural and cultural attractions is a strategic manoeuvre targeted at diversifying the tourist market and attracting higher quality, higher spending visitors. Ibiza positions itself as being able to cater to discerning cultural tourists, families and adventurers, rather than just young partyers. These are people who are likely to be seeking peaceful yet enjoyable vacations at any time of year, not only in summer.

Initial impressions

I visited Ibiza in mid-July 2014, at the peak of the clubbing season, opting to stay in Playa d'en Bossa. Having been to Paris and Barcelona in the two weeks prior to arriving in Ibiza, I could understand the appeal of the island for Europeans: the weather was sunny, warm and dry; the water was bright blue, clean and still; and each day there were spectacular sunrises and sunsets. The streets of Playa d'en Bossa were, by comparison, quite insipid. An excerpt from my field journal outlines some of my observations along the main road on which my hotel was situated (Carretera Playa d'en Bossa):

Playa d'en Bossa seems completely geared to the clubbing crowd, and I can't see how any other type of tourist would want to be here. Right next to my hotel is Ushuaia (a hotel and open air club playing house music all day long) and across the road from that is Space (one of the biggest and most famous nightclubs here). On both sides, the main road is covered in billboards and posters promoting club nights – at Space, Amnesia, Pacha, Privilege – and DJs ... [see Figure 2.25]

Figure 2.25 Club posters in Playa d'en Bossa

It seems much less built up here than the other resorts I've been to. The side of the road closer to the beach has a row of small, single-storey shops, mainly restaurants/cafes, convenience stores, nightclub merchandise stores and souvenir shops [See Figure 2.26]. There's a 'hippie' store and 'hippie' market area, which seem to be commodified throwbacks to the destination's bohemian days. The souvenir shops are just like the ones in Thailand ... fluro singlets and other clothing with phrases like 'I ♥ Ibiza', 'What happens in Ibiza stays in Ibiza', 'Ibiza All Star', 'You Only Live Once', 'I'm in Ibiza Bitch' (a reference to LMFAO's song 'I'm in Miami Bitch') and 'Sexy Bitch' (a David Guetta song).

Many of these shops and eateries are blasting dance music. I can't seem to escape it – it's in my hotel, in the streets, in cafes, and even in the corner store where I'm trying to buy milk ... Out the front of every couple of shops there's vendors selling 'disco tickets' (entry to specific events at nightclubs). They're all calling out club names to me and other passersby – 'Ushuaia, Ushuaia, Ushuaia!', 'Space, Space, Space!' ...

Apart from the vendors and other workers, there are little signs of everyday local life here. All of the people in the streets seem to be tourists. There's groups of guys walking around in shorts, loose singlets and sunnies, and groups of tanned girls in bikinis, short shorts and crop tops (some in high heels, which seems impractical at best). ... A lot of them are wearing the souvenir-style Ibiza shirts and club merch – shirts branded with Space, Sankeys, Pacha and 'F*** Me I'm Famous!' (the name of David Guetta's club night at Pacha) ... I imagine the appeal of buying these must be to wear them back home as a status symbol, to let everyone know you've been to Ibiza, that you're a part of that scene, to bolster your subcultural capital. (Field journal, 15 July 2014)

Playa d'en Bossa had a distinct party atmosphere, reminiscent of Haad Rin in Koh Phangan and the Gold Coast during Schoolies. The rhythms of the area reflected this. Throughout the night, the streets were swarming with young people, peaking at around midnight with the end of the DJ sets at Ushuaia and the opening of Space across the street. Crowds of people then lined up for 'Discobuses' (public transport infrastructure devoted to taking tourists to nightclubs around the island) to get them to other venues and hotels. Numerous food outlets stayed open late, serving up junk food like pizza to satisfy intoxicated clubbers. The quietest period was in the morning, around 6 am to 10 am. The streets and beaches were almost completely empty at this time, and finding anywhere that served breakfast before midday was a challenge. The volume of people increased throughout the day, with hungover tourists slowly emerging from their hotel rooms to sunbake or grab something to eat.

I found the leisure-dominated rhythms and atmosphere in Playa d'en Bossa were considerably different to those in the island's other tourist hubs. Both Ibiza Town and San Antonio were much quieter, with rhythms more closely approaching 'normal' everyday life than what I observed in Playa d'en Bossa. Ibiza Town, for example, was more built up, with clean, narrow streets lined with older, mid-rise buildings with shopfronts on the ground level and

Figure 2.26 A main road in Playa d'en Bossa

residents living above, indicated by flags, towels and pot plants on balconies, among other personal touches [see Figure 2.27]. The centrepiece of the area is the historic old town (Dalt Vila), featuring a castle, cathedral, museums and cobblestone walkways. The tourists here were radically different from those of Playa d'en Bossa – older couples and families with DSLR cameras and practical backpacks, clearly interested in exploring cultural attractions. There were no 'Disco Ticket' vendors on the streets, house music did not follow me everywhere I went, and promotional material for nightclubs was scarce, save for a few club merchandise stores. Overall, there seemed to be more of a sense that everyday lives of residents were being carried out here, with elderly people out for walks, young mothers pushing prams, and local businesses and services in operation.

Much like Koh Phangan, Ibiza's popular imaginaries are dominated by associations with youthful transgression, hedonism and partying. The regional and local governments of Ibiza, however, are making a concerted effort to change the island's image and promote a more sustainable tourism model, as demonstrated by official tourism narratives and recent policy initiatives. In particular, there is an emphasis on quality over quantity, and on attracting a more diverse range of visitors, such as cultural tourists and ecotourists (similar to Thailand's current objectives). This is, potentially, a somewhat

Figure 2.27 Mid-rise apartment building in Ibiza Town

precarious strategy considering not only Ibiza's reputation for partying and excess, but also the multitude of other culture- and nature-oriented destinations in Europe with which it must compete. As far as my observations of Ibiza's rhythms could indicate, this strategy has only been marginally successful as yet – there are, indeed, a few cultural tourists present in Ibiza Town and near other historical sites on the island, but Playa d'en Bossa and San Antonio remain occupied by traditional mass tourists. Clearly, in Ibiza, there are significant and various tensions between the desires of the tourists, the tourism industry, and the local and regional governments, and great disparities in how the destination is imagined, represented and lived.

Conclusion

Throughout this chapter, a number of commonalities among these resorts have emerged. Each place is an example of tourism urbanisation (Mullins 1992) in that its development has been instigated and sustained primarily by tourism and leisure industries. Despite other types of economic activity (such as farming) existing early on, these places did not start to thrive until they became holiday destinations. In contrast to more conventional cities, which have their roots in producing and trading commodities, the growth of resorts has relied on consumption, on selling *themselves* as commodities.

Each resort has loosely followed the phases of tourist area development outlined by Butler (2006) and Prideaux (2004), evolving from a small-scale local destination to a large-scale international destination. This evolution has been more rapid in some resorts than in others, with Cancún in particular moving through the initial phases very quickly. Whether development was spearheaded by governments, entrepreneurs or foreign investors, each resort started out as a relaxed beachside getaway, often for alternative tourists or travellers looking for 'authentic' experiences. As discussed in Chapter 1, while these initial visitors may have been motivated by the search for hidden, 'untouched' destinations, their actions functioned to situate these places on the mainstream tourism circuit. Through the very presence of alternative tourists, these places became 'cool', gradually attracting more visitors and prompting tourism boosters to capitalise on their emerging popularity. As accessibility, visitor numbers and tourism services and facilities increased, they became known as sites for Fordist-style mass tourism, losing their initial cachet and earning negative reputations for being 'overdeveloped' or 'touristy' (sharing similarities with Butler's [2006] consolidation and stagnation phases). Consequently, while these resorts are still generally experiencing growth in tourist arrivals, this has been punctuated by brief periods of stagnation and decline caused by natural disasters, regional or global-economic crises, outdated facilities, competition from nearby destinations or unfavourable media coverage.

The success of these resorts is due to a combination of factors, including the natural landscape and climate, a supportive government or enthusiastic entrepreneurs and developers, a carefully crafted image, and a commitment to catering to the needs and desires of tourists. Although they all offer a particular brand of sun, sand and sex mass tourism, they each receive different types of visitors – different proportions of domestic and international visitors, and of different origins, and with different motivations – and have different struggles – for example, Ibiza's problem with highly seasonal tourism, or Miami's challenge to continually reinvent itself and stay trendy.

Most of these resorts have multiple centres rather than a singular, traditional CBD. Indeed, the tourist hubs – or recreational business districts – are some of the most developed and busiest areas of each place. Although, as noted in resort morphology literature, development is centred on proximity to the coastline, how this manifests is different in each place – the Gold Coast is a series of linear strips, Ibiza and Thailand have hubs spread across the islands, and Miami and Cancún have several centres for different activities. Although still reliant on tourism, some of these places (namely, Miami and the Gold Coast) are evolving into more cosmopolitan, 'serious' cities with diverse economies and vibrant cultural scenes.

Perhaps in an attempt to rejuvenate themselves and prevent decline, these resorts are attempting to expand their offerings, moving away from solely promoting beach tourism and adopting more of a post-Fordist approach, incorporating alternatives like cultural tourism and ecotourism. Although often considered to be mutually exclusive, mass tourism and alternative tourism co-exist in these sites (Kontogeorgopoulos 2009, 2004a, 2004b; Torres 2002). The growing interest in alternative tourism may be in response to the negative effects associated with mass tourism, which progressively puts more pressure on mature destinations – for example, a perceived increase in crime (particularly drug trafficking and prostitution), traffic congestion, stress on infrastructure, pollution, environmental degradation, and, as a result, disgruntled residents (see Chapters 5 and 6). Promoting alternative, niche tourism sectors attracts types of tourists who are seen as higher-spending, more respectful,[24] and more likely to occupy areas outside of the most intensified tourism districts (in which the aforementioned problems are at their worst). In the process, resorts are capitalising on lesser known elements of their local distinctiveness and expanding imaginaries of what exactly these places are like (see Chapter 4). Advertising a variety of experiences can remedy periods of stagnation and decline by making a destination more competitive in the global market. These changes signify an interest in the long-term sustainability and growth of the tourism industry, but not necessarily any great concern for environmental sustainability. That is, strategies for sustainable tourism, rather than sustainable development, are the primary concern (Kontogeorgopoulos 1999).

The above commonalities comprise some of the characteristics and processes which have come to mark resorts as distinct kinds of urban milieux. In the following chapter, I continue to analyse these shared aspects, focusing particularly on their popular imaginaries, and how this is reflected and manifested both representationally – as dominant narratives of resort identity – and materially – as dominant rhythms.

Notes

1 However, the city council has recently been attempting to brand the suburb of Southport as the CBD (see Chapter 4).
2 A reference to the region's location in relation to Brisbane (Prideaux 2004).
3 Unlike the other resorts in this book, Thailand is largely marketed as a nation, and Phuket and Koh Phangan do not have their own official tourism websites.
4 2014 figure.
5 2015 figure.
6 2014 figure.
7 2015 figure.
8 This narrative, often applied to beach tourism in 'exotic' locations, is highly problematic as it ignores the fact that local people have occupied these sites for a long time. 'Untouched', then, means not yet significantly altered by Western development.
9 A colloquial phrase which refers to sexual acts performed on the client at the end of the massage.
10 Although most of the literature credits the Mexican government for the development of Cancún, Ambrosie (2015) critiques this narrative, instead arguing that the resort's initial success should be attributed more specifically to the efforts of the Bank of Mexico and INFRATUR.
11 Xcaret and Xel-Há offer activities such as animal encounters (swimming with dolphins, sharks or stingrays), scuba diving, snorkelling, ziplining, speed boat rides, participation in re-enactments of Maya rituals, river tours, jungle walks and shopping. Attractions include cenotes, chapels, caves, spas and Maya ruins.
12 This is unsurprising given that the city has progressed relatively rapidly through the various phases of tourism development (as outlined by Butler [2006] and Prideaux [2004]) since it was built to be an international resort from the outset.
13 2016 figures.
14 In 1970, 85 per cent of Miami Beach's population were Jewish (Desrosiers-Lauzon 2011).
15 With its expansive coastline and close proximity to South America, Miami became a hotspot for international drug trafficking (Dombrink & Thompson 1990).
16 Only 19.9 per cent of people in Florida are foreign-born, and 59.9 per cent are non-Hispanic white (United States Census Bureau 2018).
17 2016 figures. This profile is very different in Miami Beach, with roughly 40 per cent of the population being non-Hispanic white (United States Census Bureau 2010).
18 2016 figure.
19 In the Balearic Islands, as in some of Spain's other autonomous communities, Catalan and Spanish are both official languages, and thus, towns/beaches on the island may be referred to by their names in either language. Among tourists, it is more common to use the Spanish names – Ibiza, San Antonio, etc. – but most signage and official institutional websites and documents use Catalan – Eivissa, Sant Antoni, etc.
20 As such, club patrons usually arrive by bus or taxi.
21 These funds were to go directly to the Tourist and Natural Areas Restoration Fund to ensure the money would be used as intended (Serra Cantallops 2004).
22 2017 figures.
23 Songs like 'I Took A Pill In Ibiza' (Seeb Remix) by Mike Posner (2016) and 'Miami 2 Ibiza' (feat. Tinie Tempah) by Swedish House Mafia (2010).
24 This point is contested – Meethan (2001) suggests that greater disparity of wealth between hosts and (upmarket) guests causes more tensions between the two.

References

Agarwal, S & Shaw, G 2007, 'Re-engineering coastal resorts in Mexico: some management issues', in S Agarwal & G Shaw (eds), *Managing coastal tourism resorts: a global perspective*, Channel View Publications, Clevedon, pp. 216–232.

Aguiló, E, Alegre, J & Sard, M 2005, 'The persistence of the sun and sand tourism model', *Tourism Management*, vol. 26, no. 2, pp. 219–231.

Alonso, G 2007, 'Selling Miami: tourism promotion and immigrant neighbourhoods in the capital of Latin America', in J Rath (ed.), *Tourism, ethnic diversity and the city*, Routledge, New York, pp. 164–180.

Ambrosie, LM 2015, 'Myths of tourism institutionalization and Cancún', *Annals of Tourism Research*, vol. 54, pp. 65–83.

Anderson, W 2009, 'Promoting ecotourism through networks: case studies in the Balearic Islands', *Journal of Ecotourism*, vol. 8, no. 1, pp. 51–69.

Australian Bureau of Statistics 2008, 'Table 3. Estimated resident population, Local Government Areas, Queensland', *Regional population growth, Australia*, cat. no. 3218.0, viewed 23 January 2017, <http://www.abs.gov.au/AUSSTATS/subscriber.nsf/log?opena gent&SLA_1996_2001_2006.xls&3218.0&Data%20Cubes&09B5C998F4842BE9 CA2573210018BB56&0&1996%20to%202006&24.07.2007&Latest>.

Australian Bureau of Statistics 2017, 'Table 3. Estimated resident population, Local Government Areas, Queensland', *Regional population growth, Australia*, cat. no. 3218.0, viewed 10 January 2018, <http://www.abs.gov.au/AUSSTATS/abs@.nsf/ DetailsPage/3218.02016?OpenDocument>.

Bachin, R 2006, *Travel, tourism, and urban growth in Greater Miami: a digital archive*, viewed 20 August 2015, <http://scholar.library.miami.edu/miamidigital/>.

Bardolet, E & Sheldon, PJ 2008, 'Tourism in archipelagos', *Annals of Tourism Research*, vol. 35, no. 4, pp. 900–923.

Bennett, A 1999, 'Subcultures or neo-tribes? Rethinking the relationship between youth, style and musical taste', *Sociology*, vol. 33, no. 3, pp. 599–617.

Bennett, A 2001, *Cultures of popular music*, Open University Press, Buckingham.

Bennett, A 2004, '"Chilled Ibiza": dance tourism and the neo-tribal island community', in K Dawe (ed.), *Island musics*, Berg, Oxford, pp. 123–136.

Blackman, A 2013, *If only I had a heart: a history of the Gold Coast and its economy from 1823 to 2013*, Griffith Business School, Southport.

Briggs, D 2013, *Deviance and risk on holiday: an ethnography of British tourists in Ibiza*, Palgrave Macmillan, Basingstoke.

Brown, DF 2013, 'Tourists as colonizers in Quintana Roo, Mexico', *The Canadian Geographer*, vol. 57, no. 2, pp. 186–205.

Buchanan, JE 1978, *Miami: a chronological & documentary history, 1513–1977*, Oceana Publications, Dobbs Ferry.

Bush, GW 1999, 'Playground of the USA: Miami and the promotion of spectacle', *Pacific Historical Review*, vol. 68, no. 2, pp. 153–172.

Butler, RW 2006, 'The concept of a tourist area cycle of evolution', in RW Butler (ed.), *The tourism area life cycle, vol. 1: applications and modifications*, Channel View Publications, Clevedon, pp. 1–12.

Calder, S 2016, 'Mediterranean islands to slap tax on British holidaymakers. What will it mean for your trip?', *The Independent*, 26 April, viewed 26 January 2017, <http:// www.independent.co.uk/travel/mediterranean-islands-slap-tax-on-british-holidayma kers-what-will-it-mean-for-your-trip-a7000541.html>.

Cancún Convention & Visitors Bureau 2015, *The Cancun Convention & Visitors Bureau Website*, viewed 4 May 2015, <http://cancun.travel/en/>.

Cantillon, Z 2015a, 'Occupying the mainstream: performing hegemonic masculinity in Gold Coast nightclubs', in S Baker, B Robards & B Buttigieg, *Youth cultures and subcultures: Australian perspectives*, Ashgate, Farnham, pp. 183–192.

Cantillon, Z 2015b, 'Polyrhythmia, heterogeneity and urban identity: intersections between "official" and "unofficial" narratives in the socio-spatial practices of Australia's Gold Coast', *Journal of Urban Cultural Studies*, vol. 2, no. 3, pp. 253–274.

Caribbean Tourism Organization 2015, *Individual country statistics (2010, 2009, 2007, 2006, 2004) – Jamaica, Martinique, Mexican Caribbean, Montserrat, Puerto Rico, Saba*, viewed 4 May 2015, <http://www.onecaribbean.org/content/files/strep 4JAMAICAtoSABA.pdf>.

Castellanos, MB 2010a, *A return to servitude: Maya migration and the tourist trade in Cancún*, University of Minnesota Press, Minneapolis.

Castellanos, MB 2010b, 'Cancún and the campo: indigenous migration and tourism development in the Yucatán', in D Berger & AG Wood (eds), *Holiday in Mexico: critical reflections on tourism and tourist encounters*, Duke University Press, Durham, pp. 241–264.

City of Gold Coast 2014, *Gold Coast Destination Tourism Management Plan 2014–2020*, City of Gold Coast, Gold Coast.

Clancy, M 2001, *Exporting paradise: tourism and development in Mexico*, Pergamon, Oxford.

Cohen, E 1982, 'Marginal paradises: bungalow tourism on the islands of Southern Thailand', *Annals of Tourism Research*, vol. 9, pp. 189–228.

Cohen, E 2008, *Explorations in Thai tourism: collected case studies*, Emerald, Bingley.

Consejo Nacional de Población 2018, *Quintana Roo: population projections of selected towns, 2010–2030*, viewed 14 March 2018, <http://www.conapo.gob.mx/work/m odels/CONAPO/Proyecciones/Datos/Proyecciones_municipios_y_localidades/Loca lidades/QuintanaRoo_loc.xlsx>.

Consell d'Eivissa 2018, *Official Tourism Site of Ibiza*, viewed 15 March 2018, <http:// www.ibiza.travel/en/>.

Córdoba Azcárate, M, Baptista, I & Domínguez Rubio, F 2014, 'Enclosures within enclosures and hurricane reconstruction in Cancún, Mexico', *City & Society*, vol. 26, no. 1, pp. 96–116.

Council of the City of Gold Coast 2018, *City Plan*, viewed 5 June 2018, <http://www. goldcoast.qld.gov.au/thegoldcoast/city-plan-2015-19859.html>.

D'Andrea, A 2006, 'The spiritual economy of nightclubs and raves: Osho Sannyasins as party promoters in Ibiza and Pune/Goa', *Culture and Religion*, vol. 7, no. 1, pp. 61–75.

D'Andrea, A 2007, *Global nomads: techno and new age as transnational counter-cultures in Ibiza and Goa*, Routledge, New York.

Davidson, J & Spearritt, P 2000, *Holiday business: tourism in Australia since 1870*, Miegunyah Press, Carlton South.

Dedekorkut-Howes, A & Bosman, C 2015, 'The Gold Coast: Australia's playground?', *Cities*, vol. 42, pp. 70–84.

Dedekorkut-Howes, A, Bosman, C & Leach, A 2016, 'Considering the Gold Coast', in A Dedekorkut-Howes, C Bosman & A Leach (eds), *Off the plan: the urbanisation of the Gold Coast*, CSIRO Publishing, Clayton South, pp. 1–16.

84   *Resort cities and regions*

Department of Provincial Administration 2015a, *Report: demographics and houses, year 2557 – Koh Phangan* [translated], viewed 27 July 2015, <http://stat.dopa.go.th/stat/statnew/statTDD/views/showZoneData.php?rcode=8405&statType=1&year=57>.

Department of Provincial Administration 2015b, *Report: demographics and houses, year 2557 – Phuket* [translated], viewed 27 July 2015, <http://stat.dopa.go.th/stat/statnew/statTDD/views/showDistrictData.php?rcode=83&statType=1&year=57>.

Department of Tourism 2016, *Internal tourism 2015 (by region and province) – south*, viewed 19 October 2016, <http://www.tourism.go.th/farms/uploaded/00Statistic/2015/Internal/Domestic_Q1_Q4_2015_Southern.rar>.

Department of Tourism 2017, *Tourist statistics* [translated], viewed 23 January 2018, <http://www.tourism.go.th/view/1/สถิตินักท่องเที่ยว/TH-TH>.

Desrosiers-Lauzon, G 2011, *Florida's snowbirds: spectacle, mobility, and community since 1945*, McGill-Queen's University Press, Montreal.

Diken, B & Laustsen, B 2004, 'Sea, sun, sex and the discontents of pleasure', *Tourist Studies*, vol. 4, no. 2, pp. 99–114.

Dombrink, J & Thompson, WN 1990, *The last resort: success and failure in campaigns for casinos*, University of Nevada Press, Reno.

Evans, G 2005, 'Mundo Maya: from Cancún to city of culture. World heritage in post-colonial Mesoamerica', in D Harrison & M Hitchcock (eds), *The politics of world heritage: negotiating tourism and conservation*, Channel View Publications, Clevedon, pp. 35–49.

Faulkner, B & Tideswell, C 2006, 'Rejuvenating a maturing tourist destination: the case of the Gold Coast, Australia', in RW Butler (ed.), *The tourism area life cycle, vol. 1: applications and modifications*, Channel View Publications, Clevedon, pp. 306–335.

Fondo Nacional de Fomento al Turismo 2015, *Cancún: general information*, viewed 4 May 2015, <http://www.fonatur.gob.mx/en/proyectos_desarrollos/cancun/index.asp>.

Geordie Shore 2011–present, television series, MTV (UK and Ireland), London.

George, PS 1981, 'Passage to the new Eden: tourism in Miami from Flagler through Everest G. Sewell', *The Florida Historical Quarterly*, vol. 59, no. 4, pp. 440–463.

Gibbons, JD & Fish, M 1988, 'Thailand's international tourism: successes and current challenges', *International Journal of Hospitality Management*, vol. 7, no. 2, pp. 161–166.

Goulding, C & Shankar, A 2011, 'Club culture, neotribalism and ritualised behaviour', *Annals of Tourism Research*, vol. 38, no. 4, pp. 1435–1453.

Greater Miami Convention & Visitors Bureau 2017, *Greater Miami and The Beaches: 2016 visitor industry overview*, viewed 15 March 2018, <http://partners.miamiandbeaches.com/~/media/files/gmcvb/partners/research%20statistics/annual-report-2016>.

Greater Miami Convention & Visitors Bureau 2018, *Miami and The Beaches | The Official Vacation Guide*, viewed 16 March 2018, <http://www.miamiandbeaches.com/>.

Griffith Institute for Tourism 2015, *Gold Coast tourism industry report: year ending June 2015*, viewed 18 October 2016, <http://invest.moregoldcoast.com.au/wp-content/uploads/sites/2/2015/09/Gold-Coast-Tourism-Industry-Report-June-2015.pdf>.

Gross, L 1997, 'From South Beach to SoBe', in SJ Drucker & G Gumpert (eds), *Voices in the street: explorations in gender, media, and public space*, Hampton Press, Cresskill, pp. 201–210.

Gurtner, YK 2007, 'Phuket: Tsunami and tourism – a preliminary investigation', in E Laws, B Prideaux & K Chon (eds), *Crisis management in tourism*, CAB International, Wallingford, pp. 217–233.

Hiernaux-Nicolas, D 1999, 'Cancún bliss', in DR Judd & SS Fainstein (eds), *The tourist city*, Yale University Press, New Haven, pp. 124–139.

Ibiza 2018, motion picture, Netflix, Los Gatos.

Institut d'Estadística de les Illes Balears 2016, *Turisme: Flux de turistes (Frontur)*, viewed 23 October 2016, <https://www.caib.es/ibestat/estadistiques/043d7774-cd6c-4363-929a -703aaa0cb9e0/ef88f7cf-8e0b-44e0-b897-85c2f85775ec/ca/I208002_3001.px>.

Institut d'Estadística de les Illes Balears 2017, *Padrón (cifras de población)*, viewed 12 March 2018, <https://www.caib.es/ibestat/estadistiques/poblacio/padro/2acef6cf-175a -4826-b71e-8302b13c1262>.

Institut d'Estadística de les Illes Balears 2018, *Turisme: Flux de turistes (Frontur)*, viewed 14 March 2018, <https://www.caib.es/ibestat/estadistiques/043d7774-cd6c-4363-929a -703aaa0cb9e0/3f1887a5-b9b7-413b-9159-cb499cf29246/ca/I208002_n301.px>.

It's All Gone Pete Tong 2004, motion picture, Matson Films, San Francisco.

Jarvie, J & Lusher, A 2001, 'Ibiza tries to shed image as island of sun, sea and sex', *The Telegraph*, 10 June, viewed 14 October 2015, <http://www.telegraph.co.uk/ news/worldnews/europe/spain/1309913/Ibiza-tries-to-shed-image-as-island-of-sun-sea -and-sex.html>.

Jarvis, E 2011, '"Secrecy has no excuse": the Florida land boom, tourism, and the 1926 smallpox epidemic in Tampa and Miami', *The Florida Historical Quarterly*, vol. 89, no. 3, pp. 320–346.

Jones, M 1986, *A sunny place for shady people: the real Gold Coast story*, Allen & Unwin, Sydney.

Kanai, JM & Kenttamaa-Squires, K 2015, 'Remaking South Beach: metropolitan gayborhood trajectories under homonormative entrepreneurialism', *Urban Geography*, vol. 36, no. 3, pp. 385–402.

Kevin & Perry Go Large 2000, motion picture, Icon Film Distribution, Los Angeles.

Kontogeorgopoulos, N 2003, 'Keeping up with the Joneses: tourists, travellers, and the quest for cultural authenticity in southern Thailand', *Tourist Studies*, vol. 3, no. 2, pp. 171–203.

Kontogeorgopoulos, N 2004a, 'Conventional tourism and ecotourism in Phuket, Thailand: conflicting paradigms or symbiotic partners?', *Journal of Ecotourism*, vol. 3, no. 2, pp. 87–108.

Kontogeorgopoulos, N 2004b, 'Ecotourism and mass tourism in Southern Thailand: spatial interdependence, structural connections, and staged authenticity', *Geo-Journal*, vol. 61, no. 1, pp. 1–11.

Kontogeorgopoulos, N 2009, 'The temporal relationship between mass tourism and alternative tourism in Southern Thailand', *Tourism Review International*, vol. 13, no. 1, pp. 1–16.

Lavender, AD 2002, *Miami Beach in 1920*, Arcadia Publishing, Charleston.

Lonely Planet 2014, *Introducing the Gold Coast*, viewed 30 January 2014, <http:// www.lonelyplanet.com/australia/queensland/gold-coast>.

Lonely Planet 2015a, *Ibiza, Spain*, viewed 28 September 2015, <http://www.lonelypla net.com/spain/ibiza>.

Lonely Planet 2015b, *Introducing Miami*, viewed 24 August 2015, <http://www.lonelyp lanet.com/usa/miami>.

Lonely Planet 2018, *Welcome to Thailand*, viewed 12 May 2018, <http://www.lonelyp lanet.com/thailand>.

Longhurst, R 1995, *Gold Coast: our heritage in focus*, State Library of Queensland Foundation, South Brisbane.

Longhurst, R 1997, 'The Gold Coast: a history', in Allom Lovell Marquis-Kyle, Henshall Hansen Associates, Context, HJM & Staddon Consulting, *Gold Coast urban heritage & character study*, Gold Coast City Council, Surfers Paradise, pp. 24–29.

Malam, L 2004, 'Performing masculinity on the Thai beach scene', *Tourism Geographies*, vol. 6, no. 4, pp. 455–471.

Malam, L 2008, 'Geographic imaginations: exploring divergent notions of identity, power, and place meaning on Pha-ngan Island, Southern Thailand', *Asia Pacific Viewpoint*, vol. 49, no. 3, pp. 331–343.

McDowall, S & Wang, Y 2009, 'An analysis of international tourism development in Thailand: 1994–2007', *Asia Pacific Journal of Tourism Research*, vol. 14, no. 4, pp. 351–370.

McRobbie, A 1984, *The fabulous Gold Coast*, Pan News, Surfers Paradise.

Meethan, K 2001, *Tourism in global society: place, culture, consumption*, Palgrave, Basingstoke.

Mexico Tourism Board 2012, *Touristic attractions in Cancun, Mexico*, viewed 4 May 2015, <http://www.visitmexico.com/en/cancun>.

Miami Vice 1984–1989, television series, NBC, New York City.

Ministry of Tourism and Sports 2018, *Tourism statistics 2017*, viewed 23 January 2018, <http://www.mots.go.th/more_news.php?cid=414>.

Momsen, JH 2005, 'Uncertain images: tourism development and seascapes of the Caribbean', in C Cartier & AA Lew (eds), *Seductions of place: geographical perspectives on globalization and touristed landscapes*, Routledge, New York, pp. 209–221.

Mugerauer, R 2004, 'The tensed embrace of tourism and traditional environments: exclusionary practices in Cancún, Cuba, and Southern Florida', in N AlSayyad (ed.), *The end of tradition?*, Routledge, London, pp. 116–143.

Mullins, P 1992, 'Cities for pleasure: the emergence of tourism urbanization in Australia', *Built Environment*, vol. 18, no. 3, pp. 187–198.

Murray, G 2007, 'Constructing paradise: the impacts of big tourism in the Mexican coastal zone', *Coastal Management*, vol. 35, no. 2–3, pp. 339–355.

Nijman, J 2011, *Miami: mistress of the Americas*, University of Pennsylvania Press, Philadelphia.

Peleggi, M 1996, 'National heritage and global tourism in Thailand', *Annals of Tourism Research*, vol. 23, no. 2, pp. 432–448.

Pi-Sunyer, O, Thomas, RB & Daltabuit, M 2001, 'Tourism on the Maya periphery', in VL Smith & M Brent (eds), *Hosts and guests revisited: tourism issues of the 21st century*, Cognizant Communication Corporation, New York, pp. 122–140.

Polo, C & Valle, E 2008, 'An assessment of the impact of tourism in the Balearic Islands', *Tourism Economics*, vol. 14, no. 3, pp. 615–630.

Pons, A, Salamanca, OR & Murray, I 2014, 'Tourism capitalism and island urbanization: tourist accommodation diffusion in the Balearics, 1936–2010', *Island Studies Journal*, vol. 9, no. 2, pp. 239–258.

Portes, A & Stepick, A 1993, *City on the edge: the transformation of Miami*, University of California Press, Berkeley.

Prideaux, B 2004, 'The resort development spectrum: the case of the Gold Coast, Australia', *Tourism Geographies*, vol. 6, no. 1, pp. 26–58.

Re Cruz, A 1996, 'The thousand and one faces of Cancun', *Urban Anthropology and Studies of Cultural Systems and World Economic Development*, vol. 25, no. 3, pp. 283–310.

Re Cruz, A 2003, 'Milpa as an ideological weapon: tourism and Maya migration to Cancún', *Ethnohistory*, vol. 50, no. 3, pp. 489–502.

The Real Cancun 2003, motion picture, New Line Cinema, Los Angeles.

The Real World: Cancun 2009, television series, MTV, New York City.

Revels, TJ 2011, *Sunshine paradise: a history of Florida tourism*, University Press of Florida, Gainesville.

Rose, CN 2015, *The struggle for black freedom in Miami: civil rights and America's tourist paradise, 1896–1968*, Louisiana State University Press, Baton Rouge.

Rough Guides 2018a, *The Gold Coast*, viewed 20 January 2018, <https://www.rough guides.com/destinations/australasia/australia/coastal-queensland/gold-coast/>.

Rough Guides 2018b, *Miami*, viewed 14 March 2018, <https://www.roughguides.com/destinations/north-america/usa/florida/miami/>.

Rough Guides 2018c, *Thailand*, viewed 12 May 2018, <http://www.roughguides.com/destinations/asia/thailand/>.

Salmon, N 2016, 'Tourism tax to hit Ibiza and Majorca holidaymakers this summer with charges up to £70', *The Mirror*, 23 April, viewed 26 January 2017, <http://www.mirror.co.uk/news/world-news/tourism-tax-hit-ibiza-majorca-7816819>.

Sandvoss, C 2014, '"I ♥ Ibiza": music, place and belonging', in M Duffett (ed.), *Popular music fandom: identities, roles and practices*, Routledge, New York, pp. 115–145.

Scott, N, Gardiner, S & Dedekorkut-Howes, A 2016, 'Holidaying on the Gold Coast', in A Dedekorkut-Howes, C Bosman & A Leach (eds), *Off the plan: the urbanisation of the Gold Coast*, CSIRO Publishing, Clayton South, pp. 31–43.

Secretaría de Turismo del Estado de Quintana Roo 2017, *Indicadores turísticos*, viewed 14 March 2018, <http://www.qroo.gob.mx/sedetur/indicadores-turisticos>.

Serra Cantallops, A 2004, 'Policies supporting sustainable tourism development in the Balearic Islands: The Ecotax', *Anatolia: An International Journal of Tourism and Hospitality Research*, vol. 15, no. 1, pp. 39–56.

Sobot, R 2016, 'Nasty shock for holidaymakers heading to the Balearics as controversial tourist tax begins tomorrow', *Daily Mail*, 30 June, viewed 26 January 2017, <http://www.dailymail.co.uk/travel/travel_news/article-3667918/The-controversial-tourist-ta x-Balearics-starts-TOMORROW.html>.

Sobot, R 2018, 'May 1 shock for British holidaymakers arriving in Majorca and Ibiza as controversial tourist tax DOUBLES from today', *Daily Mail*, 1 May, viewed 13 June 2018, <http://www.dailymail.co.uk/travel/travel_news/article-5678017/May-1-shock-British-holidaymakers-arriving-Majorca-Ibiza-tourist-tax-DOUBLES.html>.

Soja, EW 1996, *Thirdspace: journeys to Los Angeles and other real-and-imagined places*, Blackwell Publishers, Oxford.

Surfers Paradise Alliance 2014, *Surfers Paradise, Gold Coast*, viewed 20 April 2014, <http://www.surfersparadise.com>.

Torres, R 2002, 'Cancun's tourism development from a Fordist spectrum of analysis', *Tourist Studies*, vol. 2, no. 1, pp. 87–116.

Torres, R & Momsen, JH 2006, 'Gringolandia: Cancún and the American tourist', in ND Bloom (ed.), *Adventures into Mexico: American tourism beyond the border*, Rowman & Littlefield, Lanham, pp. 58–74.

Tourism and Events Queensland 2016, *Gold Coast regional snapshot, year ending June 2016*, viewed 18 October 2016, <https://cdn-teq.queensland.com/~/media/229ae6ca c6394fb088b78db87b7ee960.ashx?vs=1&d=20161013T093747>.

Tourism and Events Queensland 2017, *Gold Coast regional snapshot, year ending June 2017*, viewed 20 January 2018, <https://cdn1-teq.queensland.com/~/media/b56f461286ac44d3bf15fca71a3855cb.ashx?vs=1&d=20171019T145059>.

Tourism Authority of Thailand 2015, *TAT News*, viewed 2 June 2015, <http://www.tatnews.org/>.

Tourism Authority of Thailand 2018, *The official travel information website for tourists visiting Thailand*, viewed 23 January 2018, <http://www.tourismthailand.org>.

TripAdvisor 2018, *2018: best of Ibiza tourism*, viewed 12 March 2018, <https://www.tripadvisor.com.au/Tourism-g187460-Ibiza_Balearic_Islands-Vacations.html>.

UNESCO World Heritage Centre 2015, *Ibiza, biodiversity and culture*, viewed 9 October 2015, <http://whc.unesco.org/en/list/417UNESCO>.

United States Census Bureau 2010, 'Miami Beach city, Florida', *Profile of general population and housing characteristics: 2010 census summary file 1*, viewed 14 March 2018, <https://factfinder.census.gov/faces/tableservices/jsf/pages/productview.xhtml?src=bkmk>.

United States Census Bureau 2018, 'Florida; Miami Beach city, Florida; Miami-Dade County, Florida; UNITED STATES', *QuickFacts*, viewed 14 March 2018, <https://www.census.gov/quickfacts/fact/table/FL,miamibeachcityflorida,miamidadecountyflorida,US/PST045217>.

Visit Florida 2018, *Miami*, viewed 13 March 2018, <http://www.visitflorida.com/en-us/cities/miami.html>.

Weaver, DB 2011, 'Contemporary tourism heritage as heritage tourism: evidence from Las Vegas and Gold Coast', *Annals of Tourism Research*, vol. 38, no. 1, pp. 249–267.

Westerhausen, K 2002, *Beyond the beach: an ethnography of modern travellers in Asia*, White Lotus Press, Bangkok.

Wilson, B 2006, *Fight, flight, or chill: subcultures, youth and rave into the twenty-first century*, McGill-Queen's University Press, Montreal.

Wilson, TD 2008, 'Economic and social impacts of tourism in Mexico', *Latin American Perspectives*, vol. 35, no. 3, pp. 37–52.

Wise, P 2006, 'Australia's Gold Coast: a city producing itself', in C Lindner (ed.), *Urban space and cityscapes: perspectives from modern and contemporary culture*, Routledge, New York, pp. 177–191.

Wise, P & Breen, S 2004, 'The concrete corridor: strategising impermanence in a frontier city', *Media International Australia*, no. 112, pp. 162–173.

The World Bank 2017, *Thailand data*, viewed 23 January 2018, <http://data.worldbank.org/country/thailand>.

World Travel & Tourism Council 2018, *Travel & tourism economic impact 2018: Thailand*, viewed 12 June 2018, <https://www.wttc.org/-/media/files/reports/economic-impact-research/countries-2018/thailand2018.pdf>.

3 Popular imaginaries, stereotypes and representations

Introduction

Resorts are constituted as much by the symbolic as the material, and how they are imagined shapes how they are lived. Through representations, inter-actions with others and subjective experiences, tourists develop mental images of destinations, which influence not only their expectations of what the place will be like, but what kinds of holidays they will have and what memories they will make. These imaginaries inform social relations and spatial practices in resorts to a significant extent, working to construct and sustain particular rhythms based on touristic consumption.

There are a number of commonalities in how each of the places in my study is imagined, and these shared imaginaries are part of what makes resorts distinct kinds of urban milieux. Additionally, the most popular elements of these imaginaries become implicated in the dominant (meta)nar-ratives of identity for each place. In this chapter, I explore the most prominent of these imagined resort characteristics, and how they manifest similarly and differently in lived spaces. Specifically, I consider resorts as escapist, extra-ordinary, paradisiacal fantasy worlds; as liminal, carnivalesque sites of lib-eration, hedonism and excessive consumption; and as sexualised, transgressive, risky, seedy and unsafe. In the second half of the chapter, I examine these themes through the example of youth tourism and nightlife.

It is important to note that while these narratives and imaginaries have arisen out of tourism, they do not exist only in the media and in the minds of tourists. On the contrary, since tourism is so pervasive in these places, touristic imaginaries, myths, behaviours and rhythms are also bound up in local experiences and understandings of space (see Chapters 5 and 6).

'Elsewhere' and 'nowhere': escapism, fantasy, spectacle and the tourist gaze

Distinctions between home and away, familiar and unfamiliar, everyday and exotic, mundane and extraordinary are central to tourism. Tourists desire spaces and experiences that are, to some degree, different from those of their everyday lives. Urry (2006) observes that tourists derive pleasure 'from the connoisseurship of difference' (p. vii). In the case of resorts, visitors may be drawn by the weather, landscape, local culture, atmosphere or 'vibe', landmarks, attractions or special events. People from colder climates flock to Miami and Ibiza to escape the winter chill; visitors to Cancún explore archaeological sites; and young people embark on journeys to Koh Phangan to attend the epic Full Moon Parties.

Existing outside of the routines and responsibilities that dominate their everyday lives, tourists imagine resorts as spatially, socially and temporally 'elsewhere'. They are places to which to escape, enabling a sense of pleasurable, temporary dislocation or displacement (Minca & Oakes 2006; Wise 2006; Rojek & Urry 1997). Resorts capitalise on this by positioning themselves in official tourism narratives as sites of fantasy – as exotic, hedonistic, playful and spectacular. This is captured by descriptions of them in scholarly literature, tourist promotion and news media as 'paradise', implying that they are idyllic, utopian and unreal. Such myths ignore the complex histories, social identities and community dynamics associated with these places, instead suggesting that they are timeless or dehistoricised spaces (Brown 2013; Bandyopadhyay & Nascimento 2010; Wise 2006). In other words, they are simultaneously imagined and portrayed as 'elsewhere' and 'nowhere' (see also Chapter 4).

Cultivating and sustaining this imaginary entails the commodification of culture and nature, people and places, as spectacles for the tourist gaze. Sightseeing is an integral practice to tourism and tourism spaces are therefore produced in ways that support visual consumption (Meethan 2001; Zukin 1991, 1995). Since tourists want to see things that are out of the ordinary, the task of the tourism industry is to 'transform places of the humdrum and ordinary into the apparently spectacular and exotic' (Bærenholdt, Haldrup, Larsen & Urry 2004, p. 2). Even where attractions (e.g. nightclubs) are similar to those that can be found at home, they are expected to be bigger, better and more extravagant (Urry 2002).

Spectacle in resorts is ubiquitous and takes many forms. The natural landscape is one of the most obvious objects of the tourist gaze in resorts, with a particular focus on beaches and forests. For example, Miami's nearby Everglades have been commodified as spectacle through the establishment of themed activities and attractions such as alligator farms, airboat rides, a 'safari park' and the Miccosukee Indian Village (Greater Miami Convention & Visitors Bureau 2015; Bush 1999). Bush (1999) describes this as the city 'exploiting the exoticism of the surroundings' (p. 157).

Maya Bay, a beach on the island of Koh Phi Phi Leh off the coast of Phuket, provides another interesting example. Made famous by the film *The Beach* (2000), Maya Bay continues to be an enormously popular day trip destination for tourists wanting a photograph in front of its iconic clear blue water, limestone cliffs and long-tail boats (see Figure 3.1). Maya Bay is a popular backdrop for the quintessential Thailand travel photo, which functions as a material artefact of memory for the self at the same time as it

Figure 3.1 Maya Bay, Koh Phi Phi Leh

signifies 'coolness', worldliness and increased cultural capital to others when shared via social media. While there, I spent my time watching people pose, taking photos of others at their request, and trying to get my own shot to post to Instagram (I was, after all, simultaneously researcher and tourist). Such practices highlight the significance of visual consumption in every stage of the tourism experience – in planning and anticipating holidays, in being there first-hand, and in creating memories and cultivating individual narratives of identity.

The built environments of resorts add another dimension to the tourism spectacle, although this is secondary to the allure of the natural environment, as visitors are typically not drawn to these destinations primarily by an interest in architecture or monuments.[1] The exception to this may be visitors to Thailand and Cancún, although even then their engagement with historic sites is often only an aside to an itinerary focused largely on beach activities and partying. Nevertheless, architecture does indeed contribute significantly to the experience of consumption in resorts, and to the sense of fantasy on which they rely. Oversized shopping malls and grand hotels emphasise the dominance of leisure, and being among Miami's colourful Art Deco facades (see Figure 3.2) or the Gold Coast's contemporary ultra-high-rises fosters a distinct feeling of being elsewhere. As Baker, Bennett and Wise (2012) observe, buildings like high-rise hotels also further encourage

Figure 3.2 Art Deco building in Miami Beach

the consumption of nature by placing a premium on rooms with 'sweeping views' of the ocean or the hinterland.

In addition to places, people are also made part of the tourism spectacle. In non-Western destinations like Cancún and Thailand, the locals – or 'natives', as they are sometimes referred to in tourism literature (Castellanos 2010; Dann 1996; Cohen 1982, 1972) – are often positioned in marketing material as the primitive, servile, exotic Other (Bandyopadhyay & Nascimento 2010; Sheller 2004). They are objectified by an orientalist, neo-colonial tourist gaze as cultural markers signifying the authenticity of the place and of the tourist experience (Bandyopadhyay & Nascimento 2010; Law, Bunnell & Ong 2007; Dann 1996). In Western destinations (such as Miami, the Gold Coast and Ibiza), the locals are notably absent from most tourism promotion, save for their possible inclusion as bodies on the beach or smiling hotel and restaurant workers.

Tourists, likewise, also become objects of the tourist gaze. It is not enough for there to be sunny beaches, mega-malls or extravagant theme parks – these spaces must be lived social spaces, occupied by others engaging in similar kinds of consumption, actively contributing to the desired atmosphere (Urry 1995). Thus, resorts are sites where the 'collective gaze' (Urry 2002) predominates, marked by the touristic equivalent of audience participation and conscious enjoyment of group experience. As Urry (2002) puts it:

what I call the *collective* tourist gaze involves conviviality. Other people also viewing the site are necessary to give liveliness or a sense of carnival or movement. Large numbers of people that are present can indicate that this is *the* place to be. These moving, viewing others are obligatory for the collective consumption of place ... (p. 150, original emphasis)

The collective gaze operates most obviously in sites of mass tourism: on crowded beaches; in nightclubs, bars and restaurants; and at theme parks and other major attractions. For Urry, this is juxtaposed to the 'romantic gaze', which is auratic, contemplative, solitary and elitist, and thus more readily associated with sites of cultural tourism, ecotourism or other forms of alternative tourism. In its most desirable form, the romantic gaze is characterised by a lack of crowds – 'the deserted beach, the empty hilltop, the uninhabited forest, the uncontaminated mountain stream' (Urry 2002, p. 150).[2] The appeal and the purpose of sites of the collective gaze, on the other hand, depends entirely on congregation and social interaction. When resorts lose their popularity, events are over or attractions close, they transform into 'sites of a lost collective gaze' (Urry 2002, p. 150). These tourist gazes, and the different styles of tourism that cater to and underpin them, are intrinsically tied to particular rhythms – to the presence of large numbers of people constituting a convivial rhythm in the case of mass tourism, and to the relative absence of people constituting a quieter, more solitary rhythm in the case of alternative tourism.

Sites of the tourist gaze can also be understood as 'temporal heterotopias' in Foucault's (1986) terms. These are spaces that are linked to disturbances in time – on the one hand, an accumulation of time, such as with museums and heritage attractions, or on the other hand, time as fleeting and transitory, such as with theme parks and festivals (Soja 1996; Foucault 1986). Resorts and their leisure spaces (including nightclubs, beaches, and main streets like Ocean Drive in Miami, Cavill Avenue on the Gold Coast, and Bangla Road in Phuket) are temporal heterotopias. The nightclubs of Ibiza, for instance, only open during the summer months when the island is filled with young tourists, and the space of the nightclub only takes on its characteristic atmosphere when occupied by people undertaking the expected practices – dancing, drinking, shouting, singing, laughing. Tourists, then, are anything but passive consumers. They in fact play an important role in the performance of space and the co-creation of spatial rhythms and spectacle.

Liminality and the carnivalesque

Resorts can be conceptualised as liminal spaces in terms of sociality, spatiality and temporality. Shields (1991) describes liminality as 'moments of discontinuity in the social fabric, in social space, and in history ... moments of "in-between-ness", of a loss of social coordinates' (p. 83). Liminality

involves 'a liberation from the regimes of normative practices and performance codes of mundane life' (Shields 1991, p. 84). Liminal spaces have
unifying effects, enabling the collective enactment of transgressive behaviours
(Shields 1991). As a concept, liminality has often referred to religious experiences like pilgrimages, or to rites of passage marking transitions from one life
stage to the next (Shields 1991; van Gennep 1977 [1960]; Turner 1974 [1969],
1973). Drawing on Victor Turner's (1974 [1969], 1973) work on pilgrimage
and *rites de passage*, Urry (2002) outlines that they entail:

> first, social and spatial separation from the normal place of residence and
> conventional social ties; second, liminality, where … conventional social
> ties are suspended, an intensive bonding 'communitas' is experienced,
> and there is direct experience of the sacred or supernatural; and third,
> reintegration, where the individual is reintegrated with the previous social
> group, usually at a higher social status. (p. 11)

Tourism in resorts shares some similarities with these experiences – tourists
temporarily escape from home, work and routine; they engage in collective
consumption of fantasy and spectacle; and upon returning home, they have
accumulated meaningful life experiences and increased their cultural capital.
Additionally, resorts can act as settings for contemporary coming-of-age rites
of passage, such as Schoolies on the Gold Coast, which is discussed in more
depth later in this chapter.

Beaches and islands have long been considered geographically liminal
(Sharpley 2004; Shaw & Williams 2004; Ryan 2002a; Urry 2002; Shields
1991). The seashore itself is an in-between, the margin between land and sea
(Preston-Whyte 2004; Ryan 2002b; Winchester, McGuirk & Everett 1999).
Resorts constitute what Turner and Ash (1976) call the 'pleasure periphery':
the collection of peripheral sites (usually warm and sunny) that act as places
for escape for people from urban centres. This is echoed in Selwyn's (1996)
argument that 'tourism may be said to be both an outcome and an expression
of the relation between centres and peripheries' (p. 10) in political, economic,
cultural, social and spatial senses.

Due in part to this spatial marginality, beaches and islands have become
strongly associated with leisure and pleasure (Sharpley 2004; Shaw &
Williams 2004; Urry 2002; Shields 1991). As Ryan (2002a) suggests,
'beaches are one of the few areas where it is socially tolerated for adults to
have fun as distinct from leisure' (p. 157). Resorts are purposeful extensions
of the beach's 'territorialized hedonism' (Crang 2014, p. 69). They are often
described as 'playgrounds', implying an atmosphere of playfulness, youth-
fulness, relaxation and 'social irresponsibility' (Ryan 2002b, p. 4). For most
adults, this is in stark contrast to their everyday experiences. Australian
writer Matthew Condon (2014) captures this effectively in his description of
the Gold Coast: 'If southeast Queensland were a body, Brisbane was the
brain and the Gold Coast a cluster of erogenous zones largely below the

waist'. Dominated by leisure industries and pleasurable pursuits, resorts are readily perceived as they are positioned: as distinct and removed from the tourist's mundane world of work, rules and obligations that take place in more conventional locations (Edensor 2007; Diken & Laustsen 2004; Meethan 1996, 2001).

During a holiday, the normative performances, routines, constraints and rules of everyday life are believed to be temporarily suspended, transcended and/or inverted (Edensor 2007; Urry 2002; Shields 1991). Thus, resorts function very effectively as liminal spaces for collective, socially sanctioned transgression, hedonism and excess. This behaviour can be understood in relation to Bakhtin's (1984) concept of the carnivalesque, which clearly shares features with liminality and rites of passage:

> carnival celebrated temporary liberation from the prevailing truth and from established order; it marked the suspension of all hierarchical rank, privileges, norms, and prohibitions. Carnival was the true feast of time, the feast of becoming, change, and renewal. It was hostile to all that was immortalized and completed. (p. 10)

In short, carnival is marked by the subversion of dominant moral codes and norms of propriety (Winchester et al. 1999; Shields 1991). Bakhtin (1984) proposes that it is a kind of *lived* spectacle, a participatory and deeply affective experience (much like Urry's collective gaze). During carnival, it feels as if 'there is no other life outside it' (Bakhtin 1984, p. 7), producing a sense of spatial, temporal and existential detachment from normal life.

Yet despite the usefulness of concepts of liminality and the carnivalesque, resorts do not exist entirely outside of the everyday. They are in some ways spectacular, and in other ways banal (Pons, Crang & Travlou 2009). Aside from the facts that resorts are everyday spaces for those who live in them, and that all holidays inevitably involve the enactment of routine daily tasks, tourism also necessarily requires a degree of control, regulation and routine (Edensor 2007). The behaviours, aesthetics and norms characteristic of liminal resort spaces are an 'extension of ... home environments' (Shaw & Williams 2004, p. 152). That is, they are sites for intensified expressions of the conventional values and consumption practices enshrined by capitalism. For example, tourists might drink alcohol at home, but may drink excessively on holiday; they might shop at home, but spend more while on vacation, and so on. As the term 'pleasure periphery' suggests, resorts are not completely *outside* of the centre (symbolic of the realm of mundane working life, dominant cultural values or norms and traditional city spaces) but on the margin, in between inside and outside. Resorts are carnival*esque*, blurring boundaries between order and disorder, freedom and constraint, home and away, and familiar and unfamiliar. It is also important to acknowledge, however, that what we conceptualise as the 'centre' is contested and problematic in itself. What is a 'normal', 'conventional' or 'serious' city? No place can ever be completely representative of a dominant Western culture, since all places are, like resorts, to greater or lesser extents liminal, hybrid, fragmented and heterogeneous.

Transgression and excess: sensuous encounters and sexualised spaces

Tourism is a sensuous experience (see Edensor 2006; Bærenholdt et al. 2004; Crouch & Desforges 2003; Crouch 2002; Saldanha 2002; Urry 2002). Places are not only seen or gazed upon, but also touched, heard, smelt and tasted. Tourists do not simply *view* space, they sense it, engage with it and perform it through their embodied encounters (Crouch & Desforges 2003; Coleman & Crang 2002; Urry 2002). Although tourists are able to see visual representations of destinations prior to their holiday – through the internet, TV, film, brochures, and photos taken by family and friends – there are certain things they can only experience by travelling to the place itself, by being immersed in its lived spaces and caught up in its rhythms.

Tourism is, then, a fundamentally embodied experience, and tourists in resorts are particularly preoccupied with bodily pleasures more so than cultural or intellectual pursuits. Sensual desires underpin and drive typical resort activities like sunbathing, swimming and surfing at the beach; dining on local cuisine at restaurants; listening to music, dancing, drinking and drug-taking in bars and nightclubs; hiking through humid rainforests; enjoying the fear and exhilaration of theme park rides or water sports; and indulging in spa treatments. This observation about embodiment also encompasses less pleasurable feelings, which are nonetheless a key part of the experience: sore feet from walking around all day, sunburn from spending too long at the beach, and hangovers from partying too hard. The tourist gaze remains important, as seeing people engage in similar ways normalises each of these socio-spatial practices and contributes to the expected atmosphere of collectively performed hedonism, indulgence and relaxation.

Many resort activities can be interpreted as performances of the undisciplined, excessive, 'grotesque' body, a concept closely connected to the carnivalesque (Shields 1991; Bakhtin 1984). In the context of resorts, Shields (1991) relates the grotesque body to that which is exposed on the beach, invades the personal space of others and transgresses norms of morality. This culture of bodily display is, in part, how resorts have come to be associated with 'sex' as much as 'sun, sand and sea' (Carson 2013; Shaw & Williams 2004; Rojek 1993). Resorts are imagined as sexualised spaces, a perception that is informed and reinforced by broader associations with pleasure, liminality, spectacle and voyeurism.

For example, this sexualised imaginary is so entrenched in the Gold Coast's identity that in 2012 the city's own art gallery curated a major exhibition entitled 'Sexualising the City: Imaging Desire and Gold Coast Identity' to document this motif throughout its history. The city has long been known to violate what is considered proper and tasteful. It is marketed as the place 'where the "bikini" was born' (Tourism Australia 2014), but as early as the 1920s, well before that icon of beach culture appeared, visitors to the Gold Coast tested the limits of modesty with their bathing suits by revealing considerably more flesh than was deemed appropriate at the time (Longhurst 1995; McRobbie 1984). Today, common sights in Surfers Paradise include scantily-clad Meter Maids, people sunbathing on the beach, and a variety of bodies in the surf and jogging down The Esplanade. A Gold Coast holiday invites tourists to gaze voyeuristically on the beach, in the street and from their high-rise balconies. After the sun goes down, bodies continue to be on display in the highly sexualised spaces of night-clubs and strip clubs (Cantillon 2015a).

Similar dynamics between bodies and voyeurism exist in each of the resorts I focus on. Walking through Playa d'en Bossa in Ibiza, I noted that tourists commonly wore nightclub-branded singlets and shirts atop their beachwear. In this context, such clothing exhibits a degree of subcultural capital (Thornton 1995) for the wearer. There is an awareness that you will be gazed upon and judged by others, and there is thus incentive to perform in ways that enable you to be deemed attractive or 'cool' by peers, or, at the very least, considered 'normal' enough to fit in.

Miami Beach, like Ibiza, was crowded with tanned, toned, barely dressed young people. This closely approximated my expectations of Miami, informed by popular cultural references and other cultural phenomena like the South Beach Diet (which metonymically associates the place with a particular life-style and aesthetic). During my fieldwork in Miami, I observed many instances of flirtatious banter between strangers on the street, as well as several instances of sexual harassment. Men catcalled women as they walked by, or shouted from afar, saying things such as: 'Hey sexy', 'You're adorable', 'You're so beautiful', 'Who you texting? You should be texting me!', 'Where are you going, pretty lady?', and offering rides in their cars. This sexualised atmosphere is markedly different from that which I had experienced in other major urban centres, except for resorts, in which a similar kind of sociality is present (albeit to less intensified degrees). What I am referring to is a more open, permissive sociality – the normalisation of superficial (and often sexually charged, aggressive or unwelcome) interactions between strangers, and a momentary reduction of the sense of anonymity or invisibility so frequently attributed to city spaces (see Tonkiss 2005).

Locals can also become sexually objectified in resort spaces, particularly in non-Western destinations like Thailand, where sex tourism is a major niche market and prostitution is a growing social issue (Berger 2007). Perceived as the exotic, erotic Other, Thai women (and to a lesser extent, men) are fetishised and sexualised as tourism commodities. In popular imaginaries and unofficial tourism narratives, Thailand is well known for its 'massage parlours' offering 'happy endings'. While there are many legitimate businesses offering Thai massages, I came across several shops in Phuket which were clearly offering sexual services – those with young Thai women waiting out the front dressed in skimpy clothing and high heels (clearly not the attire of a traditional, professional masseuse), speaking only to lone men who walked by.

Sexual encounters are just one of the many ways in which tourists can 'indulge' while on vacation. As previously mentioned, other hedonistic experiences – drinking, partying, eating, shopping – are in themselves ordinary, everyday activities, but in the context of resorts they are undertaken in excess, and are thus transformed to be more intensified and spectacular. In their imaginaries and their materiality, resorts share an emphasis on the core attributes of Bakhtin's (1984) carnivalesque: excess, hyperbole and indulgence. Wise (2012) highlights this in relation to the Gold Coast:

> In the national imagination, the Gold Coast equates with very bright sunlight, very long sandy beaches, very good waves, very high buildings, very big shopping malls, very active night life and very exciting theme parks. It equates with excess in the consumption of sun, surf, sex, shopping and the sensational. (p. 99)

In Cancún, excess is particularly exemplified in its multiple all-inclusive hotels. My hotel, for instance, had several large buffets with a range of cuisines (Mexican, Italian and American as staples, with French and Japanese themed nights), some operating 24 hours per day, in addition to five restaurants available by reservation. My room included a 'mini' bar with full size bottles of tequila, rum, vodka and brandy, which could be restocked at any time upon request. Guests were offered mimosas at breakfast, cocktails by the pool, and tequila at lunch and dinner. Excessive consumption of food and alcohol was expected and encouraged.

The all-inclusive model allows guests to stay in the confines of their hotel for the majority of their stay, limiting their zone of experience to specific spaces. Days are spent eating, drinking and lounging by the pool or on the hotel's own stretch of beach. At night, guests can venture out to the nearby clubs (which include unlimited drinks in their entry fees) before heading back to the hotel for a late night/early morning meal. Shaw and Williams (2004) argue that these practices are typical of contemporary beach resorts:

> the holiday experience is reduced to a relatively limited set of practices on the beach and at the poolside in the day-time, complemented by extensive night-life practices – often dominated by drink, music and the promise of sexual encounters. This is, in part, a reinvention of the seaside resort, in that it marks out a new form of tourist space, where extreme forms of consumption and behaviour can be experienced. (pp. 224–225)

For tourists, these excessive, hedonistic practices not only function to provide pleasure, but also to signify social status. As 'agent[s] of capitalism' (Brown 2013, p. 194), tourists engage in *conspicuous* consumption (Meethan 2001, 1996). Holidays are seen as liberating, with the potential to free oneself not only from everyday routines and responsibilities, but from everyday identities as well (Briggs 2013; Diken & Laustsen 2004; Boissevain 1996). Doing tourism involves becoming deterritorialised (Deleuze & Guattari 2004 [1987]) in that it quite literally displaces subjects from their home territories, relocating them (temporarily) to other spatial contexts. In the process, the tourists are transformed, as are their destinations of choice (during the holiday) and their localities (upon returning home). For the individual, transformation can occur through touristic consumption, with self-identity being playfully (re)constructed and performed. In the liminal space-time of a resort holiday, tourists can live out the fantasy of temporarily reinventing themselves and elevating their socio-economic status (Wise 2010; Boissevain 1996; Dann 1996). They can experience and display a more luxurious lifestyle than they are accustomed to at home, staying in opulent accommodation; eating lavish meals; devoting each day to leisure; driving fancy rental cars; mingling with the youthful, beautiful and (presumably) wealthy; and being served by hotel staff, cleaners, chefs and spa workers. Tourists consume excessively, enjoy the spectacle of other people's consumption, and capture and disseminate this shared sense of conspicuous consumption through social media. Such experiences, although temporary, have lasting effects on a tourist's sense of self in that they constitute the kinds of memories that come to shape one's life narratives.

The risky, the illicit and illegal

The transgression, excess and indulgence characteristic of resorts also gives rise to risky behaviours and acts of 'deviance' that may be avoided in other contexts, especially in the home environment. Tourists on holiday are less inhibited about partaking in illegal or potentially dangerous activities like public drunkenness, drug taking and hiring prostitutes, all of which appear to be contextually sanctioned. While such practices are obscured from official tourism narratives for obvious reasons, they have nonetheless become firmly entrenched in the popular imaginaries of resorts, due in large part to the unofficial narratives of place disseminated by the media. These are further reinforced by how often social media sites of young tourists convey representations of illegal or risky behaviours. It can readily seem as if such activities are expected, particularly in resorts associated with clubbing and partying.

On Thailand's island of Koh Phangan, it is not uncommon for tourists to ride motorbikes while intoxicated, without helmets or motorbike licences, even though the winding roads can be dangerous and difficult to navigate when sober. At Full Moon Parties, tourists may use illegal substances like magic mushrooms, marijuana, or various methamphetamines, and participate in risky activities like skipping a burning rope or limbo dancing under a burning pole. Despite the potentially severe consequences (e.g. serious injury, fines or jail time), these acts of transgression are normalised as typical parts of the tourism ritual, offering opportunities to 'let loose'. This has, in part, contributed to a strong association between resorts and crime.[3] News stories about drink spiking, alcohol-fuelled violence, drug trafficking, drug overdoses and sexual assaults occurring in tourist hubs are mainstays in national and international media. Tourists may be portrayed as the nuisance – as noisy, inconsiderate, out-of-control trouble makers; or, alternatively, as the victims – as vulnerable to local scam artists or drug dealers. Ibiza's tourists, for example, are often represented from both angles, as being potential victims of *and* potential perpetrators of crimes like sexual assault (see Alexander 2014) and drug dealing (see Couzens 2015; Reidy 2013).

In Western media, it is especially common for Thailand to be portrayed as dangerous. In addition to reporting on motorbike accidents, drug overdoses, rapes and murders, online news articles warn of an unsympathetic police force, 'bag-snatchers', drink spiking and the local 'mafia' (the 'tuk tuk mafia', as my interviewees called it) run by taxi drivers and jet ski operators who are notorious for scamming and assaulting tourists (Corderoy 2017; Daniel 2013; Paris 2013). Not surprisingly, these articles, written for a Western audience and expressing a fear of the Other, fail to reflect on how these crimes impact on the local population and *their* sense of safety.

In the case of Cancún, associations with crime pertain mostly to the drug trade and gang activity, reflecting broader issues plaguing Mexico (Argen 2018; Castellanos 2010). Over the past several years in particular, there have been an increasing number of new stories reporting drug-related murders in Cancún, with one account branding the resort as 'the world's murder capital' (Lockett 2018) and another describing it as 'one of the bloodiest high-profile battlegrounds in a turf war between drug cartels' (Martinez 2018). Incidences of violent criminal activity clearly disrupt imaginaries of Cancún as an idyllic, escapist paradise, but how this growing reputation may impact the city's tourism industry is yet to be seen.

Miami is similarly strongly associated with drugs. As outlined in Chapter 2, the ebb and flow of Miami's popularity over the years has to some extent correlated with the region's crime rates, or at least the perception that crime rates were elevated. Miami is not necessarily seen as a *dangerous* place, but a glitzy, glamorous place with a seedy underbelly, a place where pleasure and pushing boundaries easily slips into more serious transgression and risk. This image has been reinforced in popular cultural representations like the documentary *Cocaine Cowboys* (2006) and fictional films *Scarface* (1983), *Bad Boys* (1995), *Blow* (2001) and *2 Fast 2 Furious* (2003), all of which have stories based on Miami's drug trade. Other neo-noir texts like the film *Body Heat* (2001) and television series *Dexter* (2006–2013) and *Miami Vice* (1984–1989) depict violence and crime more broadly. Each of these examples stylistically plays on the juxtaposition between the idyllic tropical setting of the city and its gritty underworld.

Much like Miami, most film and television set on the Gold Coast has crime-related themes (Baker et al. 2012; Stockwell 2011) – for example, the short-lived police drama television series *The Strip* (2008), reality television series *Gold Coast Cops* (2014–2015), and animated sitcom television series

Pacific Heat (2016–2017). Due in part to sensationalist media reporting, the Gold Coast has earned labels such as Australia's 'crime capital' (Larkins 2013; Malkin 2011; Smail 2011), 'fraud capital' (Butler 2013) and 'sin city' (Potts, Dedekorkut-Howes & Bosman 2013; Griffin 1998). In particular, media reporting has focused on organised crime controlled by 'bikies' (motorcycle gangs), armed robberies, drug trafficking and rare, but highly publicised, cases of shootings and stabbings.

Bars and nightclubs in Surfers Paradise have long been rumoured as hot spots for drug trafficking in the city, involving local bikie gangs and corruption among lower-level police officers (McKenna 2010). Not long ago, a multi-million-dollar drug bust exposed the connections between several prominent Surfers Paradise nightclub owners and the trafficking of cocaine and amphetamines (see Fineran & Stigwood 2014; Stolz, Pierce & Laughlin 2014). In addition to drugs, 'millions of dollars in alleged drug assets including luxury homes, cars, boats and jewellery' were seized in the operation (Fineran & Stigwood 2014). Thus, drug trafficking was proven to be deeply implicated in both the sex and sleaze of Surfers Paradise and the extravagance of the Gold Coast's perceived luxury lifestyle.

Nightlife: an example

The nightlife scenes of resorts offer a useful example as to how the common elements outlined above – spectacle, gazing, escapism, hedonism, excess, liminality, embodiment, transgression and risk – converge and manifest socially and spatially. While the marketing of resorts tends to emphasise the beaches and warm, sunny weather of the dayscape, the sexualised clubs, bars and parties of the nightscape are equally important aspects of the tourist experience, appealing especially to the lucrative youth tourism and party tourism markets. Resorts are nodes in a shifting transnational network (Bennett 2004) of nightlife destinations, venues and events that constitute a globalised mainstream club culture. This is evident, for example, in the famous events to which these places play host, and with which they have become synonymous: Full Moon Parties in Thailand; Spring Break in Miami and Cancún; the summertime opening and closing parties of nightclubs in Ibiza; and Schoolies on the Gold Coast.

In each of these cases, hedonistic transgression and 'risky' behaviours like binge drinking, taking drugs and pursuing casual sexual encounters are considered to be the norm (Tutenges 2012; Goulding & Shankar 2011). Such aspects of the resort experience are frequently scrutinised in the literature, with studies seeking to measure levels of risk and uncover patterns of, and motivations for, these behaviours.[4] Transgressive practices vary for each event in that they have different meanings attached to them, and participants have different purposes for seeking them out. However, one key commonality is the spatial context (Briggs & Turner 2012; Litvin 2009; Sönmez, Apostolopoulos, Yu, Yang, Mattila & Yu 2006; Josiam, Hobson, Dietrich & Smeaton 1998).

Resorts offer themselves as spaces with a heightened sense of anonymity and also as spaces for socially sanctioned transgression and regulated expressions of disorder.

Full Moon Parties, Schoolies and Spring Break

The island resort of Koh Phangan, for instance, provides an exotic, marginal setting for its infamous Full Moon Parties. As mentioned in Chapter 2, the Full Moon Parties attract tens of thousands of tourists from around the world each month. Born out of the emergence of rave culture (Malam 2008; Westerhausen 2002), the events crystallise some of the most distinctive elements of the contemporary house music milieu. Young party-goers wearing fluorescent clothes and glow-in-the-dark face and body paint dance to house music, have conversations with strangers, eat junk food, throw up and hook up (see Figure 3.3). Instead of a dance floor, there is only sand, and limited (if any) security or official forms of regulation. Beachside stalls sell the iconic oversized 'bucket' drinks (filled with ice, alcohol and a mixer), and party drugs like ecstasy, LSD and magic mushrooms are easily accessible. The Full Moon Party has a carnivalesque atmosphere that has been mythologised in popular culture and mainstream youth tourism narratives, promising participants a wild, once-in-a-lifetime experience. The reality of this experience, of course, also involves serious risks associated with taking drugs of unknown origin and composition, engaging in potentially unsafe sexual activity with strangers (e.g. exposing oneself to STIs/STDs), or injury resulting from participation in dangerous activities while intoxicated (e.g. riding motorbikes).

In Australia, a similar once-in-a-lifetime experience for young people is Schoolies – the two-week period each November when Australian teenagers go on vacation to celebrate the end of their final exams and the completion of high school. The most popular Schoolies destination is overwhelmingly the Gold Coast, attracting upwards of 40,000 school leavers each year (Red Frogs 2014; Ironside 2014). The event is distinctly youthful, with participants normally being 17 to 18 years of age.[5] Colloquially and in the news media, older people who attempt to participate are branded as 'toolies' (from the derogatory term 'tool'). Toolies are assumed to be undertaking various kinds of predatory behaviour, such as providing or selling alcohol to underage Schoolies, supplying them with drugs, or trying to engage with them sexually.

A collectively enacted rite of passage, Schoolies marks the transition out of secondary school and into the next stage of life, loosely defined as 'adulthood', but incorporating many different paths (Lawton & Weaver 2015; Winchester et al. 1999; Zinkiewicz, Davey & Curd 1999). School leavers temporarily escape to the liminal space of the Gold Coast, liberating themselves from their everyday responsibilities and from parental supervision for a period of relaxation, partying and bonding with friends. Excessive alcohol consumption, drug use and sexual displays (ranging from flirting to hook ups and sex) are commonplace during Schoolies (Maticka-Tyndale, Herold &

Figure 3.3 Revellers dance at the Full Moon Party, Koh Phangan

Oppermann 2003; Winchester et al. 1999; Zinkiewicz et al. 1999). As Winchester et al. (1999) observe, the experience is one of disorder: 'The Schoolies phenomenon is highly focused on intense embodied experiences in which the physical senses are stimulated through an inversion of the norma-tively controlled body to become the out-of-control body' (p. 68).

Each year, before and during the event, there are highly publicised (although not necessarily common) incidences of rape, drink spiking, accidental death, physical assault and the destruction of public and private property (e.g. Spencer & Rudd 2017; Calligeros & Remeikis 2012; Blatchford 2011). This reporting reinforces a traditional 'youth as problem' narrative, fuelling moral panic over the threat of young people in public spaces partici-pating in risky behaviours (Baker et al. 2012; Nilan, Julian & Germov 2007; Wyn & White 1997; Thornton 1995). These media representations may serve as either a deterrent *or* a motivator to participate in Schoolies. While I chose not to 'do' Schoolies out of concern for my own safety (as well as not being able to afford it financially), many of my friends at the time were keen to have the 'out-of-control' experiences depicted in the media, intentionally seeking out what I feared.

Due to the carnivalesque disorder characteristic of the Schoolies ritual and the resulting moral panic, in recent years the Gold Coast event has become highly regulated. Schoolies now has official events (featuring DJs and an outdoor cinema) staged in Surfers Paradise with entry only permitted to people with wristbands. These are only provided to those with a valid grade 12 student ID, thus excluding toolies from events.[6] Other techniques of regulation and surveillance include a strong police presence, strict nightclub security and door policies (making it very difficult for underage patrons to gain entry) and numerous volunteer groups providing assistance[7] to young people on the ground, such as Red Frogs, Christian Youth Council, Crime Stoppers Queensland, Drug Arm Australasia, Gold Coast Youth Service, Rosies Youth Mission, and State Emergency Services (The State of Queensland 2016). Of course, these measures are largely limited to public spaces and have less capacity to influence the realm of private accommodation where activities like binge drinking, taking drugs and hooking up are most likely to take place. Consequently, acts of transgression persist despite increasing forms of regulation.

Spring Break may be considered the North American equivalent of Schoolies in that it involves large numbers of young people travelling to resorts at a specific time each year. Spring Break is a week-long break from North American university classes, usually falling in February or March depending on the institution. According to Lewis, Patrick, Mittmann and Kaysen (2014), roughly 38 per cent of college students take trips away from campus during this time, often travelling to Spring Break destinations. In addition to Cancún and Miami, other popular sites are Fort Lauderdale and Panama City Beach, Florida, USA; South Padre Island, Texas, USA; Nassau, Bahamas; and Punta Cana, Dominican Republic. Unlike Schoolies, Spring Break may be experienced several times (each year during university) and does not necessarily mark a transition[8] so much as a temporary escape in the same vein as a traditional vacation. Further, although Spring Breakers are typically older (18–22+) than Schoolies (17–18), both events feature a mixture of underage and legally sanctioned drinking due to the different legal drinking ages across these sites: 18 in Australia, 21 in the USA, 18 in Canada, and 18 in popular Spring Break destinations like Mexico, the Dominican Republic and the Bahamas.

Over the years, Spring Break has become 'firmly entrenched in the college imaginary' (Ribeiro & Yarnal 2008, p. 353) and cemented itself as a core ritual in the typical, clichéd college experience for North American youth. This myth has been perpetuated not only through word-of-mouth (the narratives of current and former college students who participated first-hand), but through pervasive media representations depicting young students in swimwear partying all day long, exemplified by MTV's annual coverage of Spring Break parties (Litvin 2009; Ribeiro & Yarnal 2008; Josiam et al. 1998). Students seek to escape the winter chill and let loose, travelling with friends to sunny resorts to be preoccupied with leisure and play rather than study and work. This is perceived as a time of liberation from the supervision of teachers and parents (Patrick, Morgan, Maggs & Lefkowitz 2010; Litvin 2009), and thus a time for transgression and indulgence.

Although some studies have found that students while on Spring Break are more likely to participate in risky behaviours such as casual sex, drug use and binge drinking (Patrick et al. 2010; Sönmez et al. 2006; Josiam et al. 1998), others have found that there is no difference between the levels of risk displayed in a Spring Break vacation than back home (Litvin 2009; Ribeiro &

Yarnal 2008). However, even if increased levels of risk-taking do not occur (which is debatable), it is clear that the *expectation* of these activities never-theless remains a significant motivating factor in taking a Spring Break vacation (Patrick et al. 2010; Ribeiro & Yarnal 2008).

Nightclubs and the clubbing milieu

As well as the special events outlined above, the more familiar spaces of nightclubs and bars also play an important role in the nightlife of resorts. The built environment provides ample evidence of nightlife's prominence in resorts, even though nightclubs are distributed differently throughout each place – appearing in clusters in Cancún, Phuket and on the Gold Coast, but scattered over greater distances in Miami and Ibiza. For example, Surfers Paradise, the bigger of the two clubbing districts on the Gold Coast,[9] has eleven nightclubs,[10] three strip clubs[11] and a number of bars, the great majority of which are located within 500 metres of each other, primarily on the main clubbing strip of Orchid Avenue. Due to the high density of venues in Surfers, the sociality characteristic of nightclubs also pervades the public areas of Orchid and Cavill Avenues (Cantillon 2015a, 2015b). As the night takes over, young people fill the sidewalks, streets and pedestrian mall, shouting, smoking, stumbling, crying, eating fast food and vomiting in the very same spaces that are occupied by holidaying families, strolling couples and tour groups during the daytime.

As sites of mass tourism, it is unsurprising that resort nightlife is dominated by mainstream venues, with alternative spaces being marginalised (Gallan 2015; Chatterton & Hollands 2002). Nightlife in resorts caters to the perceived desires and expectations of tourists, and is based on a series of elements that mark nightclubs as distinct social spaces with particular kinds of leisure experiences attached. Thus, resort nightlife venues have the poten-tial to be 'largely standardised, sanitised and non-local' (Chatterton & Hollands 2002, p. 102). In Surfers Paradise, of the eleven nightclubs there are two gay clubs (Rise and MP's) and one 'alternative'[12] club (Elsewhere), with the rest being mainstream clubs. These mainstream venues share standardised designs, spatial arrangements and aesthetics, along with social conventions and behavioural codes which are part of a globalised club culture. Some of the most notable shared characteristics among mainstream clubs are: the music, which is usually electronic dance music (trance, house, techno) and 'top 40' hits (a mixture of pop, hip hop and rap); spatial signifiers and aesthetic elements, such as being dimly lit with flashing strobe lights, brightly coloured neon lights and smoke machines; and similar kinds of dress and behavioural codes among patrons (see Cantillon 2015a).

Of all the resorts considered in this book, Ibiza is the most indelibly connected to nightlife. Since Ibiza is the global mecca of dance music, and arguably the birthplace of contemporary mainstream club culture (Goulding & Shankar 2011; Wilson 2006), I expected the nightlife to be a more intensified, more spectacular version of what I observed at home, a 'spectacle of excess' (Diken & Laustsen 2004, p. 100). In some ways, this proved true (e.g. similar club designs but larger venues, similar behaviours but larger crowds), but the Ibiza clubbing milieu had differences as well, and was not entirely 'non-local' (Chatterton & Hollands 2002, p. 102). To be specific, I had expected young tourists to be primarily motivated to go to Ibiza to party and have fun with friends, so I was surprised by the extent to which the *music* seemed to play a central role in their experiences.

As a site of innovation for electronic dance music, Ibiza attracts dance music fans and famous DJs from around the world (Sandvoss 2014; Goulding & Shankar 2011; Bennett 2004). Ibiza nightclubs act as spaces for the coming together of affective communities based on a shared taste in music, which may be characterised by fleeting, neo-tribal associations (Goulding & Shankar 2011; Bennett 2004, 2001; Malbon 1999, 1998) or more lasting and meaningful senses of affinity (Sandvoss 2014). In this context, DJs are the dance music equivalent of the more traditional 'rock star' archetype (Bennett 2001), and become key figures in tourism promotion strategies. Their faces are plastered across Ibiza's tourist hubs on billboards and posters, and their names are shouted to you by club ticket vendors on the streets – Steve Aoki, David Guetta, Afrojack, Calvin Harris, and more (see Figure 3.4). In the nightclubs, patrons are fixated on the DJ, as if worshipping (see also Briggs & Turner 2012; Goulding & Shankar 2011). On the Gold Coast, such behaviour is more akin to a music festival or live gig than a nightclub, where the gaze tends to be focused on other

Figure 3.4 Billboards advertising resident DJs at particular nightclubs in Ibiza

clubbers rather than on the DJ, and opportunities to socialise are more of a drawcard than the music itself.

Despite such differences, there are nonetheless many other similarities in the experience of clubbing that closely parallel aspects of the broader tourist experience of resorts. Clubbing is a highly sensuous activity with a strong emphasis on affective and corporeal engagements – letting go, feeling the bass, dancing to the beat, touching other bodies – often heightened by the effects of drugs and alcohol (Goulding & Shankar 2011; Malbon 1998). As a site of the collective gaze, the presence of other clubbers engaging in similar ways is essential to creating the expected atmosphere and spectacle. Collectively experienced and performed, the nightclub can be interpreted as fostering a sense of social solidarity or *communitas* characteristic of liminal, carnivalesque spaces.

Goulding and Shankar (2011) describe *communitas* among clubbers as a feeling of togetherness and equality, the disintegration of everyday structures and the emergence of a group ethos and identity that temporarily overrides the individual's identity (see also Malbon 1998). This is based on affinities arising out of shared practices and performances, and a shared desire for escapism and pleasure. The emphasis on collectivity combined with a perceived liberation from everyday life underpins the argument that the clubbing experience facilitates the momentary transcendence of normative identities and social hierarchies (Wang 1999; Shields 1991). That is, it can be argued that the carnivalesque sociality of clubs breaks down traditional divisions of class, ethnicity and gender (Goulding & Shankar 2011; Wilson 2006; Bennett 2004; Malbon 1998; Thornton 1995). This 'loss' of identity is particularly intensified by the relative sense of anonymity enabled by nightclubs (Briggs 2013; Jaimangal-Jones, Pritchard & Morgan 2010; Bennett 2004; Malbon 1999; Thornton 1995). In Melechi's (1993) terms, the nightclub affords individuals the opportunity to experience the 'ecstasy of disappearance' (p. 32). This is especially the case in places with transient populations like resorts.

Despite this apparent *communitas* and liberation, the social dynamics of the mainstream clubbing milieu are nonetheless fraught with inequalities. This is not to say that the previous arguments are invalid, but rather that there is more going on. The experience of clubbing can oscillate between feelings of immersion, togetherness, anonymity, inhibition *and* feelings of detachment, individualism, self-reflexivity, anxiety. In his analysis of nightclubs, Malbon (1999) describes a similar shift:

> the experiencing of these crowds can provide pleasurable sensations of 'in-betweenness' – or *exstasis* – as crowd members flux between awareness and sensations of their own identities on the one hand and the identifications and belongings achievable through the crowd on the other. (p. 71)

Within clubs, hierarchies exist which are contingent on the local context but often based on status, style, beauty and how much one does or does not fit in, how 'authentic' one is, or how 'cool' one might be considered (Thornton 1995). As mentioned previously, this is what Thornton (1995) calls subcultural capital. Clubbers develop specific cultural knowledges surrounding things like music and drugs, and ways of dressing, dancing, talking and interacting (Sandvoss 2014; Wilson 2006; Saldanha 2002; Malbon 1999). Individuals are then gazed upon and assessed on their subcultural competence by others in the club, which necessitates a degree of self-awareness and reflexivity on behalf of the club-goer. Individuals may deploy impression management strategies (Grazian 2008; Goffman 1969 [1956]) to ensure their performances of self are more closely aligned with the expectations of the space. Therefore, nightclubs not only encourage feelings of solidarity and sensuous embodiment, but also competitiveness, conflict and hyper-performativity (Grazian 2008; Malbon 1998). As Grazian (2009) observes, 'for many participants, such places aren't even that much fun, much less sanctuaries for social inclusion' (p. 910).

Intersecting with these subcultural hierarchies are more traditional forms of stratification based on gender, age, (dis)ability, race, ethnicity and class. For instance, since mainstream nightclubs are sites for (hetero)sexual pursuit and performances of hegemonic ideals of gender, unequal power dynamics are strongly present (Cantillon 2015a; Grazian 2009, 2008). Men are encouraged to demonstrate modes of masculinity that suggest their sexual prowess, while women's displays of sexual agency are constrained by cultural norms (such as good girl/bad girl or Madonna/whore binaries) and associated potential social sanctions (such as being called a 'slut' or a 'prude') (Cantillon 2015a). Nightclubs have also been known to use discriminatory door policies, which can operate to deselect people of certain races and ethnicities. In his work on North American nightclubs, Grazian (2009) observes that African Americans are frequently denied entry to clubs on the basis of dress codes which target fashion trends popular among black youth (e.g. baggy pants, sports jerseys, etc.).

Further, while it has been argued that association with mainstream dance cultures is not class-based as with traditional subcultures (Bennett 2004), it is evident that class and wealth remain powerful barriers to participation. A certain amount of economic capital is required to go out clubbing and to visit resort destinations, with expenses including accommodation, flights, nightclub entry, drinks, transportation and meals. As such, the clubbing experience can be marked more by exclusivity than by equality (Anderson 2009). I encountered an especially striking example of this at a popular nightclub in Miami Beach. Before going there, I had read online and been informed by some of my interviewees that the club was notoriously difficult to get into – prospective patrons will have their best chances if they are women, attractive, well-dressed and entering as a couple or with a small group of other women. Failing that, entry could be guaranteed by reserving a table with bottle service for upwards of US$1,000.

Outside the club, there was no queue, but rather a disorganised mass of people surrounding the roped-off entryway. Unlike what I was used to, gaining entry did not follow a 'first in, first served' process, but was based on a hierarchy of desirability in terms of subcultural capital as determined by the bouncers and promoters. Accompanied by a (white, young, male) friend, I waited in the crowd until a bouncer pointed to us, unhooked the rope, and escorted us to the door, despite the fact that large numbers of people who arrived before us were still waiting. We paid our gendered entry fee of US$60 for me and US$100 for my friend, and once inside spent US$39 for two serves of basic spirits. Looking for somewhere to sit, we instead encountered only roped-off VIP booths guarded by bouncers. We could not identify a clearly defined dance floor that was accessible to us, and it seemed the only spot to hang out was next to the bars and on the stairs. The club was so segregated by wealth, class and subcultural cachet that it hindered the kind of mixing and mingling that is usually a core part of the clubbing experience.

Despite the qualities of nightclubs, and of resorts, that indicate that they are spaces for the suspension and transcendence of everyday life, they are, in fact, also spaces in which very 'everyday', normative social structures, dynamics and inequalities are enacted and perpetuated. Resorts, and their nightclubs, may present as enabling people to be temporarily free from familiar social hierarchies, but markers of difference such as class, wealth, ethnicity, gender, sexuality, age, style, beauty or 'coolness' continue to operate in the spatiality, sociality and modes of consumption that these sites make available. Further, while mass tourists may be motivated by fantasies of escapism and temporarily abandoning their everyday roles, experiences of travelling and engaging in the kind of lifestyle offered by resorts are powerful modes through which to (re)negotiate one's 'everyday' self. Through anticipation, memory and storytelling, these experiences shape self-identity and consequently become very much implicated in the mundane lives of individuals.

Conclusion

Popular imaginaries of places are multiple, varied and contradictory, yet interconnected. Some myths are supported by official tourism discourses, some are sustained by sensationalised media reporting and popular cultural representations, and some are circulated through informal networks online and among acquaintances. Some imaginaries derive from the lived spatiality of resorts, while others are carefully engineered and imposed. Whatever the case, how we think about resorts – about what kinds of places they are, what they look like, what goes on there, and who occupies them – plays a powerful role in determining how we act within them. Imaginaries and representations shape social and spatial practices, and these practices in turn shape imaginaries and representations, dynamically producing the lived spatiality of resorts. While a focus on nightlife has provided some particularly intensified examples of these interactions, there is no question that they operate across the resort experience.

Resorts are characteristically liminal, being at once everyday and exotic, standardised and spectacular, ordered and disordered. Spatially marginal and socially peripheral, they are defined and experienced differently from more conventional cities, which are associated with an elusive, conceptual 'centre'. While it is important to avoid a definitional binary, since *all* cities are sites of heterogeneity and difference and each is unique, it is nevertheless the case that this distinction between resorts and conventional cities, peripheries and centres, matters. Pleasure and escapism are core to the rationale for the existence of resorts. Tourists are escaping one kind of space for another with different experiences attached. To freely enjoy themselves, and to detach from their everyday lives, they must resort to other places. Resort destinations, then, are designed to cater to the needs and expectations of the people visiting them.

Dominated by tourism and leisure, and perceived as carnivalesque 'elsewheres' or 'nowheres', resorts easily offer a striking, desirable contrast to conventional cities. However, it is far too simplistic to assume that resorts are therefore superficial, depthless and homogenous (while 'real cities' have depth, power and cultural worth). On the contrary, a great deal exists beyond the most popular imaginaries, dominant narratives of identity and tourist-centric rhythms of resorts. Although frequently positioned as peripheral in relation to any 'serious' global flows of wealth, people and meaning, resorts have unique, complex local cultures and histories, which are the focus of the next three chapters.

Notes

1 For instance, in 2015 visitors to Miami reported that their favourite features of the destinations were (in order): the beaches, weather, South Beach/Ocean Drive, shopping, restaurants, nightlife, 'attractions' (a vague category encompassing both paid and unpaid attractions), and then the Art Deco Area, followed by some other categories with smaller amounts of votes (Greater Miami Convention & Visitors Bureau 2016). For comparison, 58.6 per cent of visitors rated beaches as one of their favourite attractions, while only 22.2 per cent of visitors voted for the Art Deco Area (Greater Miami Convention & Visitors Bureau 2016).
2 The romantic and collective gazes are not necessarily mutually exclusive, and mass tourism frequently involves both.
3 This link between beach resorts and a reputation for criminality has been raised in scholarly work on other destinations as well, including Brighton (Shields 1991), Ayia Napa (Sharpley 2004) and the Caribbean (Sheller 2004).
4 See, for example, studies on young people's behaviours during Spring Break (Lewis et al. 2014; Ragsdale, Porter, Zamboanga, St Lawrence, Read-Wahidi & White 2011; Patrick et al. 2010; Sönmez et al. 2006; Josiam et al. 1998), during Schoolies (Lawton & Weaver 2015; Maticka-Tyndale, Herold & Oppermann 2003; Zinkiewicz, Davey & Curd 1999; Smith & Rosenthal 1997), and in Ibiza (Kelly, Hughes & Bellis 2014; Briggs 2013; Briggs & Turner 2011; Briggs, Turner, David & De Courcey 2011; Briggs, Tutenges, Armitage & Panchev 2011; Bellis, Hughes, Thomson & Bennett 2004; Bellis, Hale, Bennett, Chaudry & Kilfoyle 2000). Many of these studies are quantitative and aim to offer potential 'solutions' and recommendations to minimise risk and deter young people from doing these things, thus reinforcing a 'youth as problem' narrative.

5 In Queensland, people completing the final year of high school currently average 17 years old but can be as young as 16 or as old as 18. A recent change to the state's schooling system will bring Queensland school leavers into line with the other states with an average age of 18.

6 Although older people are not allowed entry into the official events, they can still easily interact with Schoolies in the surrounding streets and in nightclubs and bars.

7 By providing chill out zones, free water, first aid and counselling, as well as accompanying Schoolies back to their accommodation, cooking for them and cleaning their rooms.

8 The first Spring Break vacation one embarks on, however, may function as a rite of passage or a ritual of initiation into 'college life', a conceptual life stage marked by a series of quintessential, stereotypical college experiences (as perpetuated by popular cultural representations and people's own storytelling of what their college days entailed).

9 The other being Broadbeach, about a 10-minute drive south of Surfers. At the time of writing, Broadbeach had three nightclubs – Platinum, Love and Envy.

10 At the time of writing, these were Shooters, SinCity, The Bedroom, Melbas, Cocktails, Underground, The Avenue, Retro's, Elsewhere, MP's and Rise.

11 At the time of writing, these were Hollywood Showgirls, Toybox Showgirls and Players Showgirls.

12 What constitutes an 'alternative' club is difficult to define, but is usually marked by its differences to mainstream venues even though it is a heteronormative space. Elsewhere is different to other Gold Coast nightclubs in that it does not play top 40 hits, does not have a design aimed at appearing glitzy or opulent (rather, its aesthetic incorporates an eclectic mix of retro, industrial and street art elements), and attracts patrons with more varied senses of style (e.g. more 'hipster' clientele).

References

2 Fast 2 Furious 2003, motion picture, Universal Pictures, Universal City.

Alexander, S 2014, 'Brit girls warned not to walk home alone in Ibiza as "it could cost you your life"', *Daily Star*, 29 July, viewed 7 June 2016, <http://www.dailystar.co.uk/news/latest-news/391567/Ibiza-rape-warning-women>.

Anderson, TL 2009, 'Better to complicate, rather than homogenize, urban nightlife: a response to Grazian', *Sociological Forum*, vol. 24, no. 4, pp. 918–925.

Argen, D 2018, 'Cancún: from tourist beach paradise to hotbed of Mexico's drug violence', *The Guardian*, 14 March, viewed 19 May 2018, <https://www.theguardian.com/world/2018/mar/14/cancun-tourist-paradise-mexico-drug-violence>.

Bærenholdt, JO, Haldrup, M, Larsen, J & Urry, J 2004, *Performing tourist places*, Ashgate, Aldershot.

Bad Boys 1995, motion picture, Columbia Pictures, Culver City.

Baker, S, Bennett, A & Wise, P 2012, 'Living "the strip": negotiating neighborhood, community, and identity on Australia's Gold Coast', in C Richardson & HA Skott-Myhre (eds), *Habitus of the hood*, Intellect, Bristol, pp. 97–120.

Bakhtin, M 1984, *Rabelais and his world*, trans. H Iswolsky, Indiana University Press, Bloomington.

Bandyopadhyay, R & Nascimento, K 2010, '"Where fantasy becomes reality": how tourism forces made Brazil a sexual playground', *Journal of Sustainable Tourism*, vol. 18, no. 8, pp. 933–949.

The Beach 2000, motion picture, 20th Century Fox, Los Angeles.

Bellis, MA, Hale, G, Bennett, A, Chaudry, M & Kilfoyle, M 2000, 'Ibiza uncovered: changes in substance use and sexual behaviour amongst young people visiting an international night-life resort', *International Journal of Drug Policy*, vol. 11, no. 3, pp. 235–244.

Bellis, MA, Hughes, K, Thomson, R & Bennett, A 2004, 'Sexual behaviour of young people in international tourist resorts', *Sexually Transmitted Infections*, vol. 80, no. 1, pp. 43–47.

Bennett, A 2001, *Cultures of popular music*, Open University Press, Buckingham.

Bennett, A 2004, '"Chilled Ibiza": dance tourism and the neo-tribal island community', in K Dawe (ed.), *Island musics*, Berg, Oxford, pp. 123–136.

Berger, AA 2007, *Thailand tourism*, Haworth Hospitality & Tourism Press, New York.

Blatchford, E 2011, 'Schoolies rape victim warns', *Gladstone Observer*, 10 June, viewed 19 April 2018, <https://www.gladstoneobserver.com.au/news/schoolies-rape-victim -warns-week-gold-coast/875435/>.

Blow 2001, motion picture, New Line Cinema, Los Angeles.

Body Heat 1981, motion picture, Warner Bros., Burbank.

Boissevain, J 1996, 'Introduction', in J Boissevain (ed.), *Coping with tourists: European reactions to mass tourism*, Berghahn Books, Providence, pp. 1–26.

Briggs, D 2013, *Deviance and risk on holiday: an ethnography of British tourists in Ibiza*, Palgrave Macmillan, Basingstoke.

Briggs, D & Turner, T 2011, 'Risk, transgression and substance use: an ethnography of young British tourists in Ibiza', *Studies of Transition States and Societies*, vol. 3, no. 2, pp. 14–25.

Briggs, D & Turner, T 2012, 'Understanding British youth behaviors on holiday in Ibiza', *International Journal of Culture, Tourism and Hospitality Research*, vol. 6, no. 1, pp. 81–90.

Briggs, D, Turner, T, David, K & De Courcey, T 2011, 'British youth abroad: some observations on the social context of binge drinking in Ibiza', *Drugs and Alcohol Today*, vol. 11, no. 1, pp. 26–35.

Briggs, D, Tutenges, S, Armitage, R & Panchev, D 2011, 'Sexy substances and the substance of sex: findings from an ethnographic study in Ibiza, Spain', *Drugs and Alcohol Today*, vol. 11, no. 4, pp. 173–187.

Brown, DF 2013, 'Tourists as colonizers in Quintana Roo, Mexico', *The Canadian Geographer*, vol. 57, no. 2, pp. 186–205.

Bush, GW 1999, 'Playground of the USA: Miami and the promotion of spectacle', *Pacific Historical Review*, vol. 68, no. 2, pp. 153–172.

Butler, B 2013, 'Sun setting on fraud capital of Australia', *The Sydney Morning Herald: Business Day*, 30 March, viewed 21 April 2014, <http://www.smh.com.au/ business/sun-setting-on-fraud-capital-of-australia-20130329-2gz30.html>.

Calligeros, M & Remeikis, A 2012, 'Schoolies balcony fall victim identified as Brisbane girl Isabelle Colman', *The Sydney Morning Herald*, viewed 21 April 2018, <https://www.smh.com.au/national/schoolies-balcony-fall-victim-identified-as-brisba ne-girl-isabelle-colman-20121123-29th8.html>.

Cantillon, Z 2015a, 'Occupying the mainstream: performing hegemonic masculinity in Gold Coast nightclubs', in S Baker, B Robards & B Buttigieg, *Youth cultures and subcultures: Australian perspectives*, Ashgate, Farnham, pp. 183–192.

Cantillon, Z 2015b, 'Polyrhythmia, heterogeneity and urban identity: intersections between "official" and "unofficial" narratives in the socio-spatial practices of Australia's Gold Coast', *Journal of Urban Cultural Studies*, vol. 2, no. 3, pp. 253–274.

Carson, S 2013, 'Inside the pleasure dome: cultural tourism on Australia's Gold Coast', *AlmaTourism: Journal of Tourism, Culture and Territorial Development*, vol. 4, no. 8, pp. 32–44.

Castellanos, MB 2010, 'Cancún and the campo: indigenous migration and tourism development in the Yucatán', in D Berger & AG Wood (eds), *Holiday in Mexico: critical reflections on tourism and tourist encounters*, Duke University Press, Durham, pp. 241–264.

Chatterton, P & Hollands, R 2002, 'Theorising urban playscapes: producing, regulating and consuming youthful nightlife city spaces', *Urban Studies*, vol. 39, no. 1, pp. 95–116.

Cocaine Cowboys 2006, motion picture, Magnolia Pictures, Dallas and New York City.

Cohen, E 1972, 'Toward a sociology of international tourism', *Social Research*, vol. 39, no. 1, pp. 164–182.

Cohen, E 1982, 'Marginal paradises: bungalow tourism on the islands of Southern Thailand', *Annals of Tourism Research*, vol. 9, pp. 189–228.

Coleman, S & Crang, M 2002, 'Grounded tourists, travelling theory', in S Coleman & M Crang (eds), *Tourism: between place and performance*, Berghahn Books, New York, pp. 1–17.

Condon, M 2014, 'Gold Coast's past in the flesh', *The Courier-Mail*, 29 September, viewed 27 October 2015, <http://www.couriermail.com.au/news/special-features/gold-coasts-past-in-the-flesh/story-fnl1b568-1227074209173>.

Corderoy, J 2017, *Our favourite travel destinations have a serious problem with drink spiking*, 3 May, viewed 19 May 2018, <http://www.news.com.au/travel/travel-updates/warnings/our-favourite-travel-destinations-have-a-serious-problem-with-drink-spiking/news-story/6d7b9bf205fd38c424cd328485c53965>.

Couzens, G 2015, 'San Antonio: British cops to patrol Ibiza resort plagued by drug dealers this summer', *The Mirror*, 6 March, viewed 7 June 2016, <http://www.mirror.co.uk/news/world-news/san-antonio-british-cops-patrol-5281150>.

Crang, M 2014, 'Cultural geographies of tourism', in AA Lew, CM Hall & AM Williams (eds), *The Wiley Blackwell companion to tourism*, Wiley Blackwell, Hoboken, pp. 66–77.

Crouch, D 2002, 'Surrounded by place: embodied encounters', in S Coleman & M Crang (eds), *Tourism: between place and performance*, Berghahn Books, New York, pp. 207–218.

Crouch, D & Desforges, L 2003, 'The sensuous in the tourist encounter: introduction: the power of the body in tourist studies', *Tourist Studies*, vol. 3, no. 1, pp. 5–22.

Daniel, Z 2013, 'Phuket introduces "safety zones" to protect tourists', *ABC News*, 1 April, viewed 7 June 2016, <http://www.abc.net.au/news/2013-04-01/phuket-safety-zones-introduced-to-protect-tourists/4603562>.

Dann, G 1996, 'The people of tourist brochures', in T Selwyn (ed.), *The tourist image: myths and myth making in tourism*, John Wiley & Sons, Chichester, pp. 61–81.

Deleuze, G & Guattari, F 2004 [1987], *A thousand plateaus: capitalism and schizophrenia*, trans. B Massumi, Continuum, London.

Dexter 2006–2013, television series, Showtime Networks, New York City.

Diken, B & Laustsen, B 2004, 'Sea, sun, sex and the discontents of pleasure', *Tourist Studies*, vol. 4, no. 2, pp. 99–114.

Edensor, T 2006, 'Sensing tourist spaces', in C Minca & T Oakes (eds), *Travels in paradox: remapping tourism*, Rowman & Littlefield, Lanham, pp. 23–45.

Edensor, T 2007, 'Mundane mobilities, performances and spaces of tourism', *Social & Cultural Geography*, vol. 8, no. 2, pp. 199–215.

Fineran, L & Stigwood, E 2014, 'Dark depths of the Gold Coast's own seedy underworld exposed as an alleged drug kingpin fights for bail', *Gold Coast Bulletin*, 19 April, viewed 20 April 2014, <http://www.goldcoastbulletin.com.au/news/crime-court/dark-depths-of-the-gold-coasts-own-seedy-underworld-exposed-as-an-alleged-drug-kingpin-fights-for-bail/story-fnje8bkv-1226889293334>.

Foucault, M 1986, 'Of other spaces', *Diacritics*, vol. 16, no. 1, pp. 22–27.

Gallan, B 2015, 'Night lives: heterotopia, youth transitions and cultural infrastructure in the urban night', *Urban Studies*, vol. 52, no. 3, pp. 555–570.

Goffman, E 1969 [1956], *The presentation of the self in everyday life*, Pelican Books, London.

Gold Coast Cops 2014–2015, television series, Network Ten, Prymont.

Goulding, C & Shankar, A 2011, 'Club culture, neotribalism and ritualised behaviour', *Annals of Tourism Research*, vol. 38, no. 4, pp. 1435–1453.

Grazian, D 2008, *On the make: the hustle of urban nightlife*, University of Chicago Press, Chicago.

Grazian, D 2009, 'Urban nightlife, social capital, and the public life of cities', *Sociological Forum*, vol. 24, no. 4, pp. 908–917.

Greater Miami Convention & Visitors Bureau 2015, *Miami and The Beaches | The Official Vacation Guide*, viewed 20 August 2015, <http://www.miamiandbeaches.com/>.

Greater Miami Convention & Visitors Bureau 2016, *Greater Miami and The Beaches: 2015 Visitor Industry Overview*, viewed 21 October 2016, <http://partners.miamiandbeaches.com/~/media/files/gmcvb/partners/research%20statistics/annual-report_2015>.

Griffin, G 1998, 'The good, the bad and the peculiar: cultures and policies of urban planning and development on the Gold Coast', *Urban Policy and Research*, vol. 16, no. 4, pp. 285–292.

Ironside, R 2014, 'Gold Coast to remain a hot spot for Schoolies as risks of celebrating abroad highlighted', *Gold Coast Bulletin*, 11 October, viewed 28 June 2016, <http://www.goldcoastbulletin.com.au/news/gold-coast-to-remain-a-hot-spot-for-schoolies-as-risks-of-celebrating-abroad-highlighted/news-story/fb11c06cdd0b9b7c106e01f8ae43b368>.

Jaimangal-Jones, D, Pritchard, A & Morgan, N 2010, 'Going the distance: locating journey, liminality and rites of passage in dance music experiences', *Leisure Studies*, vol. 29, no. 3, pp. 253–268.

Josiam, BM, Hobson, JP, Dietrich, UC & Smeaton, G 1998, 'An analysis of the sexual, alcohol and drug related behavioural patterns of students on spring break', *Tourism Management*, vol. 19, no. 6, pp. 501–513.

Kelly, D, Hughes, K & Bellis, M 2014, 'Work hard, party harder: drug use and sexual behaviour in young British casual workers in Ibiza, Spain', *International Journal of Environmental Research and Public Health*, vol. 11, no. 10, pp. 10051–10061.

Larkins, F 2013, 'Police union stands by Gold Coast "crime capital" label', *ABC Gold Coast*, 6 June, viewed 21 April 2014, <http://www.abc.net.au/local/stories/2013/06/06/3776125.htm>.

Law, L, Bunnell, T & Ong, C-E 2007, 'The Beach, the gaze and film tourism', *Tourist Studies*, vol. 7, no. 2, pp. 141–164.

Lawton, LJ & Weaver, DB 2015, 'Using residents' perceptions research to inform planning and management for sustainable tourism: a study of the Gold Coast

Schoolies Week, a contentious tourism event', *Journal of Sustainable Tourism*, vol. 23, no. 5, pp. 660–682.

Lewis, MA, Patrick, ME, Mittmann, A & Kaysen, DL 2014, 'Sex on the beach: the influence of social norms and trip companion on Spring Break sexual behavior', *Prevention Science*, vol. 15, no. 3, pp. 408–418.

Litvin, SW 2009, 'A comparison of student Spring Break and their "normal" behaviors: is the hype justified?', *Tourism Review International*, vol. 13, no. 3, pp. 173–181.

Lockett, J 2018, 'Murder in paradise: how Mexico's party hotspot Cancun has become one of the world's murder capitals', *The Sun*, 13 March, viewed 18 May 2018, <https://www.thesun.co.uk/news/5789294/crime-wave-murder-mexico-cancun-spring-break/>.

Longhurst, R 1995, *Gold Coast: our heritage in focus*, State Library of Queensland Foundation, South Brisbane.

Malam, L 2008, 'Geographic imaginations: exploring divergent notions of identity, power, and place meaning on Pha-ngan Island, Southern Thailand', *Asia Pacific Viewpoint*, vol. 49, no. 3, pp. 331–343.

Malbon, B 1998, 'The club: clubbing: consumption, identity and the spatial practices of every-night life', in T Skelton & G Valentine (eds), *Cool places: geographies of youth cultures*, Routledge, London, pp. 266–286.

Malbon, B 1999, *Clubbing: dancing, ecstacy and vitality*, Routledge, New York.

Malkin, B 2011, 'Gold Coast tourist hub becomes Australia's crime capital', *The Telegraph*, 21 July, viewed 6 June 2016, <http://www.telegraph.co.uk/news/worldnews/australiaandthepacific/australia/8652342/Gold-Coast-tourist-hub-becomes-Australias-crime-capital.html>.

Martinez, M 2018, 'Are tourists at risk? Cancun murders spike as drug cartels wage a bloody turf war', *Miami Herald*, 12 April, viewed 18 May 2018, <http://www.miamiherald.com/article208720004.html>.

Maticka-Tyndale, E, Herold, ES & Oppermann, M 2003, 'Casual sex among Australian schoolies', *The Journal of Sex Research*, vol. 40, no. 2, pp. 158–169.

McKenna, M 2010, 'Dark side of Glitter Strip exposed', *The Australian*, 28 August, viewed 20 April 2014, <http://www.theaustralian.com.au/news/nation/dark-side-of-glitter-strip-exposed/story-e6frg6nf-1225911091843>.

McRobbie, A 1984, *The fabulous Gold Coast*, Pan News, Surfers Paradise.

Meethan, K 1996, 'Place, image and power: Brighton as a resort', in T Selwyn (ed.), *The tourist image: myths and myth making in tourism*, John Wiley & Sons, Chichester, pp. 179–196.

Meethan, K 2001, *Tourism in global society: place, culture, consumption*, Palgrave, Basingstoke.

Melechi, A 1993, 'The ecstasy of disappearance', in S Redhead (ed.), *Rave off: politics and deviance in contemporary youth culture*, Avebury, Aldershot, pp. 29–40.

Miami Vice 1984–1989, television series, NBC, New York City.

Minca, C & Oakes, T 2006, 'Introduction: traveling paradoxes', in C Minca & T Oakes (eds), *Travels in paradox: remapping tourism*, Rowman & Littlefield, Lanham, pp. 1–21.

Nilan, P, Julian, R & Germov, J 2007, *Australian youth: social and cultural issues*, Pearson Education, Frenchs Forest.

Pacific Heat 2016–2017, television series, The Comedy Channel, Melbourne.

Paris, N 2013, 'Fears over safety of tourists in Phuket', *The Telegraph*, 14 March, viewed 7 June 2016, <http://www.telegraph.co.uk/travel/news/Fears-over-safety-of-tourists-in-Phuket/>.

Patrick, ME, Morgan, N, Maggs, JL & Lefkowitz, ES 2010, '"I got your back": friends' understandings regarding college student Spring Break behavior', *Journal of Youth and Adolescence*, vol. 40, no. 1, pp. 108–120.

Pons, PO, Crang, M & Travlou, P 2009, 'Introduction: taking Mediterranean tourists seriously', in PO Pons, M Crang & P Travlou (eds), *Cultures of mass tourism: doing the Mediterranean in the age of banal mobilities*, Ashgate, Farnham, pp. 1–20.

Potts, R, Dedekorkut-Howes, A & Bosman, C 2013, 'Gold Coast is not only all that glitters: understanding visitor and resident perceptions of the Gold Coast', *Australian Planner*, vol. 50, no. 4, pp. 316–327.

Preston-Whyte, R 2004, 'The beach as a liminal space', in AA Lew, CM Hall & AM Williams (eds), *A companion to tourism*, Blackwell Publishing, Malden, pp. 349–359.

Ragsdale, K, Porter, JR, Zamboanga, BL, St Lawrence, JS, Read-Wahidi, R & White, A 2011, 'High-risk drinking among female college drinkers at two reporting intervals: comparing Spring Break to the 30 days prior', *Sexuality Research and Social Policy*, vol. 9, no. 1, pp. 31–40.

Red Frogs 2014, *Gold Coast | Red Frogs Australia*, viewed 22 April 2014, <http://au.redfrogs.com/schoolies/im-a-volunteer/gold-coast>.

Reidy, T 2013, 'Ibiza: "nothing is innocent and dealing is normal"', *The Guardian*, 17 August, viewed 7 June 2016, <http://www.theguardian.com/world/2013/aug/17/ibiza-drugs-dark-side>.

Ribeiro, NF & Yarnal, CM 2008, '"It wasn't my sole purpose for going down there" – an inquiry into the Spring Break experience and its relation to risky behaviors and alcohol consumption', *Annals of Leisure Research*, vol. 11, no. 3–4, pp. 351–367.

Rojek, C 1993, *Ways of escape: modern transformations in leisure and travel*, Macmillan Press, London.

Rojek, C & Urry, J 1997, 'Transformations of travel and theory', in C Rojek & J Urry (eds), *Touring cultures: transformations of travel and theory*, Routledge, London, pp. 1–19.

Ryan, C 2002a, 'Memories of the beach', in C Ryan (ed.), *The tourist experience*, 2nd edn, Continuum, London, pp. 156–171.

Ryan, C 2002b, 'Stages, gazes and constructions of tourism', in C Ryan (ed.), *The tourist experience*, 2nd edn, Continuum, London, pp. 1–26.

Saldanha, A 2002, 'Music tourism and factions of bodies in Goa', *Tourist Studies*, vol. 2, no. 1, pp. 43–62.

Sandvoss, C 2014, '"I ♥ Ibiza": music, place and belonging', in M Duffett (ed.), *Popular music fandom: identities, roles and practices*, Routledge, New York, pp. 115–145.

Scarface 1983, motion picture, Universal Pictures, Universal City.

Selwyn, T 1996, 'Introduction', in T Selwyn (ed.), *The tourist image: myths and myth making in tourism*, John Wiley & Sons, Chichester, pp. 1–32.

Sharpley, R 2004, 'Islands in the sun: Cyprus', in M Sheller & J Urry (eds), *Tourism mobilities: places to play, places in play*, Routledge, London, pp. 22–31.

Shaw, G & Williams, AM 2004, *Tourism and tourism spaces*, SAGE Publications, London.

Sheller, M 2004, 'Demobilizing and remobilizing Caribbean paradise', in M Sheller & J Urry (eds), *Tourism mobilities: places to play, places in play*, Routledge, London, pp. 13–21.

Shields, R 1991, *Places on the margin: alternative geographies of modernity*, Routledge, London.

Smail, S 2011, 'Gold Coast "the crime capital of Australia"', *ABC News*, 22 July, viewed 23 April 2014, <http://www.abc.net.au/news/2011-07-21/gold-coast-becoming-crime-capital/2803830>.

Smith, AMA & Rosenthal, D 1997, 'Sex, alcohol and drugs? Young people's experience of Schoolies Week', *Australia and New Zealand Journal of Public Health*, vol. 21, no. 2, pp. 175–179.

Soja, EW 1996, *Thirdspace: journeys to Los Angeles and other real-and-imagined places*, Blackwell Publishers, Oxford.

Sönmez, S, Apostolopoulos, Y, Yu, CH, Yang, S, Mattila, A & Yu, LC 2006, 'Binge drinking and casual sex on spring break', *Annals of Tourism Research*, vol. 33, no. 4, pp. 895–917.

Spencer, K & Rudd, M 2017, 'Out of their minds: Schoolies completely destroy their luxury Gold Coast penthouse apartment and then boast about the damage in latest 2017 celebration atrocity', *Daily Mail Australia*, 25 November, viewed 20 April 2018, <http://www.dailymail.co.uk/news/article-5116025/Schoolies-trash-Gold-Coast-Mantra-Sun-City-penthouse-room.html>.

The State of Queensland 2016, *Schoolies: be safe & watch your mates*, viewed 28 June 2016, <https://www.schoolies.qld.gov.au>.

Stockwell, S 2011, 'Crime capital of Australia: the Gold Coast on screen', *Studies in Australasian Cinema*, vol. 5, no. 3, pp. 281–292.

Stolz, G, Pierce, J & Laughlin, S 2014, 'Nightclub owner Jamie Pickering, top DJ Joseph "JoeyMojo" Sandagon and senior bikie Josh Downey arrested in Gold Coast drug raids', *Gold Coast Bulletin*, 6 April, viewed 20 April 2014, <http://www.goldcoastbulletin.com.au/news/crime-court/nightclub-owner-jamie-pickering-top-dj-joseph-joeymojo-sandagon-and-senior-bikie-josh-downey-arrested-in-gold-coast-drug-raids/story-fnje8bkv-1226875954745>.

The Strip 2008, television series, Nine Network, Willoughby.

Thornton, S 1995, *Club cultures: music, media and subcultural capital*, Polity Press, Cambridge.

Tonkiss, F 2005, *Space, the city and social theory*, Polity Press, Cambridge.

Tourism Australia 2014, *Gold Coast*, viewed 20 April 2014, <http://www.australia.com/explore/cities/gold-coast.aspx>.

Turner, L & Ash, J 1976, *The golden hordes: international tourism and the pleasure periphery*, St. Martin's Press, New York.

Turner, V 1973, 'The center out there: pilgrim's goal', *History of Religions*, vol. 12, no. 3, pp. 191–230.

Turner, V 1974 [1969], *The ritual process: structure and anti-structure*, Penguin, Harmondsworth.

Tutenges, S 2012, 'Nightlife tourism: a mixed methods study of young tourists at an international nightlife resort', *Tourist Studies*, vol. 12, no. 2, pp. 131–150.

Urry, J 1995, *Consuming places*, Routledge, London.

Urry, J 2002, *The tourist gaze*, 2nd edn, SAGE Publications, London.

Urry, J 2006, 'Preface: places and performances', in C Minca & T Oakes (eds), *Travels in paradox: remapping tourism*, Rowman & Littlefield Publishers, Lanham, pp. vii–xi.

van Gennep, A 1977 [1960], *The rites of passage*, trans. MB Vizedom & GL Gaffee, Routledge, London.

Wang, N 1999, 'Rethinking authenticity in tourism experience', *Annals of Tourism Research*, vol. 26, no. 2, pp. 349–370.

Westerhausen, K 2002, *Beyond the beach: an ethnography of modern travellers in Asia*, White Lotus Press, Bangkok.

Wilson, B 2006, *Fight, flight, or chill: subcultures, youth and rave into the twenty-first century*, McGill-Queen's University Press, Montreal.

Winchester, HP, McGuirk, PM & Everett, K 1999, 'Schoolies Week as a rite of passage: a study of celebration and control', in EK Teather (ed.), *Embodied geographies: spaces, bodies and rites of passage*, Routledge, London, pp. 59–77.

Wise, P 2006, 'Australia's Gold Coast: a city producing itself', in C Lindner (ed.), *Urban space and cityscapes: perspectives from modern and contemporary culture*, Routledge, New York, pp. 177–191.

Wise, P 2012, 'Solar flow: the uses of light in Gold Coast living', in A Ballantyne & CL Smith (eds), *Architecture in the space of flows*, Routledge, New York, pp. 99–116.

Wyn, J & White, R 1997, *Rethinking youth*, Allen & Unwin, St Leonards.

Zinkiewicz, L, Davey, J & Curd, D 1999, 'Sin beyond Surfers? Young people's risky behaviour during Schoolies Week in three Queensland regions', *Drug and Alcohol Review*, vol. 18, no. 3, pp. 279–285.

Zukin, S 1991, *Landscapes of power: from Detroit to Disney World*, University of California Press, Berkeley.

Zukin, S 1995, *The cultures of cities*, Blackwell Publishers, Oxford.

4 Culture and tourism

Global trends, local specificity and the symbolic economy

Introduction

The dominant touristic narratives of resorts are based on their existence as long-standing sites for mass tourism and party tourism. As such, resorts are perceived and lived (to an extent) as liminal and carnivalesque, predominantly attracting tourists seeking escapist, hedonistic, sensuous experiences through vacations centred on excessive consumption in spaces like hotels, beaches, shopping malls, theme parks or nightclubs. While this narrative is powerful and highly influential, there are numerous other narratives shaping the spatiality of resorts. In this chapter, I focus on some of the *emerging* narratives implicated in resorts' increasingly diverse tourism offerings. Each of these resorts is attempting to move beyond its 'sun, sand and sex' reputation to attract a broader range of visitors seeking alternative experiences, particularly those related to an interest in heritage, nature and/or culture. These types of tourists are assumed to be motivated primarily by a desire for intellectual (rather than bodily)[1] pleasures and to have 'authentic' experiences through encountering sites like landmarks, museums, galleries or urban precincts.

Below, I explore the role of cultural tourism[2] in resorts. In particular, I consider how cultural tourism initiatives play out in spaces which are saturated by mass tourism and, thus, often assumed to be antithetical to the tastes and principles of high culture. Despite having long supported tourism narratives which portray them as the opposite – as 'elsewhere', 'nowhere' or 'anywhere' – resorts are now striving to capitalise on their local specificity and distinctiveness. In this context, culture and heritage are being staged in the face of pervasive stereotypes of resorts as ahistorical, inauthentic, depthless, transient, superficial, fake and homogenous (stereotypes which themselves constitute another dominant narrative of resort identity and spatiality). These stereotypes stem from wider discourses regarding the influence of globalising processes – like tourism – on local cultures. Throughout the chapter, I aim to critique the assumptions underpinning such stereotypes by destabilising binaries of real/fake, authentic/inauthentic, difference/familiarity and local/global.

Culture, capitalism and the symbolic economy

Culture and capitalism have traditionally been conceived as counterposed ideas (Zukin 1995). Culture is often associated with 'high arts, literature, music, theatre' and the 'social exclusivity and superior knowledge' that these interests may afford (Meethan 2001, p. 115). Similarly, cultural heritage is typically understood as artistic forms, architecture, landmarks, traditions and customs that originate from a 'distant past' (Weaver 2011, p. 249). 'Culture' is thus concerned with what is unique, singular, authentic or intellectual (Meethan 2001). Capitalism is seen to threaten these qualities – it is associated with the cycles of mass production and consumption that give rise to popular culture, which 'provides commodified, unsophisticated, throwaway instant gratification' and is 'neither elitist, nor does it require [the] development of a highly refined aesthetic sensibility' (Meethan 2001, p. 116). Clearly, the term culture is used interchangeably with what we can more accurately designate as *high* culture.[3] This lack of specificity is indicative of how popular/mass culture is often conceptualised as existing outside of the realm of culture or, at most, on its margins. It is unsurprising, then, that the highly capitalistic spaces of resorts are frequently misunderstood as *lacking* culture.

However, as Sharon Zukin (1995) argues in *The Cultures of Cities*, culture and capital are very much entwined in contemporary cities. Tourism, for example, necessarily involves the commodification and packaging of a place's culture – its histories, architecture, rituals, festivals, traditional cuisine, lifestyles – for capitalistic ends (Shaw & Williams 2004; Chhabra, Healy & Sills 2003; Cohen 1988). Zukin (1995) posits that this process is part of what produces a city's 'symbolic economy'. She observes that with the decline of manufacturing and the intermittent instability of government and financial industries, 'culture is more and more the business of cities' (Zukin 1995, p. 2). Cities are increasingly mobilising their local distinctiveness – their history, arts scene, cultural enclaves or other forms of symbolic capital – as a means to sell themselves (Salazar 2011; Alonso 2007; Zukin 1995). Through urban tourism sites such as historic buildings, art galleries, museums, opera theatres and upmarket dining precincts, culture is used to revitalise derelict city districts and attract visitors to bolster the regional economy. Just as more conventional cities are cultivating their symbolic economies through tourism, so too are resorts.

Touristic desire for the 'real'

Many tourists have grown dissatisfied with the standardised, generic, Fordist-style mass tourism conventionally exemplified by resorts, and are increasingly interested in post-Fordist, niche tourism experiences (Boissevain 1996; MacCannell 2001). As Boissevain (1996) puts it:

More and more [tourists] are seeking holidays that cater to their desire for learning, nostalgia, heritage, make-believe, action, and a closer look at the Other. Not sun, sand, and sea, but culture, nature, and 'traditional' rural life have become the objects of the postmodern tourist. (p. 3)

Those occupied by such pursuits can be loosely defined as cultural tourists. In tourism literature, it is often claimed that cultural tourists (and, likewise, academic researchers) are seeking to experience the 'real' through their engagements with the cultures and landscapes of other places (Minca & Oakes 2006; Fainstein & Judd 1999; MacCannell 1999 [1976]; Desforges 1998). That is, some tourists want 'to share in the real life of the places visited, or at least to see that life as it is really lived' (MacCannell 1999 [1976], p. 96) as typified by the wish to travel 'off the beaten path' or 'get in with the natives' (p. 97). In Urry's (2002) terms, these tourists are after sites of the romantic gaze – that which is auratic, solitary, elitist and free of mass tourists. In other words, cultural tourists apparently seek the 'authentic'.

Although authenticity is a highly contested concept, it is nonetheless useful to the discussion at hand because of its significance for tourists as a framing device for how they perceive particular tourism spaces and experiences. As Zukin (2010) points out, the matter of whether or not authenticity actually exists is less important than how authenticity 'becomes a tool of power' (p. 3). Much like high culture, authenticity is commonly defined in terms of uniqueness, tradition, a sense of continuity and the appearance of stasis. Consequently, authenticity has been more closely associated with 'primitive' cultures, while modern cultures are perceived as inauthentic and alienating (Buchanan 2005; Meethan 2001; MacCannell 1999 [1976]).

It follows, then, that the modern cultural tourist must find authenticity elsewhere than home. In Meethan's (2001) words, 'Modernity is dystopia and tourism the search for utopia' (p. 91). Tourists who seek the real are motivated by a search for authentic experiences with authentic places, people and objects, and a desire for self-improvement (e.g. acquiring knowledge, cultural capital and life experience) (Meethan 2001; MacCannell 1973). In their quest for finding out what a place is 'really' like, these tourists (and, to some degree, all tourists) compare different destinations, and different sites within the same destination, to make assessments about what is real and what is fake or hyperreal (Minca & Oakes 2006). For example, I chose to stay in accommodation booked through Airbnb rather than hotels in some of my fieldwork sites. Being a tourist (not only a researcher), I wanted to feel as if I was 'living like a local' for a week by staying in an apartment on a 'normal' residential street, rather than in the contrived space of a hotel or tourist-centric strip.

Cultural tourists – those who actively seek authenticity – are typically regarded as preferable to mass tourists (Crang 2014; Boissevain 1996), with supposedly superior taste, greater respect for the host culture and more 'honourable' aims.[4] Destinations like resorts hence attempt to cater to the needs of both types of tourist. As Fainstein and Judd (1999) observe:

tourists do not always want to be humoured or amused. Instead, they often seek immersion in the daily, ordinary, *authentic* life of a culture or place that is not their own. Thus, the tourism industry is preoccupied with shaping and responding to the desire for carnival-like diversion, on the one hand, and a yearning for extraordinary, but 'real', experience on the other. (p. 7, original emphasis)

Cultural tourism and mass tourism, then, occupy the same spaces. One of my interviewees in Thailand (an expatriate who previously lived on the Gold Coast) reflected on this in relation to his town of residence near Phuket's Patong Beach:

JAKUB: Look, there are tourists who just live on the beach and that's all they come here for – sun, sand and surf, or sea. But there are tourists who try and get a feel for the place ... There are people who come here, enclose themselves in 5-star hotels or some beautiful villas with services, maids, cleaners, chefs and live in the paradise situation, but are not really touching or getting involved in Thai life. On the other hand, you see tourists who come to the market in my village who look around and try the different foods.

(Phuket, 9 December 2013)

Further, in contemporary resorts, tourists have the option to experience *both* of these in the same vacation. Despite what the dualism implies, individual tourists can possess the qualities and motivations of both cultural and mass tourists, and in varying combinations.

The challenge for resorts is that, unlike urban tourism destinations, their visitors have traditionally expressed more interest in consuming the destination's beaches and purpose-built tourism facilities than experiencing its local cultures. This varies somewhat among the resorts I focus on. The local cultures of Thailand and Cancún are fairly prominent in tourism imageries and promotion, even if only to evoke a sense of the exotic for the Western traveller. However, in the case of Miami, Ibiza and the Gold Coast, local cultures are, despite recent efforts to highlight them in official marketing material, still largely inconsequential to one's vacation. Such destinations may be less appealing to cultural tourists seeking the real in the conventional sense, and are commonly stereotyped as being fake or hyperreal.

Staged authenticity

As a result, the real is *staged* in resorts. Tourist spaces are carefully constructed and manipulated to provide visitors (especially cultural tourists) with the sense of authenticity that they demand. This is what MacCannell (1999 [1976], 1973) calls 'staged authenticity', a concept he develops in terms of Goffman's (1969 [1956]) work on dramaturgy. MacCannell (1999 [1976]) proposes that tourist sites are like sets or stages with front and back regions featuring different social performances. Front regions are those designed specifically for tourism purposes and are occupied by both hosts and guests – for instance, hotel lobbies, restaurants or theme parks (MacCannell 1999 [1976]). Back regions, on the other hand, are dominated by the hosts, and can range from spaces like kitchens or back offices (which keep the front regions running smoothly) to residential areas predominantly occupied by local lives and activities.

The existence of back regions suggests to tourists that 'there is something more than meets the eye' (MacCannell 1999 [1976], p. 93) or that there is 'a hidden realness somewhere just out of view' (Minca & Oakes 2006, p. 8). Thus, front regions are seen as contrived, performative and false, whereas back regions are seen as organic, intimate and real (MacCannell 1999 [1976]). However, the distinctions 'between false fronts and intimate reality' (MacCannell 1999 [1976], p. 95) are not as clear-cut as they may seem. MacCannell (1999 [1976], 1973) contends that there is, rather, a front-back continuum instead of a dichotomy, and that 'front' and 'back' function most effectively as conceptual tools if they are treated as 'ideal poles of touristic experience' (MacCannell 1999 [1976], p. 101) which do not manifest in their pure form. MacCannell (1973) identifies six stages on the continuum to illustrate that different dynamics between front and back (or staged and real) may be present; for instance:

> Stage 2: a touristic front region that has been decorated to appear, in some of its particulars, like a back region: a seafood restaurant with a fish net hanging on the wall; a meat counter in a supermarket with three-dimensional plastic replicas of cheeses and bolognas hanging against the wall. Functionally, this stage (two) is entirely a front region, and it always has been, but it is cosmetically decorated with reminders of back-region activities: mementos, not taken seriously, called 'atmosphere'. (p. 598)

This example details how front regions can be endowed with qualities of difference and authenticity, but back regions can be staged as well. The practice of making sites and cultures available for tourist consumption always requires them to be organised, manipulated, represented and packaged in some way (Salazar 2009; Urry 2002; Selwyn 1996; Cohen 1972). As tourists increasingly expect the spectacular, it is no longer enough for a culture, tourist site or product to *be* real, it must also *act* real, it must perform authenticity (Mac-Cannell 1999 [1976]; Rojek & Urry 1997; Cohen 1988). Further, it does not even have to *be* real if it can masquerade as such and create the *experience* of authenticity (Zukin 2010; Wang 1999). It is my contention that this subjective experience of authenticity is more important to an analysis of tourism than any kind of objective notion of authenticity. Material objects and places cannot be essentialised as authentic or inauthentic in themselves – what matters is how they are perceived differently by different people in relation to these concepts. In short, authenticity is a fluid, dynamic and contextually-contingent concept (Meethan 2001; Wang 1999; Craik 1997). If something seems real, then it is real. Wang (1999) explains that from this perspective:

> the experience of authenticity is pluralistic, relative to each tourist type who may have their own way of definition, experience, and interpretation of authenticity … In this sense, if mass tourists empathically experience the toured objects as authentic, then, their viewpoints are real in their own right, no matter whether experts may propose an opposite view from an objective perspective. (p. 355)

What researchers and experts might view as deceptive, superficial or inauthentic might be experienced by the tourist as real, meaningful and authentic (Shaw & Williams 2004; Cohen 1988). Further, what is authentic to one tourist might be inauthentic to another; what is authentic to a tourist might be inauthentic to a local, and so on. These differing judgments are inevitable considering the varied and multiple preconceptions, expectations, imaginaries, tastes, ideologies and motivations that inform each individual's encounter with the same site or object.

Cultural tourism initiatives

The types of cultural tourism attractions in each resort vary substantially because they have different histories, geographies and cultural backgrounds. Thailand, Ibiza and Cancún have quite conventional cultural attractions – namely, very old, tangible, officially recognised heritage in the form of architectural structures protected by bodies like the UNESCO World Heritage Centre. Miami, on the other hand, promotes more recent forms of heritage, including its preserved Art Deco facades and the rich cultural history and diversity of its local people. Additionally, Miami has a flourishing arts scene, with cultural attractions such as ballets, theatres, museums and galleries, particularly centred around Downtown Miami and the Wynwood and Design District/Buena Vista neighbourhoods (rather than in the tourist hub of Miami Beach itself). The Gold Coast is altogether different to these other resorts in that over the course of its history as a tourism destination, the city has invested little energy in mobilising its culture and heritage as potential attractions. Below, I discuss cultural tourism in both Cancún and the Gold Coast as disparate examples that nonetheless share some important commonalities.

Cancún: an example

Being a relatively 'new' city in terms of its Western development, Cancún itself has little in the way of cultural activities like galleries, museums or theatres, but it is located within two and a half hours drive of major Maya archaeological sites like Chichén Itzá, Tulum and Cobá. The destination is also close to several eco-archaeological theme parks, such as Xcaret and Xel-Ha, which are built around Maya ruins and offer additional activities like water sports, animal encounters and Mexican and Maya cultural experiences. These attractions fuse the interests of cultural tourism and ecotourism with the packaged, full service model characteristic of mass tourism (Torres 2002).

Torres and Momsen (2006) argue that cultural tourists interested in learning about Maya cultural heritage are unlikely to stay in mass tourism destinations like Cancún. Although 'genuine'[5] cultural tourists (or travellers) may not be drawn to the resort, many of its mass tourists nonetheless choose to punctuate their sun, sand and sex holidays with cultural activities. Indeed, visiting sites like Chichén Itzá has become almost an imperative to under-taking a 'proper' Cancún holiday,[6] by virtue of its promotion as a 'must see' icon (Evans 2005), a famous UNESCO World Heritage Site and one of the 'New Seven Wonders of the World'[7] (Cancún Convention & Visitors Bureau 2015). Cultural heritage has thus become a core component of the destination's mass tourism model, a process referred to by Muñoz-Fernández (2014) as the 'Mayanization' of Cancún's imaginary.

Tour operators offer day trips to the nearby archaeological sites, with each marketed somewhat differently. One of my interviewees, Felipe, advised me that Chichén Itzá is the most popular heritage site to tour, but that Cobá offered more authentic experiences. As he put it, Cobá was popular among European tourists, who he thought showed more interest in history and culture than Americans. Unlike Chichén Itzá, Cobá is not on the UNESCO World Heritage List, and is therefore less populated by tourists and less strictly regulated. This allows greater access to the ruins, with visitors being permitted to climb the pyramids. By doing so, they are able to feel that they have had an opportunity to have a more intimate engagement with the site, but they are also demonstrating disregard for how their practices may be compromising the integrity of the built heritage. In effect, this renders them no more respectful or 'sound' in their decisions than mass tourists.

Capitalising on this desire for authentic cultural experiences, tours to Cobá often also include a visit to a Maya community. For example, the company Alltournative[8] (whose website offers 'ecoarchaeological adven-tures') advertises a Maya encounter including traditional food and an authentic blessing ceremony performed by a shaman (Alltournative 2016). Tourists can get a sense that they are experiencing a back region, a glimpse of how Mexico's indigenous people really live. In actuality, it is a series of staged, superficial displays packaged for touristic consumption, emphasising a selection of what might seem to be the most exotic elements of Maya culture. This can satisfy the tourists' desire to experience difference by making it available to them in a manner that is not onerous, inconvenient or uncomfortable.

My day trip to Chichén Itzá was similar in many ways, providing a breadth of experiences without any depth of education. The journey there was in itself a kind of tourism spectacle – immediately after leaving the modernised city limits of Cancún, we drove through seemingly more 'real' rural areas, taking photos of rustic homes and churches that stood in stark contrast to the polished, opulent hotels in which we stayed. Our first stop was the city of Valladolid, where our tour guide instructed us to take note of the Spanish-style architecture as he elaborated on Mexico's colonial history.

Back on the bus, the tour guide prepared us for our next stop, a nearby cenote (sinkhole). Of course, it was not just a cenote, but a more elaborate, staged tourist attraction with numerous activities and services, including a tequila distillery and a Western buffet. The guide informed us that at the cenote we could find authentic crafts like jewellery representing ancient Maya glyphs or trinkets made of obsidian (a type of black rock traditionally used by Maya people). On arrival, we walked through a maze-like gift shop displaying these items. As we exited the shop, the staff stopped each of us to take a photo, which we later found is printed onto the label of a bottle of liquor and sold to us on the tour bus as a novelty item. The cenote itself featured the usual juxtaposition of natural wonders and manmade additions – visitors can go inside the cenote and swim in the water, but there are queues to maintain order, and railings and life jackets for safety. At the entrance to the cenote were two men dressed as traditional Maya warriors, stationed there to pose for photos with tourists (see Figure 4.1).

Chichén Itzá was a similar kind of experience, showcasing the spectacle of the ruins of an ancient Maya city, roped off to protect them from visitors and set among landscaped grounds to facilitate gazing. Even the ruins themselves are staged in the sense that they have been excavated and restored. The space was occupied by tour groups with guides repeating the same historical narratives; tourists taking selfies with Chichén Itzá's iconic pyramid (see Figure 4.2); and local Mexican and Maya people lining each pathway selling souvenirs (see Figure 4.3), shouting things like 'One dollar! Just one dollar!' or 'Almost free!' as we walked by. These vendors touted items like miniature versions of the monuments (commodified representations of their own cultural heritage), wood carved ornaments, painted plates, musical instruments, jewellery, shirts and sombreros. Whether they were handmade or mass produced, made locally or elsewhere, was unclear. Presumably, what mattered most for the buyer was the memorialising of the experience and the *feeling* of authenticity, regardless of the item's origins.

Clearly, the symbolic economy of places like Chichén Itzá and the cenote rely on the commodification of Maya culture, catering to a desire for the exotic and the ancient. Sites like these exhibit an awareness of the importance of souvenirs – however staged, kitschy or inauthentic – to the tourist experience. They are sought out, collected and treasured by tourists. Back home, such items become material resources for the representation of cultural capital and the cultivation of autobiographical narratives through the reminiscing and retelling of holiday memories.

Figure 4.1 Men dressed as Maya warriors at the cenote

Figure 4.2 The El Castillo pyramid at Chichén Itzá

Figure 4.3 Souvenir vendors at Chichén Itzá

Gold Coast: an example

Unlike Cancún, the Gold Coast area has few major cultural attractions. If the built environment is one of 'the most obvious manifestations of heritage' (Chhabra et al. 2003, p. 704), this is where the Gold Coast is sorely lacking. The city has a habit of continually transforming and reinventing itself, knocking down older buildings rather than preserving them, and rebuilding with taller and more stylish structures. Skyscrapers, theme parks and shopping centres are the closest equivalents to any kind of architectural landmarks. The material past is treated as disposable and, as a result, the Gold Coast is often assumed to be bereft of history in a conventional sense (Wise 2012; Symes 1997).

The Gold Coast is also disparaged – both colloquially and in the media – as a 'cultural desert' (Smith 2018; Blackman 2013; Baker, Bennett & Wise 2012; Ditton 2010; Wise 2010, 2006). Despite Indigenous Australians having a long history in the area, there are few attractions focusing on this aspect of the region's heritage. In Surfers Paradise, the only symbols of this history that are present are an Indigenous busker playing the didgeridoo, cultural objects and artworks that have been commodified for sale in souvenir shops, and a single Indigenous art gallery (which sells typical Australian souvenirs like stuffed koalas, opals and UGG boots in addition to its certified artworks). Further, visitors have typically expressed little interest in the city's back regions or engaging with everyday local life. Beesley (2005) suggests that the inattention to both cultural heritage and contemporary local cultures on the Gold Coast may be due to the city's primarily domestic, and especially

regional, tourism market. International visitors, for whom the city is somewhat foreign and exotic, are more likely to want to experience the Gold
Coast's culture and learn about its history.

Residents lament the apparent lack of culture, internalising popular
discourses about the city, and attributing this to the tourist-centric nature of
development, which has tended to be geared towards catering to the needs of
mass tourists. This is not to say that cultural activities or an active arts scene
do not exist, but rather that these have conventionally been dislocated,
undervalued and underfunded on the Gold Coast (Ditton 2010; Beesley
2005). Some current examples of cultural events and spaces active in the city
include: the Swell Sculpture Festival, held each year since 2003 along the
beach in Currumbin, about a 35-minute drive south of Surfers Paradise;
Bleach* Festival, held annually since 2012, taking place in a variety of locations across the Gold Coast, and featuring art exhibitions, interactive work-
shops and film screenings as well as theatre, dance, circus and musical
performances; and Miami Marketta, operating since 2011, a popular venue
among locals that hosts live music performances and street food events
several times per week.

In the lead up to the 2018 Commonwealth Games, the Gold Coast's city
council attempted to support more of these kinds of cultural initiatives, and
to stage authenticity. In addition to programming an extensive array of music,
dance, theatre and circus performances, film screenings and art installations
during the Games, the city also invested in several redevelopment projects. An
outdoor amphitheatre was constructed as an expansion to the existing arts
centre (formerly the Gold Coast Arts Centre, recently rebranded as Home of
the Arts or HOTA) located west of Surfers Paradise, creating a more
comprehensive and spectacular cultural attraction. This addition is the first
stage in a multi-year cultural precinct redevelopment plan, which will also
include an 'art hotel' and new performing and exhibition facilities (Council of
the City of Gold Coast 2018; Simonot 2018).

Further north, in the suburb of Southport, the city has recently imposed a
Chinatown (see Figure 4.4) on a cluster of streets that were previously occupied by a mixture of Western, Japanese, Korean and Thai (rather than
Chinese) businesses. A range of spatial signifiers were added to indicate a
sense of authenticity, including a Confucius statue, strings of colourful
lanterns, and three Paifang gateways (Potts 2014). This initiative is part of the
larger rebranding of Southport as the Gold Coast's CBD (despite the resort's
decidedly *de*centred formation and commercial activities), with Chinatown
functioning to symbolise 'maturity, urban life and global identity', and to
appeal to growing numbers of Chinese tourists and international students
(Council of the City of Gold Coast 2015). This initiative also serves to complement the city's attempts to reposition itself in popular imaginaries as a
vibrant, cosmopolitan city, rather than only a resort town. Whereas in a
conventional urban centre a Chinatown may emerge organically, on the Gold
Coast it is blatantly staged to infer cultural diversity. Nevertheless, in true

Gold Coast style, the precinct is cementing itself as a 'real' Chinatown, with increasing numbers of Chinese shops and restaurants, and events like Lunar New Year celebrations and weekly street markets attracting a diverse range of people.

Notions of cultural identity and heritage on the Gold Coast are deeply implicated in the city's history as a tourism destination. Thus, among the few things the city *does* preserve are narratives and artefacts relating to its development alongside the tourism industry (Wise & Breen 2004). This is what Weaver (2011) calls 'contemporary tourism heritage' – the history *of* mass tourism as a legitimate form of heritage that can be mobilised for further touristic consumption. After all, this heritage is what makes the Gold Coast unique. In spite of the city's attempts to diversify its image, its symbolic economy nonetheless capitalises on its status as an icon of Australia's much valued beach culture (Davidson & Spearritt 2000).

Although there is no museum devoted to contemporary tourism heritage, the city is home to sites like Surf World, a museum displaying a collection of surfboards and other surfing memorabilia, photographs and oral histories (Surf World Gold Coast 2018). The Gold Coast City Art Gallery has held several exhibitions documenting the city's history in terms of tourism: for example, 'Sexualising the City' (Gold Coast City Art Gallery 2012) focused on the city's narratives of identity in relation to sex, bikinis and bare bodies; 'Learning from Surfers Paradise' (Gold Coast City Art Gallery 2013) compared one photographer's shots of the same

Figure 4.4 Chinatown, Southport

spots taken in 1973 and again in 2013 to illustrate the tourist hub's rapid development; while 'Flesh: Gold Coast in the 60s, 70s and 80s' (Burstow 2014) provided a look back at the resort's beach culture through a photographer's collection of pictures from his own annual family vacations. Such exhibitions have also featured kitsch ephemera including postcards, promotional posters, swimwear and photographs of locally iconic figures like Meter Maids and lifeguards. The Meter Maids are in themselves a form of living heritage – no longer topping up parking meters as they initially did, they persist as mainstays in the visual spectacle of Surfers Paradise, chatting to passersby and selling merchandise.

In terms of built heritage listed on the Gold Coast Local Heritage Register, there are tourism facilities like the Main Beach Pavilion (constructed in 1934); Southport Surf Lifesaving Club (constructed in 1936); the first high-rise hotel, Kinkabool (constructed 1959–60); and the Pink Poodle Motel signs (constructed in the mid-1960s, with the neon sign replaced in 1987 and relocated in 2011; see Figure 4.5) (Gold Coast City Council 2013a, 2013b). These are seen to symbolise particularly significant trends in the evolution of the city's tourism industry. The latter two examples, for instance, are positioned as emblematic of the influence of American styles and standards on regional architecture, aesthetics and consumer tastes. In the case of the Pink Poodle, the motel was demolished in 2003 yet the iconic signs were retained as a symbol of 'the Gold Coast fun and fantasy phase' (Gold Coast City Council 2013b, p. 98). In typical postmodern fashion, the city opted to

Figure 4.5 Pink Poodle Motel sign, Surfers Paradise

Figure 4.6 Billboard with a retro photograph in Surfers Paradise

preserve *traces* of its material past rather than the substance of it, appealing to local and touristic desires for heritage without compromising the opportunity for more modern developments on the same site.[9]

The redevelopment several years ago of the pedestrian walkway along The Esplanade, bordering the beach in Surfers Paradise, included the addition of old photographs of the area on display boards (see Figure 4.6) and on the sides of public toilet buildings. These nostalgic images (primarily from the 1930s–1960s) feature women in bikinis, men with surfboards, Meter Maids and surf life savers, functioning to impose a sense of heritage on the contemporary built environment. This kind of initiative, which stages tourism culture as heritage, signals a growing recognition of the advantages that may be provided by historicising place for tourists. In particular, it offers the sense of authenticity that places like resorts are so frequently purported to lack.

Impermanence, simulacra and hyperreality

As the examples above highlight, resorts are perceived as disembedded (Featherstone & Lash 1995; Giddens 1990) from the historical and cultural contexts in which they actually exist. Even a city like Cancún, which has numerous conventional cultural tourism sites available nearby, is still seen as a banal tourist trap, disconnected from the authenticity and 'real' lives which saturate its surrounds. Through producing (and reproducing) a metanarrative that promotes them as escapist, liminal spaces that are dislocated from the mundane nature of everyday life, resorts have positioned themselves as dehistoricised spaces (Wise 2006; Wise & Breen 2004). As Wise and Breen (2004) explain in relation to the Gold Coast:

> This is not to say there are not histories, but from the time of its spectacular expansion, the most obvious characteristic of the Gold Coast was that it imagined its main purpose as somewhere that others came to enjoy, and leave. Its project has been to give visitors respite from their own historically located and determined daily lives. That is, its project has been to be outside history. (p. 164)

This dehistoricisation is further heightened by the impermanence characteristic of resorts. Being mature destinations dependent on mass tourism, resorts are perpetually changing and rejuvenating themselves, staving off or reducing periods of decline by adapting to global trends and consumer demands. This is true of both their materiality – ensuring tourism facilities and attractions are modern and well maintained – and their imaginaries – altering, managing and diversifying their official tourism narratives. Very little stays the same for very long. Whether tourists or residents, people tend to be transient, as do social spaces and senses of belonging (Baker et al. 2012; Nijman 2011). This lack of continuity is assumed to produce inauthenticity, since the authentic is generally considered as that which emerges organically, remains stable and 'accumulate[s] the patina of age' (Zukin 2010, p. 2). In a contradictory movement, the only sense of continuity or permanence in resorts is to be found in their transience, and in ongoing, unpredictable shifts and transformations, not only in the built environment, but in lifestyles, identities, imaginaries, narratives and rhythms. Even their spectacular natural landscapes – the core reason for their presence as tourism destinations – are subject to constant change from the impacts of weather, tides, seasons and human use.

Due to the staged nature of both cultural and mass tourism, resorts can be read as hyperreal spaces composed of simulacra. The need to cater to a touristic demand for the real and the exotic has required destinations to package their local distinctiveness for mass consumption, raising questions regarding the dynamics between genuine and false, representation and reality. According to Baudrillard (1994 [1981]), under postmodernism the real is progressively being replaced by simulations of the real – what he calls 'the precession of simulacra'. Simulacra are signs, symbols or copies with no referent or original counterpart. Simulacra do not *hide* the truth, because there is no truth (Baudrillard 1994 [1981]). With the proliferation of simulacra, Baudrillard (1994 [1981]) argues, the postmodern world is increasingly becoming hyperreal, a 'desert of the real' (p. 1).

Common examples of the hyperreal include spaces like theme parks and shopping malls, and cultural products like advertising and reality television (Soja 2000; Belk 1996; Eco 1986). It can also be argued that simulacra have become so pervasive that they now permeate our everyday lives. As Soja (1996) observes, 'Now you do not just choose to visit these hyperreality factories at your leisure, *hyperreality visits you* every day wherever you choose to be' (p. 251, original emphasis). Even some cities can be conceptualised as hyperreal environments. Soja (2000, 1996) considers this specifically in terms of urban formations like the exopolis,[10] which he posits are 'spin-doctored "scamscapes"' (Soja 1996, p. 9) constituted by 'thick layers of simulations' (Soja 2000, p. 343), much like theme parks. Similarly, Hannigan's (1998) concept of the 'fantasy city' suggests that urban precincts are being progressively redeveloped to function as intensively branded, themed, eclectic and hyperreal enclaves for entertainment consumption. Much like the fantasy city and the exopolis, resorts can also be understood as hyperreal, although this is more of an appropriate description of the tourist hubs specifically. Indeed, Surfers Paradise has been blatantly marketed as such, at one stage adopting a tourism campaign that branded it as the Gold Coast's sixth theme park (Surfers Paradise Alliance 2015).

While some aspects of Baudrillard's theories are problematic – particularly the suggestion that a romanticised notion of the real once existed, but has now been eroded under postmodernism – they are nonetheless useful for understanding certain aspects of what is occurring in resorts. I am less concerned with the *disappearance* of the real than with the emerging recognition that representations, signs, spectacle and imaginaries are themselves dimensions of the real (see also Olalquiaga 1992). This is reflected in Baudrillard's example of maps. The map is supposedly only a representation of the real territory, but in hyperreality this distinction has disintegrated to the point where the map *is* real (Soja 2000; Baudrillard 1994 [1981]). In Baudrillard's (1994 [1981]) words, 'It is no longer a question of imitation, nor duplication, nor even parody. It is a question of substituting the signs of the real for the real' (p. 2).

For the purposes of this book, I am most interested in how hyperreality collapses the distinctions between real and imaginary, original and copy, fact and fiction, authentic and inauthentic. One of the most obvious ways this plays out in resorts is in the dynamics between reality and representation and, similarly, the material and the imagined. That is, how places like resort are imagined and represented is informed by reality, and, in a reciprocal loop, imaginaries and representations inform reality and materiality as well (e.g. through providing cues as to what expected or normalised spatial practices are).

Representations of resorts – in tourism brochures, travel websites, film and television, news media, photographs and stories on social media – are assumed by tourists to be depicting reality (even if only partially), and these inform popular imaginaries and myths of place as well as more personalised fantasies of individual vacations. Further, by taking their own photographs and accumulating souvenirs to signify their real, material, lived experiences of the destination, multiple layers of simulacra proliferate for tourists. In the hyperreal spaces of resorts, reality – what is actually going on there, spatially and socially – cannot be separated from fantasy, imaginary or representation, which have transformed into aspects of the real themselves.

Hyperreality confuses the boundaries between front and back regions, and authenticity and inauthenticity, as evidenced in the previous discussion of Cancún and the Gold Coast. Certain tourists may seek out authentic back regions and experiences – a concealed reality – and in doing so they may be met with staged, contrived spaces, performances, objects and other simulacra. Nevertheless, these may *feel* real to the tourist, and therefore cannot be considered completely fake. In relation to these touristic simulacra, it is important to make a distinction, too, between the fake or staged that purports to be real (a front region masquerading as a back region, for instance) and that which makes no such claims. Chichén Itzá would be an example of the former, whereas the Gold Coast's theme parks are an example of the latter. Sites like theme parks are blatantly artificial, exaggerated, kitschy and hyper-real (Symes 1995; Olalquiaga 1992), but are authentic in the sense that they are not feigning to be anything else.

Simulacra exist in resorts with the purpose of creating the experience of authenticity. Sites, peoples and objects are manipulated and staged to feel more real than the 'original', to more closely approximate the tourist's expectations and fantasies of what the real is (Urry 2002; Eco 1986). As MacCannell (1999 [1976]) suggests, 'Settings are often not merely copies or replicas of real-life situations but copies that are presented as disclosing more about the real thing than the real thing itself discloses' (p. 102). For example, Thailand's Maya Bay was carefully landscaped for the film *The Beach* (2000), involving the replacement of native vegetation with palm trees to make the beach look more like a tropical paradise as imagined by Westerners (Law, Bunnell & Ong 2007). Similarly, Miami and the Gold Coast have transformed their swamplands/wetlands into exclusive islands and canal estates, creating a landscape of spectacle which spatially extends the appeal of the beach and, despite appearing natural, is actually a manufactured, more ideal version of the real. Thus, the real in resorts is often hyperreal.

It is also important to remember that not all tourists are necessarily seeking the real – indeed, some desire the kitsch, the inauthentic and the simulacral (Torres 2002; Rojek & Urry 1997; Ritzer & Liska 1997; Feifer 1985). These types of visitors are most commonly referred to as post-tourists (Feifer 1985), although any kind of tourist may exhibit these desires. Qualities associated with post-tourists are reflexivity, eclecticism and playfulness, epitomising the postmodern consumer (Fahmi 2008; Shaw & Williams 2004; Rojek 1993; Feifer 1985). They are aware of the constructed nature of tourism and their role within it – they know that marketing material is illusory, that culture has been packaged and commodified, that hyperreal environments have been staged, and that their experience will be as much about travel delays, queues and schedules as about fun and escapism (Urry 2002; Rojek 1993; Feifer 1985). In the literature, post-tourists are associated more with self-conscious detachment than with the naïve immersion that is supposedly characteristic of mass tourists and cultural tourists.[11] As Feifer (1985) puts it:

> Above all, though, the post-tourist knows that he [sic] is a tourist: not a time traveller when he goes somewhere historic; not an instant noble savage when he stays on a tropical beach; not an invisible observer when he visits a native compound. Resolutely 'realistic', he cannot evade his condition of an outsider. (p. 271)

Instead of resenting this position, as many mass or cultural tourists might, post-tourists embrace it, delighting in the inauthenticity of tourism (Torres 2002; Urry 1995; Rojek 1993). Post-tourists can enjoy a diversity of experiences, from visiting museums and gazing on ancient ruins to visiting theme parks, purchasing tacky souvenirs and people-watching (Rojek 1993). They are more concerned with having fleeting pleasurable experiences than any kind of quest for authenticity or self-realisation (Rojek 1993).

Although post-tourists may be less interested than others in encountering authentic places, people and things (in the objective, conventional sense), they may still experience authenticity in other forms, such as existential authenticity (Wang 1999). This refers to the ways in which tourism is implicated in the cultivation of self-identity, autobiographical narratives and memories through experiencing one's 'true' or 'real' self, whatever that may be to the individual (Wang 1999). This is especially intensified by the sensuous, liminal experiences and spaces that tourism offers. In destinations like resorts, tourists have very real feelings of pleasure, desire, excitement, relaxation, anxiety and disappointment, as well as engaging sensuously with sights, sounds, smells, tastes, other bodies and atmospheres – what Wang (1999) terms intra-personal authenticity. As Sheller and Urry (2004) observe, 'If tourism sometimes feels "unreal", it nevertheless still mobilizes bodies in sensuous encounters with the physical world' (p. 4). When travelling with family and friends, vacations can also be authentic on an inter-personal level through providing meaningful bonding opportunities (Wang 1999). What these varying interpretations highlight is that the real, and authenticity, can be a part of *any* tourism experience or site, even those that are disparaged as staged, fake or hyperreal.

As apparently escapist, disembedded, impermanent, transient and hyperreal places, resorts are regularly described as postmodern cities (Nijman 2011; Ditton 2010; Symes 1997). As Gladstone (1998) remarks, 'tourist cities and their attractions [are] often held out as the apotheosis of postmodernity' (p. 4). Specifically, they are frequently derided as epitomising the 'worst' characteristics of postmodernism. This relates to the high culture/popular culture binary outlined earlier – resorts are products of capitalist-driven tourism urbanisation, and are thus intensified sites for manifestations of popular culture, mass consumption and spectacle in excess. Far from being seen as sophisticated or elitist, resorts are stereotyped as banal, tacky, trashy and tasteless, which problematically equates mass culture with 'bad' taste and high culture with 'good' taste (a dichotomy undone by the very nature of postmodernism).

Because of the pervasiveness of staged, hyperreal tourism spaces and experiences, resorts are often labelled as manufactured or engineered, artificial and phony (Revels 2011; Ditton 2010; Shaw & Williams 2004; Goad 1997; Eco 1986). By extension, the people living in resorts are perceived as fake as well (e.g. Colagrande 2014). As a Gold Coast local, this apparent artificiality is something I have heard others express great disdain for over the years. My interviewees communicated similar sentiments, referring to both the people and the landscape:

INTERVIEWER: So what don't you like about the Gold Coast?

ALYSSA: GC guys and girls – you know what I mean – the fake bimbos ... the girls with the fake orange tan and the bleach blonde hair and the fake tits and their fake personalities. And the guys are always trying to assert their masculinity and dominance or something. It's just like – you walk into any club on the GC and you would know what I mean. That's what I don't like.

(Gold Coast, 24 September 2014)

INTERVIEWER: How do you feel about Miami's tourism presence and the tourism industry?

LUCIANA: Well, I feel it makes Miami fake. Just because Miami thrives on the tourism and they kind of built the city around tourism. I mean, knowing a little bit of history about Miami, it used to be nothing but swampland. Well not necessarily swampland, but just an area where there really wasn't anything here. And they, you know, imported the sand. Everything's fake to me, but they need it. They need it. That's what brings the money. I mean, it's nice, but I always think about how it's not real.

(Miami, 13 March 2014)

These sentiments reflect dissatisfaction with what is felt to be an excessive concern for money, appearances, surfaces and spectacle, with regard to spaces, people's values and their bodies. This echoes yet another set of inter-related stereotypes of resorts as being superficial and depthless (Ditton 2010; Wise 2010), a critique also associated with postmodernism itself (Savage, Bagnall & Longhurst 2005; Buchanan 2005; Rojek 1993).

Globalisation, generic spaces and non-places

As the preceding discussion makes clear, tourism can be interpreted as a destructive force that contaminates cultures and erodes authenticity (Crang 2014, 2006; Shaw & Williams 2004; Coleman & Crang 2002; Meethan 2001; Abram & Waldren 1997; Cohen 1988). This is seen to occur, for example, through the commodification of places and cultures for touristic consumption, which necessarily involves complex assemblages being simplified, manipulated and staged. Crang (2014) observes that tourists (rather than larger forces like local governments or developers) are typically blamed for this, being seen as 'agents of anticulture that destroys culture with which it comes into contact' (p. 66).

As a result, one of the main perceived impacts of tourism on places like resorts is the homogenisation of local cultures (Crang 2014; Relph 2008 [1976]; Macleod 2004; Shaw & Williams 2004; Meethan 2001; Belk 1996). This idea is implicated in a broader series of debates which theorise globalisation as producing homogenising effects or cultural convergence (Guillén 2010; Augé 2008 [1995]; Robertson 1992). Such perspectives argue that the world is becoming increasingly uniform, with local cultures being threatened by a world culture or global monoculture (Guillén 2010; Lechner & Boli 2010, 2005; Massey 2007, 1994; Holmes 2001; Belk 1996). As Belk (1996) asserts:

> Music is increasingly becoming world music. Food is increasingly succumbing to an international cuisine. Clothing styles are becoming a pastiche of worldwide influences. Our heroes are decreasingly likely to be local and increasingly likely to be selected from around the globe. Our shopping malls, franchise outlets, hotels, airports, banks, and gambling casinos are quickly becoming indistinguishable, whether they are in Australia, Europe, Asia, or the Americas. (p. 27)

Tourism is one mode through which world culture is manifested and proliferated, and is subsequently considered to contribute to cultural homogenisation (Hopkins & Becken 2014; Shaw & Williams 2004). Tourist-centric places like resorts, for instance, feature a high concentration of multinational hotel chains, international fast food chains, retail stores for global brands, restaurants serving cuisine from a range of other nations, and a pastiche of architectural styles from around the world. Zukin (2010) observes that these expressions of standardisation in development are sometimes met with hostility. They are seen to mark a loss or destruction of local distinctiveness, replaced by supposedly depthless, globalised signs.

Scott Lash (2002) refers to sites marked by such characteristics as 'generic spaces' – those which are 'a-contextual' (p. 4), lacking a distinct identity, and interchangeable with other spaces around the globe. Disembedded or 'lifted out' from their social, historical and spatial contexts, they could, theoretically, be anywhere (Lash 2002, p. 161; Urry 1995). Generic spaces are thus characterised by a degree of placelessness (Relph 2008 [1976]; Lash 2002). Another term used to refer to a similar spatiality is 'non-place' (Augé 2008 [1995]). Examples of non-places include transient spaces such as airports, shopping malls and hotels, all of which are sites associated with tourism.[12] Like generic spaces, non-places are disembedded and 'cannot be defined as relational, or historical, or concerned with identity' in the same way that 'places' are (Augé 2008 [1995], p. 63).[13] As Augé (2008 [1995]) explains it,

'There is no room there for history unless it has been transformed into an element of spectacle, usually in allusive texts. What reigns there is actuality, the urgency of the present moment' (p. 83). He argues that, consequently, occupants of non-places experience 'the passive joys of identity-loss, and the more active pleasure of role-playing' (Augé 2008 [1995], p. 83) afforded by these ahistorical, acontextual spaces. There are clear parallels, then, between such generic non-places and the liminal, carnivalesque spaces of resorts.

Shaw and Williams (2004) suggest one of the impacts of globalisation on pleasure periphery resorts has been the espousal of this sense of placelessness. By routinely obscuring or reducing (until quite recently) the prominence of their local cultures in tourism promotion, resorts have been able to disconnect (to an extent) the fantasy world of the tourist hubs from their other 'real' spaces and the less-than-utopian aspects of everyday local lives (e.g. visible social problems and inequalities; see also Chapter 6). In other words, resorts have tended to disembed themselves in order to facilitate the escapist, hedonistic experiences that tourists seek out. However, resorts are no longer officially being sold as generic anywheres. Rather, they actively 'expend effort on creating ideas of places' (Coleman & Crang 2002, p. 4) through tourism promotions that emphasise local specificity and cultural and historical activities. As such, analyses stressing how globalisation and tourism engender cultural homogeneity and placelessness do not adequately attend to other opposing forces and processes that are clearly at work in the lived spaces of resorts.

Americanisation and Westernisation

In addition to the perceived threats of globalisation to places and cultures, scholarly literature frequently debates specific concerns related to Westernisation and Americanisation. These concepts deal with processes of homogenisation by way of neo-colonialism and cultural imperialism, contending that nations around the world are becoming more like the West (particularly America) (Lechner & Boli 2010; Pieterse 2010a; Berger 2002; Appadurai 1996; Featherstone 1993). The American influence is particularly obvious in resorts like Cancún, which attract visitors predominantly from the USA (see Torres & Momsen 2006 for a more detailed exploration). However, even an English-speaking Western city like the Gold Coast can be read as Americanised. As well as being habitually compared to locations in the USA, such as Las Vegas, California and Florida,[14] American influences are readily observable in the city's aesthetics – a landscape of high-rises, canal estates and theme parks made famous by cities like Miami and Orlando – and its nomenclature – with suburbs and neighbourhoods named Miami, Miami Keys, Florida Gardens, Palm Beach and Santa Barbara.

Since international resorts typically attract many Western visitors, they benefit from providing brands, aesthetics, infrastructure, services and amenities familiar to Westerners. For example, Patong Beach in Phuket has McDonald's, KFC, Subway, Starbucks and Coffee Club, along with a number of Australian- and American-themed bars. In Cancún, you can eat at Hooters, Hard Rock Café, Chilli's and Applebee's; shop at Calvin Klein, Coach, Guess and Zara; speak to almost anyone in English; and use American currency instead of the Mexican Peso. Across all of the resorts on which I focus, you can find Best Westerns, Holiday Inns, Hard Rock Hotels and Hiltons offering standard Western comforts, from basics like electricity and running water to more bourgeois facilities like air conditioning, mini bars, room service (with American staples such as cheeseburgers and Caesar salads), free WiFi, flat screen televisions, fresh linens and towels, pillow menus, and concierges to demystify any confusion about the locality. Thus, it is no surprise that mass tourism in resorts has been interpreted as somewhat standardised, homogenised and predictable (Minca & Oakes 2006).

The movement towards packaged, 'sterilized, sanitized' (Belk 1996, p. 23) consumption experiences is often referred to in the literature as McDonaldisation (Ritzer 2011). As a particular form of Americanisation, the theory of McDonaldisation claims that social practices and institutions around the world are increasingly modelled on the principles of American corporations (namely, McDonald's). That is, they are becoming more efficient, calculable, predictable and controlled (Ritzer 2011; Ritzer & Liska 1997). Ritzer (2011) argues that these fast food chain principles have come to shape a range of sectors including education, religion, politics and health care systems. In terms of tourism, this means that many tourists supposedly still desire Fordist-style vacations: efficiency provided by travel agents and tours (e.g. Contiki) that fit as many activities and sights as possible in short periods of time; calculability offered by value-for-money package deals and all-inclusive options; predictability from stringently organised itineraries and chains that promise consistency across international locations; and control via orderly lines and well-trained staff (Ritzer & Liska 1997).

McDonaldisation 'is not an all-or-nothing process', but is expressed to different degrees in different sites (Ritzer 2011, p. 21). Perhaps the most obvious examples of McDonaldised tourism spaces are theme parks.[15] These attractions are highly regulated, exemplifying the McDonaldised characteristics outlined above, as well as being highly stylised and sanitised to be hyperreal (Belk 1996). As Zukin (1995) observes:

> Disney World … uses a visual strategy that makes unpleasant things – like garbage removal, building maintenance, and pushing and shoving – *invisible*. Disney World uses *compression* and *condensation*, flattening out experience to an easily digestible narrative and limiting visualization to a selective sample of symbols. Despite all the rides and thrills, Disney World relies on *facades*. (p. 64, original emphasis)

McDonaldised tourism sites like theme parks are, then, 'a sanitized version of reality, cleansed of strife, world problems, dirt, prejudice, exploitation, or other problems of everyday life' (Belk 1996, p. 29). As discussed above, this phenomenon is evident in resorts more broadly as their touristic narratives attempt to position them as safe, pristine, carefree fantasy worlds. This manifests spatially through the emergence of tourism enclaves (Edensor 2000) or tourism bubbles (Craik 1997). These types of spaces involve the subdivision of destinations into micro and macro environments (Cohen 1972), with the former being the disembedded, staged tourism hubs and the latter being the wider socio-spatial context of the city, region or nation. This segregation between tourist and local is perhaps most striking in Cancún, with its clearly demarcated 'Hotel Zone'. Insulated from the alien environment, the tourist enclave is purposely controlled and monitored to meet tourists' expectations and ensure safety, familiarity and reliability, and to minimise risk or any undesirable realities, including unwanted sights, smells and sounds (Edensor 2007, 2000; Fainstein & Judd 1999; Cohen 1972).

Familiarity and difference

Ritzer and Liska (1997) note that McDonaldisation processes undermine the central purpose of tourism. Travelling for leisure is usually motivated by a desire to escape one's mundane life and experience the 'variety, novelty, and strangeness' of other places and cultures (Cohen 1972, p. 172). Paradoxically, due to globalisation, destinations are in some ways exhibiting greater uniformity and standardisation to the point where the places to which tourists travel are not all that unlike home. Demand for predictability and control also undercuts motivations for escaping routine. In this sense, contemporary tourism blurs distinctions between home and away, and our travel experiences have the potential to be increasingly more like our everyday lives[16] (Ritzer & Liska 1997; Rojek & Urry 1997; Rojek 1993).

This is not to say that difference no longer exists or matters, or that a sense of familiarity is privileged over difference. Even if a site like Chichén Itzá is staged and sanitised, it is nonetheless unique to Mexico and something one can only experience first-hand by physically travelling to the Yucatán. Tourists still desire novelty – even if only in climate, landscape, cuisine or superficial symbolism – and this is clear in the ways resort destinations are marketed. As Belk (1996) illustrates, elements of local distinctiveness are fundamental to touristic place-myths, which are in themselves caricatures of the destination:

> there is little to draw the European tourist to South America if the sights and services there are totally indistinguishable from those at home. Rather, the culture that represents Brazil or Peru in the European's mind is likely to be stylized, exaggerated, and subtly Europeanized. Brazil thus becomes year-round Carnival and samba, while Peru becomes Inca-land and the Andes. (p. 32)

Clearly, whether these aspects of local specificity are real or staged is less important than the feeling of authenticity, or the resort's ability to 'offer the illusion or fantasy of otherness' (Craik 1997, p. 114). Contemporary tourism is less about the desire for *either* difference *or* familiarity, and more about the pleasure derived from the tensions between them. This varies depending on individual tourists and their cultural backgrounds,[17] needs, desires and motivations, as well as the particular temporal and spatial contexts of their holidays. Some tourists (usually assumed to be mass tourists) want a high degree of predictability, safety and comfort, or to 'observe without actually experiencing' the host culture (Cohen 1972, p. 169). Others (such as cultural tourists) may be actively seeking difference and adventure and avoiding complete immersion in tourist enclaves, but could also want 'McDonaldized stops along the way, and to retreat to at the end of the day' (Ritzer & Liska 1997, p. 101). The business of the tourism industry, then, is to attempt to stage 'ordered disorder' (Minca & Oakes 2006, p. 11) or 'riskless risk' (Hannigan 1998, p. 71) for visitors.

Localisation, hybridity and complexity

Just as difference is not being replaced by familiarity, the local is not being destroyed by the global. Such dystopian arguments operate on the problematic assumption that cultures (more specifically regarded as non-Western cultures) are geographically bounded, static, homogenous, 'coherent and closed systems of meaning' (Coleman & Crang 2002, p. 1; see also Crang 2014; Hannerz 2010; Lechner & Boli 2010; Pons, Crang & Travlou 2009; Meethan 2001; Appadurai 1996). On the contrary, cultures are produced through interactions with other regions, nations and people (Huddart 2006). Like money, ideas, information and images, cultures are also mobile and travel across the globe, adapting and transforming over time through various fluid processes and networks.[18] Cultures are always already hybrid (Pieterse 2010a; Huddart 2006; Massey 1998), characterised as much by shared experiences, continuity and unity as by differences, transience and ruptures (Hall 2006 [1990]; Savage et al. 2005). The same is true of places more generally. Since spaces are already multiple and contested, and produced through a series of flows, interconnections and relations (involving that which exists 'outside' of them), they are never really homogenous, bounded or closed either (Pons et al. 2009; Massey 2005, 1994). Thus, places and cultures being toured cannot necessarily be 'contaminated' since they were never 'pure' to begin with. Similarly, tourism cannot eliminate culture since it is one of the forces actively producing and re-producing culture (Crang 2014).

Urry (2003) observes that there is no 'single centre of global power' (p. 93) exerting a universal influence. Any kind of world culture that has emerged exists in tandem with, and interacts with, other cultures (Lechner & Boli 2010, 2005). Further, this world culture is distinct (Lechner & Boli 2010, 2005) and not necessarily only American or Western. As Appadurai (1996) points out, 'the United States is no longer the puppeteer of a world system of images but is only one node of a complex transnational construction of imaginary landscapes' (p. 31). While Americanisation and McDonaldisation are very real phenomena, they are only two processes – among many – that are occurring. Non-Western cultures can, and do, influence Western cultures as well as other non-Western cultures, so we must acknowledge that beyond Americanisation there is also Easternisation, Japanisation, and so on (Appadurai 1996; Featherstone & Lash 1995). On the Gold Coast, for example, the impact of a steady flow of international visitors from Asia (previously mostly Japanese and now mostly Chinese) is evident in the increasing number of tourism providers and shopping and dining precincts (e.g. Chinatown) catering specifically to them. Miami, on the other hand, has been influenced quite significantly by processes of Latinisation as a result of its geographic location and patterns of migration, both forced and elective, over the past several decades (Rose 2015; Olalquiaga 1992).

If there is no single dominant culture, then globalisation (or any of its sub-processes) cannot be conceptualised as having a set of uniform, linear, predictable effects like cultural homogenisation (Hannerz 2010; Robertson 2010; Urry 2003, 1995). It is far too simplistic to argue that places around the world are becoming more alike, or more like America (or any other nation), since what is 'global' or 'American' does not signify something unified and uncontested, but is hybrid, fragmented, heterogeneous and constituted by a wide range of cultural influences and competing discourses. Berger (2002) illustrates this well:

> Western 'culture wars' are exported as part and parcel of the globalization process. Thus a Hungarian, for instance, looking west for cultural inspiration, comes on free market ideology versus environmentalism, freedom of speech verses 'politically correct' speech codes, Hollywood machismo versus feminism, American junk food versus American health foods, and so on. In other words, 'the West' is hardly a homogenous cultural identity, and its conflict-laden heterogeneity is carried along by its globalization. (p. 15)

The same is true for the cultures and places that globalisation is said to be influencing. Since all places have their own particularities, ideological conflicts, trajectories and spatial specificity, global trends will manifest differently in these different contexts (Robertson 2010; Massey 2005, 1998). Moreover, global elements are not merely imposed on and passively absorbed by cultures – they can also be resisted, rejected, embraced, reappropriated and reassembled in idiosyncratic ways (Huddart 2006; Minca & Oakes 2006; Berger 2002; Meethan 2001; Belk 1996; Bhabha 1994), and these responses may vary between different groups within a place or culture (Urry 1995). Following Massey's (1994) approach towards a progressive or global sense of place, one that is more 'outward-looking' (p. 14), we can notice that local specificity is something produced in *interaction with* the global, with internal *and* external forces.

These complex, uneven engagements also mean that the global becomes localised or indigenised. Even a global fast food chain like McDonald's has different practices and meanings in different places (Watson 2006; Meethan 2001). Not only are menus adapted to cater to local tastes, but the spaces of the restaurants vary in use. In East Asia, for example, the value of efficiency in the dining experience is subverted because many customers prefer to linger (Watson 2006; Berger 2002). Additionally, no two restaurants can be the same because each is situated in a different spatial, historical, political and social context, and is run by staff who are connected to and live out these differences. Far from being 'non-people' occupying 'non-places' (Ritzer 2003), those working at McDonald's can have meaningful engagements with it as an integral space in their everyday lives in which they construct their identities, develop skills, build social relationships or engage in conflict. Supposedly generic spaces can never really be disembedded, and multi-national corporations like McDonald's can only exercise a limited degree of control in maintaining standardisation and uniformity: local particularities inevitably assert themselves and disrupt these ideals. The global, therefore, does not abolish the local, and can even provide opportunities for local distinctiveness to be reaffirmed (Meethan 2001; Soja 2000; Urry 1995). Indeed, heritage and cultural tourism may provide one such means of differentiation (Meethan 2001).

These various local manifestations also influence how global elements evolve (Massey 1998, 2007). This is unsurprising considering that what comes to be designated as 'global' originates in local contexts (Massey 2007; Urry 1995) and is circulated around the world through practices like tourism. As Urry (2003) explains:

> while people know little about the global connections or implications of their particular actions, these local actions nevertheless do not remain local. They are captured, represented, transported, marketed and generalized elsewhere. They get carried along the scapes and flows of the emerging global world, mobilizing ideas, people, images, moneys and technologies to potentially everywhere. (p. 80)

Clearly, the global and the local cannot be treated as a binary opposition. Local cultures are indeed shaped by global trends and flows, but these are always already being adapted, altered and formed in local contexts. Like products of *bricolage*, resorts are heterotopic spaces that represent and juxtapose several globalised sites and symbols while simultaneously recontextualising and inverting them (Foucault 1986). They are unique, localised singularities that are nonetheless connected to the globalised totality.

Globalisation and localisation are mutually constitutive and mutually transformative, and neither can be easily distinguished let alone privileged as more powerful. Consequently, the effects of globalisation cannot be assumed to be as straightforward as cultural homogenisation. Nothing can become completely staged, sanitised, fake or McDonaldised. Disorder, difference and the messiness of the real will always emerge, disrupting any attempt at standardisation and control. Instead of deploying hierarchical either/or logics, it is more productive to consider interconnections (Massey 2005, 1998, 1994; Urry 1995), exchanges and multiplicities – the *movements between* the conceptual (not actual) poles of fake and real, familiarity and difference, global and local, homogeneity and heterogeneity, universal and particular. These dynamics lead to processes of hybridisation – the synthesis of global and local[19] – rather than domination and erasure (Pieterse 2010b; Fahmi 2008; Huddart 2006; Berger 2002; Meethan 2001). Through creating these hybrid forms, globalisation can be understood as generative of diversity more than sameness (Guillén 2010; Lechner & Boli 2010; Featherstone 1993). Resorts, then, cannot simply be read as impermanent, transient or depthless. They are always hybrid and in a perpetual state of becoming, marked by complex, shifting arrangements of fluidity and stasis, difference and sameness, local and global.

Conclusion

In this chapter, I have problematised the parallel dichotomies of culture/ capitalism, real/staged, authentic/fake, different/familiar and local/global, which have long framed scholarly and popular discourses surrounding tourism destinations, especially mass tourism destinations. In each of these dichotomies, the former terms – culture, real, authentic, different, local – have been privileged as being meaningful, valuable, organic, diverse and heterogeneous. The latter terms – capitalism, staged, fake, familiar, global – have been perceived as devoid of these qualities, instead being characterised as depthless, empty, superficial, contrived and homogeneous. Places like resorts, as sites for intensified expressions of capitalist processes, values and mass consumption practices, have thus been negatively stereotyped as representing all that is apparently bad about globalisation, and all that is threatening to a romanticised, idealistic notion of culture and authenticity.

As this chapter made clear, such distinctions become blurred when considering the lived spatiality of resorts. All of these concepts are inter-implicated and mutually constitutive – one cannot eradicate the other, nor can any exist in pure form. Tourists may indeed seek the 'real' or the 'authentic', but what this means will vary greatly among individual visitors. Therefore, people – tourists and locals alike – can have very real, meaningful, significant life experiences in supposedly 'fake' or hyperreal settings. Similarly, sites, objects and practices widely considered to be authentic in the traditional sense may also be staged and packaged to facilitate touristic consumption. All tourism attractions combine aspects of the exotic and the familiar in various ways to cultivate the experience of authenticity.

Globalisation and capitalism are not necessarily at odds with culture. Cities around the world, including resorts, are increasingly relying on their natural and cultural assets – their local distinctiveness – to sell themselves, to capitalise on their symbolic economies. As my examples of Cancún and the Gold Coast showed, this may be through the marketing of culture in a traditional, modern sense (high culture and heritage in the form of ancient ruins and the continued existence of ancient cultures) or in a more unconventional, postmodern sense (heritage commemorating contemporary mass consumption of beach culture). The existence of distinct cultural forms in each resort highlights that they can never truly be disembedded, placeless or generic anywheres. Resorts have complex, multiple, heterogeneous imaginaries, narratives of identity, histories, communities, everyday practices and lived local experiences, as are explored in the next chapter.

Notes

1 This distinction reinforces a false Cartesian (mind/body) split – in reality, all tourist experiences involve the sensuous (body) and the imaginary (mind) in different ways.
2 For the purposes of this book, 'cultural tourism' refers to the consumption of both material and symbolic, and past and present, aspects of culture (Meethan 2001).
3 'High' culture and 'mass' culture do not actually exist in a binary, but they are perceived as such, with high culture regarded as the privileged term.
4 Such as seeking insight, knowledge, self-realisation and self-improvement rather than only seeking pleasure.
5 A term equally as problematic as 'authentic', but in this context, I am referring to those who are emphatically disinterested in mass tourism and do not *seek* experiences that fuse cultural tourism and mass tourism (even if they may not be able to completely avoid such hybrid forms).
6 In much in the same way that visitors to destinations like Paris 'must' see iconic attractions like the Eiffel Tower or The Louvre in order to have 'properly' experienced the city.
7 This initiative, organised by the privately-funded 'New7Wonders Foundation', aimed to promote a different set of monuments than those of the Seven Wonders of the Ancient World. Decided by popular vote, the monuments selected included The Great Wall of China, the Taj Mahal and Machu Picchu.
8 An obvious reference to 'alternative' rather than mainstream tourism experiences.
9 Thus, simultaneously appealing to the touristic desire for up-to-date facilities.
10 An urban formation lacking a singular, distinct centre, such as the Gold Coast or Los Angeles.
11 However, any kind of tourist can experience *both* immersion and detachment.
12 Similarly, Relph (2008) suggests that tourism spaces are prime examples of placelessness.
13 Augé (2008) also notes that concepts of 'place' and 'non-place' do not exist in pure form. In his words, 'Place and non-place are rather like opposed polarities: the first is never completely erased, the second never totally completed ...' (p. 64).
14 See, for example, comparisons made by Davidson & Spearritt (2000), Griffin (1998), Symes (1995, 1997), Goad (1997), Longhurst (1995) and Jones (1986).
15 A parallel concept to McDonaldisation is 'Disneyisation' or 'Disneyification', which has developed based on the notion that the principles that dominate theme parks have spread to other spaces as well (Relph 2008; Bryman 2006; Rojek & Urry 1997).
16 Of course, this has always been the case, to an extent. Our daily lives involve touristic practices – shopping, people watching, gazing upon spectacle – just as our

holidays necessarily involve daily tasks – grooming ourselves, caring for children, eating regular meals (Crang 2006).

17 That is, what is 'familiar' and what is 'different' will be different for each tourist since they come from different localities, speak different languages, and so on.

18 These flows and networks have also enabled the formation (and/or strengthening) of other cultures and affinities, including those of transnational and imagined communities.

19 This is also often referred to as glocalisation.

References

Abram, S & Waldren, J 1997, 'Introduction: tourists and tourism – identifying with people and places', in S Abram, J Waldren & DVL Macleod, *Tourists and tourism: identifying with people and places*, Berg, Oxford, pp. 1–11.

Alltournative 2016, *Coba Maya encounter*, viewed 21 July 2016, <https://www.all tournative.com/tours-expeditions/coba-maya-encounter/>.

Alonso, G 2007, 'Selling Miami: tourism promotion and immigrant neighbourhoods in the capital of Latin America', in J Rath (ed.), *Tourism, ethnic diversity and the city*, Routledge, New York, pp. 164–180.

Appadurai, A 1996, *Modernity at large: cultural dimensions of globalization*, University of Minnesota Press, Minneapolis.

Augé, M 2008 [1995], *Non-places: an introduction to supermodernity*, 2nd edn, trans. J Howe, Verso, London.

Baker, S, Bennett, A & Wise, P 2012, 'Living "the strip": negotiating neighborhood, community, and identity on Australia's Gold Coast', in C Richardson & HA Skott-Myhre (eds), *Habitus of the hood*, Intellect, Bristol, pp. 97–120.

Baudrillard, J 1994 [1981], *Simulacra and simulation*, trans. SF Glaser, University of Michigan Press, Ann Arbor.

Beesley, L 2005, *The potential role of cultural tourism on the Gold Coast*, CRC for Sustainable Tourism, Gold Coast.

Belk, RW 1996, 'Hyperreality and globalization: culture in the age of Ronald McDonald', *Journal of International Consumer Marketing*, vol. 8, no. 3–4, pp. 23–37.

Berger, PL 2002, 'Introduction: the cultural dynamics of globalization', in PL Berger & SP Huntington (eds), *Many globalizations: cultural diversity in the contemporary world*, Oxford University Press, New York, pp. 1–16.

Bhabha, HK 1994, *The location of culture*, Routledge, London.

Blackman, A 2013, *If only I had a heart: a history of the Gold Coast and its economy from 1823 to 2013*, Griffith Business School, Southport.

Boissevain, J 1996, 'Introduction', in J Boissevain (ed.), *Coping with tourists: European reactions to mass tourism*, Berghahn Books, Providence, pp. 1–26.

Bryman, A 2006, 'McDonald's as a Disneyized institution', in G Ritzer (ed.), *McDonaldization: the reader*, 2nd edn, Pine Forge Press, Thousand Oaks, pp. 54–62.

Buchanan, I 2005, 'Space in the age of non-place', in I Buchanan & G Lambert (eds), *Deleuze and space*, University of Toronto Press, Toronto, pp. 16–35.

Burstow, G 2014, *Flesh: the Gold Coast in the 1960s, 70s and 80s*, University of Queensland Press, St Lucia.

Cancún Convention & Visitors Bureau 2015, *The Cancun Convention & Visitors Bureau Website*, viewed 4 May 2015, <http://cancun.travel/en/>.

Chhabra, D, Healy, R & Sills, E 2003, 'Staged authenticity and heritage tourism', *Annals of Tourism Research*, vol. 30, no. 3, pp. 702–719.

Cohen, E 1972, 'Toward a sociology of international tourism', *Social Research*, vol. 39, no. 1, pp. 164–182.

Cohen, E 1988, 'Authenticity and commoditization in tourism', *Annals of Tourism Research*, vol. 15, no. 3, pp. 371–386.

Colagrande, JJ 2014, 'Miami is so fake it's frustrating', *Huffpost Miami*, 29 January, viewed 1 February 2014, <http://www.huffingtonpost.com/jj-colagrande/miami-is-so-fake_b_4684267.html?ncid=edlinkusaolp00000009>.

Coleman, S & Crang, M 2002, 'Grounded tourists, travelling theory', in S Coleman & M Crang (eds), *Tourism: between place and performance*, Berghahn Books, New York, pp. 1–17.

Council of the City of Gold Coast 2015, *Gold Coast Chinatown unveils Confucius statue*, viewed 21 May 2018, <http://www.goldcoast.qld.gov.au/gold-coast-china town-unveils-confucius-statue-25333.html>.

Council of the City of Gold Coast 2018, *Gold Coast Cultural Precinct*, viewed 22 May 2018, <http://www.goldcoast.qld.gov.au/gold-coast-cultural-precinct-13122.html>.

Craik, J 1997, 'The culture of tourism', in C Rojek & J Urry (eds), *Touring cultures: transformations of travel and theory*, Routledge, London, pp. 113–136.

Crang, M 2006, 'Circulation and emplacement: the hollowed-out performance of tourism', in C Minca & T Oakes (eds), *Travels in paradox: remapping tourism*, Rowman & Littlefield Publishers, Lanham, pp. 47–64.

Crang, M 2014, 'Cultural geographies of tourism', in AA Lew, CM Hall & AM Williams (eds), *The Wiley Blackwell companion to tourism*, Wiley Blackwell, Hoboken, pp. 66–77.

Davidson, J & Spearritt, P 2000, *Holiday business: tourism in Australia since 1870*, Miegunyah Press, Carlton South.

Desforges, L 1998, '"Checking out the planet": global representations/local identities and youth travel', in T Skelton & G Valentine (eds), *Cool places: geographies of youth cultures*, Routledge, London, pp. 175–192.

Ditton, S 2010, 'Gold Coast: realigning community, culture and development in dispersed urban settings', *Local-Global*, vol. 7, pp. 164–183.

Eco, U 1986, *Travels in hyperreality: essays*, trans. W Weaver, Harcourt Brace & Company, San Diego.

Edensor, T 2000, 'Staging tourism: tourists as performers', *Annals of Tourism Research*, vol. 27, no. 2, pp. 322–344.

Edensor, T 2007, 'Mundane mobilities, performances and spaces of tourism', *Social & Cultural Geography*, vol. 8, no. 2, pp. 199–215.

Evans, G 2005, 'Mundo Maya: from Cancún to city of culture. World heritage in postcolonial Mesoamerica', in D Harrison & M Hitchcock (eds), *The politics of world heritage: negotiating tourism and conservation*, Channel View Publications, Clevedon, pp. 35–49.

Fahmi, WS 2008, '"Glocal" heterotopias: neo-flâneur's transit narratives', in PM Burns & M Novelli (eds), *Tourism and mobilities: local-global connections*, CABI, Wallingford, pp. 33–64.

Fainstein, SS & Judd, DR 1999, 'Global forces, local strategies, and urban tourism', in DR Judd & SS Fainstein (eds), *The tourist city*, Yale University Press, New Haven, pp. 1–17.

Featherstone, M 1993, 'Global and local cultures', in J Bird, B Curtis, T Putnam, G Robertson & L Tickner (eds), *Mapping the futures: local cultures, global change*, Routledge, London, pp. 169–187.

Featherstone, M & Lash, S 1995, 'Globalization, modernity and the spatialization of social theory: an introduction', in M Featherstone, S Lash & R Robertson (eds), *Global modernities*, SAGE Publications, London, pp. 1–24.

Feifer, M 1985, *Tourism in history: from imperial Rome to the present*, Stein and Day, New York.

Foucault, M 1986, 'Of other spaces', *Diacritics*, vol. 16, no. 1, pp. 22–27.

Giddens, A 1990, *The consequences of modernity*, Polity Press, Cambridge.

Gladstone, DL 1998, 'Tourism urbanization in the United States', *Urban Affairs Review*, vol. 34, no. 1, pp. 3–27.

Goad, P 1997, 'The Gold Coast: architecture and planning', in Allom Lovell Marquis-Kyle, Henshall Hansen Associates, Context, HJM & Staddon Consulting, *Gold Coast urban heritage & character study*, Gold Coast City Council, Surfers Paradise, pp. 40–45.

Goffman, E 1969 [1956], *The presentation of the self in everyday life*, Pelican Books, London.

Gold Coast City Art Gallery 2012, *Sexualising the city: imaging desire and Gold Coast identity*, exhibition catalogue, 20 October–2 December, Gold Coast City Art Gallery, Surfers Paradise.

Gold Coast City Art Gallery 2013, *Learning from Surfers Paradise: a rephotography project, 1973 to 2013*, John Gollings exhibition catalogue, 22 June–4 August, Gold Coast City Art Gallery, Surfers Paradise.

Gold Coast City Council 2013a, *Gold Coast Local Heritage Register, A–M*, viewed 23 July 2016, <http://www.goldcoast.qld.gov.au/documents/bf/local-heritage-register-a-m.pdf>.

Gold Coast City Council 2013b, *Gold Coast Local Heritage Register, N–Z*, viewed 23 July 2016, <http://www.goldcoast.qld.gov.au/documents/bf/gc-local-heritage-r egister-n-z.pdf>.

Griffin, G 1998, 'The good, the bad and the peculiar: cultures and policies of urban planning and development on the Gold Coast', *Urban Policy and Research*, vol. 16, no. 4, pp. 285–292.

Guillén, MF 2010, 'Is globalization civilizing, destructive or feeble? A critique of five key debates in the social science literature', in G Ritzer & Z Atalay (eds), *Readings in globalization: key concepts and major debates*, Blackwell Publishing, Chichester, pp. 4–17.

Hannigan, J 1998, *Fantasy city: pleasure and profit in the postmodern metropolis*, Routledge, London.

Hall, S 2006 [1990], 'Cultural identity and diaspora', in B Ashcroft, G Griffiths & H Tiffin (eds), *The post-colonial studies reader*, 2nd edn, Routledge, London, pp. 435–438.

Hannerz, U 2010, 'Flows, boundaries and hybrids: keywords in transnational anthropology', in G Ritzer & Z Atalay (eds), *Readings in globalization: key concepts and major debates*, Blackwell Publishing, Chichester, pp. 324–326.

Holmes, D 2001, 'Monocultures of globalization: touring Australia's Gold Coast', in D Holmes (ed.), *Virtual globalization: virtual spaces/tourist spaces*, Routledge, London, pp. 175–191.

Hopkins, D & Becken, S 2014, 'Sociocultural resilience and tourism', in AA Lew, CM Hall & AM Williams (eds), *The Wiley Blackwell companion to tourism*, Wiley Blackwell, Hoboken, pp. 490–498.

Huddart, D 2006, *Homi K. Bhabha*, Routledge, New York.

Jones, M 1986, *A sunny place for shady people: the real Gold Coast story*, Allen & Unwin, Sydney.

Lash, S 2002, *Critique of information*, SAGE Publications, London.

Law, L, Bunnell, T & Ong, C-E 2007, 'The Beach, the gaze and film tourism', *Tourist Studies*, vol. 7, no. 2, pp. 141–164.

Lechner, FJ & Boli, J 2005, *World culture: origins and consequences*, Blackwell Publishing, Malden.

Lechner, FJ & Boli, J 2010, 'World culture: origins and consequences', in G Ritzer & Z Atalay (eds), *Readings in globalization: key concepts and major debates*, Blackwell Publishing, Chichester, pp. 410–421.

Longhurst, R 1995, *Gold Coast: our heritage in focus*, State Library of Queensland Foundation, South Brisbane.

MacCannell, D 1973, 'Staged authenticity: arrangements of social space in tourist settings', *American Journal of Sociology*, vol. 79, no. 3, pp. 589–603.

MacCannell, D 1999 [1976], *The tourist: a new theory of the leisure class*, University of California Press, Berkeley.

MacCannell, D 2001, 'Remarks on the commodification of cultures', in VL Smith & M Brent (eds), *Hosts and guests revisited: tourism issues of the 21st century*, Cognizant Communication Corporation, New York, pp. 380–390.

Macleod, DVL 2004, *Tourism, globalization, and cultural change: an island community perspective*, Channel View Publications, Clevedon.

Massey, D 1994, *Space, place, and gender*, University of Minnesota Press, Minneapolis.

Massey, D 1998, 'Spatial constructions of youth cultures', in T Skelton & G Valentine (eds), *Cool places: geographies of youth cultures*, Routledge, London, pp. 121–129.

Massey, D 2005, *For space*, SAGE Publications, London.

Massey, D 2007, *World city*, Polity Press, Cambridge.

Meethan, K 2001, *Tourism in global society: place, culture, consumption*, Palgrave, Basingstoke.

Minca, C & Oakes, T 2006, 'Introduction: traveling paradoxes', in C Minca & T Oakes (eds), *Travels in paradox: remapping tourism*, Rowman & Littlefield, Lanham, pp. 1–21.

Muñoz-Fernández, C 2014, 'Sun, sand, and … sacred pyramids: the Mayanization of Cancun's tourist imaginary', *Archeological Papers of the American Anthropological Association*, vol. 25, no. 1, pp. 68–73.

Nijman, J 2011, *Miami: mistress of the Americas*, University of Pennsylvania Press, Philadelphia.

Olalquiaga, C 1992, *Megalopolis: contemporary cultural sensibilities*, University of Minnesota Press, Minneapolis.

Pieterse, JN 2010a, 'Globalization and culture: three paradigms', in G Ritzer & Z Atalay (eds), *Readings in globalization: key concepts and major debates*, Blackwell Publishing, Chichester, pp. 309–318.

Pieterse, JN 2010b, 'Globalization as hybridization', in G Ritzer & Z Atalay (eds), *Readings in globalization: key concepts and major debates*, Blackwell Publishing, Chichester, pp. 326–333.

Pons, PO, Crang, M & Travlou, P 2009, 'Introduction: taking Mediterranean tourists seriously', in PO Pons, M Crang & P Travlou (eds), *Cultures of mass tourism: doing the Mediterranean in the age of banal mobilities*, Ashgate, Farnham, pp. 1–20.

Potts, A 2014, 'Chinese gates to be built in Southport by council', *Gold Coast Bulletin*, 2 December, viewed 20 May 2018, <https://www.goldcoastbulletin.com.au/news/gold-coast/chinese-gates-to-be-built-in-southport-by-council/news-story/966a 5a2c929edf158dca387b609e439b>.

Relph, E 2008 [1976], *Place and placelessness*, Pion Limited, London.

Revels, TJ 2011, *Sunshine paradise: a history of Florida tourism*, University Press of Florida, Gainesville.

Ritzer, G 2003, 'Rethinking globalization/grobalization and something/nothing', *Sociological Theory*, vol. 21, no. 3, pp. 193–209.

Ritzer, G 2011, *The McDonaldization of society*, 6th edn, Pine Forge Press, Thousand Oaks.

Ritzer, G & Liska, A 1997, '"McDisneyization" and "post-tourism": contemporary perspectives on contemporary tourism', in C Rojek & J Urry (eds), *Touring cultures: transformations of travel and theory*, Routledge, London, pp. 96–109.

Robertson, R 1992, *Globalization: social theory and global culture*, SAGE Publications, London.

Robertson, R 2010, 'Glocalization: time-space and homogeneity-heterogeneity', in G Ritzer & Z Atalay (eds), *Readings in globalization: key concepts and major debates*, Blackwell Publishing, Chichester, pp. 334–343.

Rojek, C 1993, *Ways of escape: modern transformations in leisure and travel*, Macmillan Press, London.

Rojek, C & Urry, J 1997, 'Transformations of travel and theory', in C Rojek & J Urry (eds), *Touring cultures: transformations of travel and theory*, Routledge, London, pp. 1–19.

Rose, CN 2015, *The struggle for black freedom in Miami: civil rights and America's tourist paradise, 1896–1968*, Louisiana State University Press, Baton Rouge.

Salazar, NB 2009, 'Imaged or imagined? Cultural representations and the "tourismification" of peoples and places', *Cahiers d'Études Africaines*, vol. 49, no. 193/194, pp. 49–71.

Salazar, NB 2011, 'Studying local-to-global tourism dynamics through glocal ethnography', in CM Hall (ed.), *Fieldwork in tourism: methods, issues and reflections*, Routledge, New York, pp. 177–187.

Savage, M, Bagnall, G & Longhurst, B 2005, *Globalization and belonging*, SAGE Publications, London.

Selwyn, T 1996, 'Introduction', in T Selwyn (ed.), *The tourist image: myths and myth making in tourism*, John Wiley & Sons, Chichester, pp. 1–32.

Shaw, G & Williams, AM 2004, *Tourism and tourism spaces*, SAGE Publications, London.

Sheller, M & Urry, J 2004, 'Places to play, places in play', in M Sheller & J Urry (eds), *Tourism mobilities: places to play, places in play*, Routledge, London, pp. 1–10.

Simonot, S 2018, 'First look at Gold Coast's incredible new outdoor stage', *Gold Coast Bulletin*, 6 February, viewed 22 May 2018, <https://www.goldcoastbulletin.com.au/entertainment/its-showtime-as-gold-coast-reveals-cultural-precincts-new-name-and-star-attractions/news-story/8af1558f438e0504a65aa6dfd225f5c4>.

Smith, A 2018, 'How the Gold Coast games transformed a resort region into a city', *The Conversation*, 18 April, viewed 22 May 2018, <https://theconversation.com/how-the-gold-coast-games-transformed-a-resort-region-into-a-city-94877>.

Soja, EW 1996, *Thirdspace: journeys to Los Angeles and other real-and-imagined places*, Blackwell Publishers, Oxford.

Soja, EW 2000, *Postmetropolis: critical studies of cities and regions*, Blackwell Publishers, Oxford.

Surf World Gold Coast 2018, *Surf World Gold Coast*, viewed 23 May 2018, <http://surfworldgoldcoast.com>.

Surfers Paradise Alliance 2015, *6th theme park*, viewed 23 November 2015, <http://www.surfersparadise.com/things-to-do/attractions/surfers-paradise,-the-6th-theme-park>.

Symes, C 1995, 'Taking people for a ride: Dreamworld, Sea World and Movieworld as excursive practice', *Journal of Australian Studies*, vol. 19, no. 44, pp. 1–12.

Symes, C 1997, 'Strange alchemy: the Gold Coast as a cultural phenomenon', in Allom Lovell Marquis-Kyle, Henshall Hansen Associates, Context, HJM & Staddon Consulting, *Gold Coast urban heritage & character study*, Gold Coast City Council, Surfers Paradise, pp. 33–38.

The Beach 2000, motion picture, 20th Century Fox, Los Angeles.

Torres, R 2002, 'Cancun's tourism development from a Fordist spectrum of analysis', *Tourist Studies*, vol. 2, no. 1, pp. 87–116.

Torres, R & Momsen, JH 2006, 'Gringolandia: Cancún and the American tourist', in ND Bloom (ed.), *Adventures into Mexico: American tourism beyond the border*, Rowman & Littlefield, Lanham, pp. 58–74.

Urry, J 1995, *Consuming places*, Routledge, London.

Urry, J 2002, *The tourist gaze*, 2nd edn, SAGE Publications, London.

Urry, J 2003, *Global complexity*, Polity Press, Cambridge.

Wang, N 1999, 'Rethinking authenticity in tourism experience', *Annals of Tourism Research*, vol. 26, no. 2, pp. 349–370.

Watson, JL 2006, 'Transnationalism, localization, and fast foods in East Asia', in G Ritzer (ed.), *McDonaldization: the reader*, 2nd edn, Pine Forge Press, Thousand Oaks, pp. 292–297.

Weaver, DB 2011, 'Contemporary tourism heritage as heritage tourism: evidence from Las Vegas and Gold Coast', *Annals of Tourism Research*, vol. 38, no. 1, pp. 249–267.

Wise, P 2006, 'Australia's Gold Coast: a city producing itself', in C Lindner (ed.), *Urban space and cityscapes: perspectives from modern and contemporary culture*, Routledge, New York, pp. 177–191.

Wise, P 2010, 'Life, style and the capture of code', paper presented at Crossroads in Cultural Studies, Hong Kong, 17–21 June.

Wise, P 2012, 'Solar flow: the uses of light in Gold Coast living', in A Ballantyne & CL Smith (eds), *Architecture in the space of flows*, Routledge, New York, pp. 99–116.

Wise, P & Breen, S 2004, 'The concrete corridor: strategising impermanence in a frontier city', *Media International Australia*, no. 112, pp. 162–173.

Zukin, S 1995, *The cultures of cities*, Blackwell Publishers, Oxford.

Zukin, S 2010, *Naked city: the death and life of authentic urban places*, Oxford University Press, Oxford.

5 Living in sites of leisure
Local experiences and impacts of tourism

Introduction

It is easy to imagine resorts only in terms of tourism. Due to the industry's prominence, resorts are often perceived as merely 'destinations' – places that one goes to, temporarily – and not 'real' or 'serious' cities (Dedekorkut-Howes & Bosman 2015) where everyday lives, routines and non-touristic commercial and cultural endeavours take place. On the contrary, resorts have been localities, neighbourhoods, hometowns for as long they have been destinations, and much longer for those indigenous to the areas. They are places to play, but also places to live and work (Sheller 2004). As they have grown more populated, attracting residents drawn by the lifestyle and landscape as much as by job opportunities, the local cultures of resorts have become increasingly rich, complex and varied. Far from being only tourism sites, resorts are constituted by a range of diverse communities, activities, spaces and services.

Up until this point in the book, I have primarily examined how resorts are represented, imagined and experienced by 'outsiders' (tourists, the media and academics). In the next two chapters, I aim to create a more holistic understanding of resorts by focusing on local perspectives and experiences. I acknowledge that 'local' is an ambiguous concept given that people's attachments to place can be complicated, pluralistic, and in the case of resorts, fraught with ambivalence. Some residents have lived in a particular resort their entire lives; some migrated from elsewhere for job opportunities; some are exiles whose families fled political persecution (as with Cubans in Miami) or refugees from various other forms of conflict; some are higher education students, seeing themselves as people who will only stay for a few years and then leave again; some are expatriates; some desperately want to move elsewhere; some want to 'settle down' there; and so on. Each of these kinds of residents have varying understandings of what 'home' is, where they feel they belong, which places they have a sense of ownership over, and how invested they are in where they live. What they all have in common, and what defines them as locals, is that they carry out much of their everyday lives in the social and spatial contexts of resorts. They are immersed in the particular material and symbolic life-worlds of these places, and this comes to shape their biographical narratives and their *habitus*.

Drawing on interviews conducted with residents of resorts, this chapter and the next discuss some of the impacts of tourism on local people and places. Although much scholarly work has been devoted to mass tourism's environmental, ecological and economic impacts, less attention has been paid to the socio-spatial manifestations and effects that are core to this book. This chapter focuses on how resort residents engage with and feel about their localities, and how living in a tourist-centric place influences their socio-spatial practices and everyday routines. First, I outline the context in which these local experiences take place, emphasising the multiple, and often competing, discourses of resort identity.

Beyond the metanarratives

The urban identities of resorts have been largely defined by how they are imagined by – and how they have been represented for – tourists. They are typically perceived and presented as exotic, escapist, excessive, hedonistic and carnivalesque places in which to relax, indulge, have fun and push boundaries. Simultaneously, there are other unofficial, but still dominant, narratives which position resorts as sexualised, risky, hyperreal, culturally depthless, tacky, Americanised and homogenous. These popular imaginaries and stereotypes constitute the metanarrative of resort identity, which functions to make the illegible city legible, regulate complexity and dispel 'the exceptional and the wayward' urban rhythms (Highmore 2005, p. 7).

Despite its totalising implications, the most familiar metanarrative is only one facet of resort identity. Beyond this, there are a multiplicity of other localised experiences, rhythms, communities and narratives of identity that are marginalised by 'louder' expressions. The tourist hubs – Surfers Paradise, Miami Beach, Cancún's Hotel Zone, Playa d'en Bossa, Patong, Haad Rin – are only small, specialised spaces within large, diverse urban formations, and cannot be taken to represent a resort in its entirety. Outside these zones, there are universities, hospitals, parks, libraries, charity shops, grocery stores, banks, welfare offices, small businesses, and neighbourhoods with different built environments, social relations, spatial usages, historical contexts and reputations. Many of my interviewees, like Jakub, stressed that there was much more to their localities than just tourism:

JAKUB: Patong, Karon, Kata – totally touristy, there's nothing else happening there, right? If you move out [inland] – like I live in Kamala, which is a village in the next bay, there is also normal life – like not touristy life, where people have other businesses, do other things ... there is a city called Phuket Town which has nothing to do with tourism. It's a normal city functioning with its own life, it has universities, it has schools, hospitals, shopping centres, business – it is totally normal life. Tourism is very important, but it's not everything. And if you drive up north to the other side of the island, you will see fishermen, you will see rubber tree plantations, you will see other things that happen which are not tourist-dependent.

(Phuket, 9 December 2013)

This heterogeneity is something that can be readily observed when one ventures away from the tourist hub of any resort.

The major failing of the resort metanarrative is that it focuses on how resorts are represented and imagined, largely ignoring how they are *lived*. The livedness of these places unsettles any coherent myths or narratives of place, and transforms not only how we perceive them, but how we act within them. That is, we are responsive to the materiality of space. At many points during my fieldwork, *in situ*, I experienced moments of surprise when I encountered things for which the myths, tourism marketing and my own travel research had not prepared me. I did not expect to see small shrines to the king along the streets in Patong, nor abandoned hotels in Cancún, nor all of the diverse neighbourhoods located inland from Miami Beach. This even happened in my own locality. For example, I was surprised at how many women wearing hijabs and niqabs were in Surfers Paradise among the other Western, swim-suit-clad tourists and sexualised Meter Maids. The unexpected encompassed more than the visual as well, with other sensorial particularities contributing to the overall atmosphere of place, something that representations could not capture, and that could only fully be grasped through embodied experience.

I am not suggesting that the metanarrative is a facade that conceals the 'reality' of a resort, or a somehow more authentic identity hidden beneath the surface. Even the most contrived narrative can nonetheless become internalised, made concrete through spatial practice and repeatedly enacted to become a 'natural' city rhythm. Tourism (and all of its associated individuals, groups, spaces, imaginaries, representations and repercussions) is integral to resorts, seeping into and affecting every part of their lived existence, and thus many local formations, experiences and understandings are mediated by or engage with tourism in some way, as explored below. Conversely, symbolic and material aspects of local cultures have recently been incorporated into the dominant tourism narratives. The touristic and the local, the dominant and the marginal, the official and the unofficial, and everything in between, shape the lived spatiality of resorts.

Competing discourses

CORY: I think Miami in general has the perception around the world, and not just the US, of being like a sexy, glamorous place – on one hand. But also kind of like a dangerous, crime-ridden place.

(Miami, 14 March 2014)

Like conventional cities, resorts are assemblages constituted by multiplicities, difference and eclecticism, which creates contrasts, juxtapositions and conflicting narratives. Pile (1999) describes this aspect of cities in terms of paradox:

> what is characteristically urban is that it is paradoxical; paradoxical, both in the sense that it embodies elements that are seemingly opposed at one and the same time, and in the sense that the seemingly opposed elements are brought together, intensified and concentrated in the city. (p. 45)

How these differences overlap and intersect can be understood in terms of Elspeth Probyn's (1996) description of the heterotopic as 'the coexistence of different orders of space, the materiality of different forms of social relations and modes of belonging' (p. 10). In traditional urban formations, this produces what Robert E Park (1967) calls 'moral regions', 'moral milieux' or 'social worlds', which compose a mapping of the city as 'a mosaic of little worlds which touch but do not interpenetrate' (p. 40). These somewhat segregated areas, which can never be fully cohesive or pure, and which are occupied by particular social milieu, do indeed exist in resorts (e.g. Little Haiti and Little Havana in Miami), but much more common are spaces of mixture, *bricolage* and hybridity.

Resorts are at once home and away, everyday and exotic, familiar and unfamiliar, for tourists and locals alike. Their landscapes combine the artificial and the natural, with high-rises and mega-malls set against the vast ocean and lush forests. They are positioned as family-friendly, fun-in-the-sun destinations, but are simultaneously famous for partying, transgression and crime. They are sites for liberation, hedonism and *communitas*, but are also highly regulated and exclusionary. McDonald's restaurants sit side-by-side with opulent five-star hotels, and the excessive displays of wealth and conspicuous consumption characteristic of the tourist hubs stand in stark contrast to the poverty and low-income residential areas found on the fringes. Sexy and sleazy slide together, spectacle has a tendency to appear tacky or banal, and there is a fine line between adventurous and out-of-control. Resorts undermine binaries, always being both, being in-between, hybrid, liminal.

These competing discourses manifest spatially in resorts as polyrhythmia (Lefebvre 2004 [1992]) – multiple rhythms which may co-exist harmoniously, interplay or clash. For instance, in resorts, there are local rhythms – people travelling to and from work each day, dropping their kids off at school, going to the grocery store, and engaging in leisure practices in their free time; and there are tourist rhythms – the seasonal flows of visitors, daily tours to popular sites and attractions, and the shifts in activity from day to night in entertainment zones. While local rhythms dominate the suburbs and residential areas further inland, tourist and local rhythms often intermingle in more urbanised areas. In the tourist hubs, for instance, the dominant rhythm is composed of tourists (and to a lesser extent residents) shopping, eating, sightseeing and going to the beach, and this converges with the less noticeable rhythms of locals undertaking paid labour.

Impacts of tourism

There is, then, much more to resorts than simply tourism. To understand resorts more fully and conceptualise them as distinct urban formations, it is crucial to consider local perspectives, experiences and practices, which are frequently obscured by the touristic metanarrative. The remainder of this chapter elucidates some of these local experiences, focusing particularly on how residents are affected by, respond to, engage with and feel about tourism in their localities. A range of economic, social, political, environmental and geological impacts of tourism in various resorts have been well documented in scholarly literature. Here, I briefly outline some of the most pressing issues common to the destinations on which this book concentrates before shifting focus to my own observations and what emerged from my interviews.

The commodification of culture is seen to be one of the major social changes instigated by tourism development (Hall & Lew 2009; Boissevain 1996). This can be viewed negatively, as with the assumption that commodification inevitably leads to homogenisation or Westernisation (see Chapter 4). For instance, Castellanos (2010) describes how Maya communities living around Cancún express fears that the modernised, 'vulgar' (p. 255), excessive consumerist culture of the resort will threaten their traditional rural lifestyle. In contrast, commodification can also be perceived as potentially positive. Preserving and protecting cultural and natural heritage, for example, can renew interest and pride in local (or regional, or national) practices, traditions and landmarks, and thus (re)shape and strengthen collectively shared identities, histories and attachments to place (Salazar 2009; Boissevain 1996; Cohen 1988). In other words, commodification may work to reaffirm local specificity and difference rather diminish it (Meethan 2001).

Although tourism has proved to be a successful route to economic prosperity for the resorts in this study, it has also led to: increased costs of living and property prices (Bosman 2016; Sakolnakorn, Naipinit & Kroeksakul 2013; Tourism and Events Queensland 2013; Agarwal & Shaw 2007; D'Andrea 2007; Murray 2007); higher crime rates, gang activity, drug trafficking and acts of delinquency, especially in Cancún (Sakolnakorn et al. 2013; Tourism and Events Queensland 2013; Castellanos 2010; Mugerauer 2004; Minca 2000); problems associated with prostitution and sex tourism, especially in Thailand (Hobbs, Na Pattalung & Chandler 2011; Hall & Lew 2009; Kontogeorgopoulos 2009; Berger 2007; Henkel, Henkel, Agrusa, Agrusa & Tanner 2006; Mugerauer 2004); and overcrowding of public spaces and traffic congestion across all resorts, but with particular intensity in seasonal destinations like Ibiza (Sakolnakorn et al. 2013; McDowall & Choi 2010; D'Andrea 2007; Boissevain 1996; Smith 1991; Jones 1986).

In terms of infrastructure and resources, some of these destinations – notably Cancún, Phuket, Koh Phangan and Ibiza – have experienced overwhelming demands for energy and fresh water, as well as extreme pressures on waste management and disposal methods (which has further contributed to pollution) (Sakolnakorn et al. 2013; Córdoba Azcárate 2011; Kontogeorgopoulos 2009; Anderson 2009; Fortuny, Soler, Cánovas & Sánchez 2008; Murray 2007; Agarwal & Shaw 2007). As with overcrowding and traffic, these problems are exacerbated in seasonal destinations, those with small resident populations compared to tourism arrivals, and those with rapidly expanding resident populations, since local infrastructure is typically not designed to keep up with the highest volume of users. Consequently, residents can be disadvantaged and inconvenienced during peak times.

Environmental and ecological impacts due to unconstrained development have been multiple and severe, including damage to coral reefs from over-fishing, water sports and boat anchors (Córdoba Azcárate 2011; McDowall & Wang 2009; Murray 2007; Agarwal & Shaw 2007); deforestation, the clearing of mangroves and the destruction of sand dunes to make way for tourism facilities in prime coastal locations (Brenner, Engelbauer & Job 2018; Sakolnakorn et al. 2013; Cohen 2008; Agarwal & Shaw 2007; Kontogeorgopoulos 2009, 2004; Murray 2007; Mugerauer 2004; Smith 1991); the degradation of natural ecosystems, which has threatened local plant and animal life (Agarwal & Shaw 2007; Murray 2007); and air and water pollution (McDowall & Choi 2010; Hall & Lew 2009; McDowall & Wang 2009; Cohen 2008; D'Andrea 2007; Murray 2007; Henkel et al. 2006; Smith 1991). These ongoing issues are evidence of the ways in which supporting rapid development and generating tourism revenue has consistently been privileged over long-term environmental sustainability. This can cause resentment among locals by damaging the natural assets that attracted them to live there in the first place (McDowall & Choi 2010; Mugerauer 2004). Beyond this, it can also harm the long-term sustainability of the tourism industries themselves, since the appeal and successful operation of resorts principally relies on the natural landscape and its resources. Beaches seem much less like 'paradise' with garbage strewn across the sand and the stench of petrol emanating from hordes of jet skis and tour boats.

While many of the impacts listed here are undoubtedly negative, and certainly require intervention, my aim is not simply to make judgments regarding whether tourism is good or bad – a 'blight' or a 'blessing' (Smith 2001, p. 109; Poon 1993, p. 287). The effects of tourism on resort destinations are varied and complex, which is why my interest below is predominantly in how resort residents *feel* about living among those effects. I have set out to glean something of their micro-level perspectives on macro-level influences, as well as their responses and resistances to them. The findings I discuss are examples, and are not intended to be representative of all possible attitudes. Rather,

I draw on my personal experiences and observations along with those of my interviewees to speak to the ways in which residing in a resort may create unique circumstances for particular ways of living, belonging and interacting.

Local lifestyles

Living in a resort myself, what I hear most often from other locals are complaints – that tourists are 'annoying', that the city has 'no culture', and that all anyone cares about is looks and money. In my nearly 10 years of residing on the Gold Coast, I have seldom stopped to ask myself, or others, what it is that people actually *like* about living here. If so many of us express such disdain for the city, why are we even here? And why do we stay? When I put these questions to my interviewees in different locations, their answers were expectedly varied: for the job opportunities, to attend university, and, most commonly, because of ties to family and friends.

Regardless of what brought them to these places, all of my interviewees expressed some degree of appreciation for what their locality has to offer them. They frequently mentioned the weather as the best part about living in a resort – even if only because it lets their clothes dry faster on the washing line – along with the beaches and the wide variety of dining options. Most significantly, however, was the 'lifestyle', something that almost every participant cited as their favourite thing about where they live. This lifestyle is seen to be relaxed and connected to nature:

NICOLE: I love the beach and the water, I'm a water person … And the fact that there is that outdoor kind of culture of being able to have a barbeque … That aspect, and the relaxed kind of nature of our city. So, it's a city, but it's not like Sydney where you feel like you're gonna get run over by people on the street with their briefcases because it's so busy.

(Gold Coast, 4 November 2014)

ALYSSA: It's hard to put into words. … Like the atmosphere, the vibe … it's like, more relaxed, I guess, and it's sort of got the beach vibe to it. It's like, really chill, whereas – the only other place I'd move is Brisbane or Melbourne and it's sort of busy, and big cities don't have that same sort of relaxed, chill thing.

(Gold Coast, 24 September 2014)

SETH: I think after travelling a bit, I've decided that I like the lifestyle here. Not the typical lifestyle, but I like the fact that it's – there's not a lot of people here, it's not like when you go to somewhere like Japan, and after 10 days you want to come home because you can't breathe because there's so many people.

(Gold Coast, 24 November 2014)

Thus, what residents like about the Gold Coast is not dissimilar to what tourists like. As Baker, Bennett and Wise (2012) observe, locals' strong identification with lifestyle unsettles conventional notions of belonging characterised by citizenship or community in that it is shaped to a large extent by tourism representations aimed at outsiders. Wise (2010) expands on this: 'The discourses of leisure and "lifestyle" so pervade the milieux of ordinary life – through media, social interaction and retail engagements – that they constitute the most available vocabulary to express local belonging' (p. 2). Resorts are seen as not governed by the same corporate, fast-paced rhythms as conventional cities, which reinforces their liminal status. Further, they have a feeling of spatial openness: since their aesthetic is so dependent on providing expansive views of the beaches, buildings are spread out rather than densely packed together as in a traditional CBD. Seth elaborated on this theme, explaining that he appreciates that the Gold Coast has a small town feel but with all the amenities of a big city:

SETH: … it's big enough that it has everything that I need, you know? I like small towns but the thing they lack is employment and jobs and some of the luxuries that we have here … there's at least one of everything here. And not like it is in a city where there's a hundred of it. So, I like that there might be a local shop that I can go to just down the street, but then if I need to I can go to somewhere like Pacific Fair or Robina [major shopping malls] and there's a lot of the things that I want to get access to … It's just the right size, the right amount of population.

(Gold Coast, 24 November 2014)

The fact that a relaxed lifestyle is something that residents value reinforces the importance of managing issues like overcrowding, overdevelopment and environmental degradation to ensure that this way of life can be maintained.

For residents of Miami, lifestyle is also bound up in the city's cultural diversity. My interviewees there each expressed a deep fondness for this aspect of the city, which, to them, sets it apart from the state (which is predominantly white) and the nation:

DAMLA: I did my undergrad in Pennsylvania and I was very unhappy and very disappointed [laughs]. It was very – at least where I was, where I went to college – was very homogenous and not much diversity. And so I definitely like that about here – the diversity.

(Miami, 11 March 2014)

LUCIANA: I like the diversity of it, there's a lot of Caribbean people, and back home [San Francisco] we have a different kind of diversity. Here it's very Caribbean or Latin American people, so it's really interesting all these different restaurants and different foods.

(Miami, 13 March 2014)

EMILIO: What I like about the city is there is some diversity. There is a
sense of diversity, at least for me as an insider. I have close friends
from all over Latin America, and you know, for a white person up
north, that might mean it's all full of Hispanics, but you know, we're
all different in one way or another. There's good food from everywhere, good access to music, and literature and arts from all over
Latin America.

(Miami, 12 March 2014)

MIGUEL: The plastic, materialistic image gets pushed more than the diversity. I
know a lot of people who were born and raised in Miami as well, parents
born outside of the United States, and they say that Miami lacks culture. I
had a particular friend of mine who just moved back to New Jersey and
she claimed that New Jersey has more culture than Miami, yet she's
Cuban, her boy's Irish-Puerto Rican, the boy next door's Ecuadorian. I'm
like, hello? How's there no culture here? ... I think the diversity is really the
best ... because that allows you [the] opportunity to see everybody's
perspective, you know?

(Miami, 11 March 2014)

Miami's diversity was also something I noticed and appreciated as an
outsider visiting temporarily. One day, for instance, I went from my apartment to a fieldwork site and then to meet an interviewee, and along the way
saw young Spring Breakers and Art Deco architecture in South Beach; people
in corporate wear waiting in line for Cuban take away in downtown; hipsters
among warehouses covered in street art in Wynwood; families with young
children walking through the predominantly black neighbourhood of Little
Haiti; and streets lined with leafy trees and Mediterranean revival and Spanish Mission style homes in Buena Vista. Although cultural diversity was not
explicitly mentioned by interviewees in other resorts, it is clearly present in
each place. Being sites for continuous flows of transient visitors from around
the world, and appealing places for others to migrate to, resorts are becoming
increasingly hybrid, heterogeneous and eclectic, transforming and adapting as
different groups of people come into contact with them and territorialise them
(whether briefly or longer term).

In places like Phuket, for my white expatriate interviewees, the concept of
lifestyle also encompassed a perceived relaxation of the rules and
regulations characteristic of everyday life in the West. For Jakub and Jeff,
the decision to live in Phuket stemmed from a desire to make the carefree,
permissive elements of the resort vacation a permanent part of their everyday lives:

JAKUB: Phuket itself, it's beautiful. Great weather all year round, excellent food.
And probably one of the things I would mention more importantly is the
people's freestyle attitude. People don't judge – well, if they judge they don't

express it ... people live and let live, basically. It's a very, very tolerant society in many, many areas, so that's part of the big attraction for me.

(Phuket, 9 December 2013)

JEFF: [on why he moved from Australia to Thailand]: I got a bit tired of all the rules and regulations and taxes and the cameras, and I can't say this and I can't say that ... I got sick of paying 58 cents on the dollar of tax, I got sick of cameras watching everything I was doing, I got sick of being not able to tell a joke and it might offend someone. All the bullshit started to get to me ... Here, it's different, the pace is relaxed. When I arrived, I was quite highly strung and stressed out, I wasn't a happy person ... But here, I don't need to keep 9 to 5 type hours. I like the pace of life.

(Phuket, 9 December 2013)

More specifically, they both relayed stories to explain why they perceive normalised 'corruption' (as defined from a Western perspective) as allowing for greater freedom and flexibility:

JEFF: ... if something happens, you can fix it just with a smile, a sorry, sometimes 100 baht under the table ... In Australia if I had a problem I'd call my lawyer at 600 dollars an hour, I'd be in court for 2 years. Look, sometimes I'd rather just go bang, it's fixed, and it's fixed instantly ... Like, we're sitting here having a drink. If we had two of these in my country [Australia], I wouldn't be allowed to drive the car. Not that it's a good thing, but I could have 10 of them sitting here and I wouldn't think twice about it, because no one's going to do anything to me. And even if they do, even on the million in one chance that some policeman says 'have you had something to drink?', my answer would be 'okay, yeah, but what's it gonna cost to fix this?', and that's our rules ... Doesn't mean you behave like an idiot, no, of course you don't. But it's still nice to know that it's a bit more flexible, a bit more freedom with things like that ... Every rule here is deliberately ambiguous to allow for flexibility and allow for negotiation. Most of the government workers are so underpaid that it's an accepted part of society here, that if you're a policeman, or if you're some sort of authority somewhere, that you expect to make some money on something on the way through.

(Phuket, 9 December 2013)

What this points to is not so much a *lack* of rules, but a *different* set of rules. Individuals are still accountable for their actions, but in less official, less conventional ways than in the West. Similarly, local businesses and vendors in Phuket may not have to be as concerned about meeting standards and regulations set by government authorities, but they are still overseen by, and at the mercy of, what my interviewees called the 'beach mafia' or 'tuk tuk mafia' – the notorious group known to run tourist scams and restrict the activities of other tourism operators.

These systems based on bribery are far more advantageous for those who have the economic capital necessary to offer bribes on a regular basis. As such, wealthy expatriate and Thai elites may enjoy this flexibility more than the lower and working-class locals, for whom this system may be disproportionately unreliable and unjust. Further, as Jakub explained, not having conventional bureaucratic policies has a downside for all residents as well:

JAKUB: ... because of the free lifestyle, they don't plan too much ahead. So sometimes in my village we will have [a] blackout because they need some repairs for electrical cables, but they will never announce it, so you'll be sitting at home and suddenly there's no power for six hours or so. There is not enough communication about things which may affect you, from the public authorities ... on the Gold Coast, as far as I can recall, you wouldn't see one beach vendor, no restaurants, nothing is on the beach ... here, there are no lifeguards or there are few and far apart; safety is your own problem. The whole system here in Thailand is based on – you take care of yourself, the government doesn't take care of you. There is no social security or hardly any. Medical help is very minimum, or a very low level if it's the public health system. In Australia, you have – you pay, and you get. Here, nobody pays, and you get nothing.

(Phuket, 9 December 2013)

Again, this has far greater negative impacts for the poorest locals. Clearly, the capacity to which lifestyle can appeal to residents is mediated by their economic and social standing.

Frustrations and tensions

Despite generally liking where they live, most of my interviewees expressed some negative attitudes towards tourists and tourism. In addition to identifying specific inconveniences like traffic congestion, noise pollution and overcrowding, interviewees also revealed general feelings of resentment, frustration and annoyance. These kinds of attitudes, which signify prolonged tensions between tourists and locals, are typical of intensively developed mature destinations (Lawton 2005; Minca 2000). Asking my interviewees 'How do you feel about the tourist presence?' elicited responses such as these:

ALYSSA: It's annoying as shit.

(Gold Coast, 24 September 2014)

JAKUB: Well, in low season, it's peaceful, it's ours. In high season, the tourists ... they take over, and also then the locals, I mean Thai people who live here – everybody gets really ... I wouldn't say stressed, but grabby, pushy for business, hassling, etc., etc., especially in areas like Patong ... Patong is hell.

(Phuket, 9 December 2013)

JEFF: ... when you live here, it [high season] gets annoying too, because the roads are full, the restaurants are full, you can't see the beach. I mean in 3 months' time, you look up that beach, you won't see one umbrella, you'll just see sand ... And there's a lot of meatheads here at the time, basically, especially the Russians, but Australians too. ... They're uneducated, they don't have social skills, they're just annoying people ... they get drunk a lot, they start fights, they treat the girls badly.

(Phuket, 9 December 2013)

NICOLE: I accept that it's there, but I don't like it ... Because I've lived in high-rises most of my life, and those high-rises have all been half residential, half tourist ... they [tourists] have this perception that no one actually lives here, everyone that's here is on holiday. So they're completely astounded that I live here, that I'm a resident, and that I'm not on holiday. As a result of that, because they do have this misconception that we're on holidays, they're loud, they're noisy, they overtake the space and they don't respect that we have our day-to-day lives that we go about ... like at the moment, sometimes I work from home ... and I'm trying to concentrate and people are being really loud. Or they're coming home from going out partying in the middle of the week because they're on holidays, and they're slamming doors and yelling in the lift, or they park in your parking space, or they park across the driveway ... They're like, 'We're all on holiday, so you've got plenty of time for me to move my car because you're going nowhere'. No, I'm going to work, get out of my fucking driveway ... So I do feel suffocated around tourist time. It's a burden.

(Gold Coast, 4 November 2014)

Residents see tourists as noisy, rowdy, messy, rude, inconsiderate and overbearing. Just as tourists objectify, essentialise and stereotype local people, locals also do this to tourists, viewing them as a homogenous mass with shared characteristics and behaviours. Castellanos (2010) argues that this is the function of the 'native gaze', which encompasses 'the universalizing ways local people "see" tourism and tourists and construct them as other' (p. 242). These perceptions are shaped by individual encounters with tourists and reinforced in the media (Shaw & Williams 2004). Importantly, although resentment is usually directed at *tourists* and their behaviours, there are a range of other groups, policies and processes (e.g. local governments and their marketing strategies and tourism development policies) implicated in the production of how tourists understand and use space. Therefore, frustrations with 'tourists' reflect problems with the tourism industry's presence more broadly, rather than the individual visitors themselves.

One of the major sources of tension, as the above quotes demonstrate, arises when tourists interfere with the everyday socio-spatial practices of residents – when tourist rhythms and local rhythms clash. Given that residents and visitors can often occupy the same spaces within resorts, whether because of leisure, labour or mixed-use residences, these clashes are inevitable. The discontent this causes is further aggravated by the fact that tourists are perceived as having a sense of entitlement – as Jakub put it, 'they think that they own the place' (Phuket, 9 December 2013). Mass tourists, in particular, are renowned for behaving carelessly and disrespectfully towards these places – places to which residents, to varying degrees, have affective attachments. Such tourists behave as if resorts really *are* disembedded, hyperreal fantasy lands with no rules and no restrictions.

As a consequence of these strained relations, residents of resorts actively avoid the tourist hubs as much as they can. In this way, the presence of tourists, and tourism sites and activities, significantly shapes how locals perceive and use space in their own localities. Along with the overcrowding and congestion noted above, residents deplore tourist hubs for being fake, tacky,[1] overpriced and low in quality.[2] Locals instead tend to head for quieter beaches and trendy cafes away from the tourist hubs. On the Gold Coast, we say 'locals don't go to Surfers Paradise'. This is not exactly true, of course, as while many of us make a concerted effort to stay away, opting for more local beaches and dining precincts, many others still work in Surfers (e.g. in retail and hospitality). Moreover, since nightlife scarcely exists outside of tourist hubs, many of us find ourselves there for specific social events at bars, restaurants or clubs. However, these leisure spaces are designed to appeal to the tastes of mass tourists, and thus do not cater for the many locals who prefer alternative or subcultural experiences.

My interviewees shared similar observations, noting that they usually only go to these areas to entertain visitors, thereby enacting their position as 'host' on a micro level:

JEFF: ... look, Patong, we still go there sometimes. Of course, whenever I have visitors here they always want to go check it out, so I go and show them the girly bars and the ladyboy bars ... They all wanna see it. I don't really enjoy my time there, but I've had some fun there as well ...

(Phuket, 9 December 2013)

EMILIO: It's easy to get lost on a weekend in South Beach, and whatever that means – drugs and sex and alcohol and party, and that still attracts some of us as much as we dislike it ... But we do understand that it's superficial and annoying, so when we go it's either because there's something really good happening or because we are taking a family member to like, see the city. But not as often. I rarely go to the beach anymore ... even when we go to the beach with friends, we usually end up going to areas of the beach that are more secluded.

(Miami, 12 March 2014)

MIGUEL: If somebody comes, we're going to take them to South Beach, of course. The beach or the club or the bars, you know. And again, the locals live a little bit more inland. There's cool stuff to do there too, but where's the go-to place you're gonna take your family or friends to show them a good time? It's down here.

(Miami, 11 March 2014)

LUCIANA: It's interesting because [with] my boyfriend ... he doesn't really like all of the tourists coming in all the time and he doesn't like to do touristy things, he stays away from it. He likes the different side of Miami, where the tourists aren't at. I was like, oh, that's interesting, because I'm the opposite ... I love South Beach. Even though it's fake and everything, I still love it ... I like that the beach is right there. So when our friends come to visit, of course, [we] have to take them to South Beach and to the clubs there ... I kind of consider myself in a sense a tourist here because I'm not from here, so I'm kind of drawn to touristy areas. But even then, I sort of think about it, like, oh, this is so fake, it's not even real, or a lot of these plants and things aren't even native to Florida. It kind of ruins it.

(Miami, 13 March 2014)

JAKUB: ... the life of the expats or the locals has shifted from, let's say, Patong – if you wanted to go out the only place was Patong, but now we all go out in this area here [Kamala Beach] because the tourists or – let's say, I don't mean it bad, but the white trash – doesn't come here ... the locals go out here. Patong? Never, never, never. It's a big brothel, basi-cally ... when I used to live in Runaway Bay [a northern Gold Coast suburb] – I would never, ever, ever go to Surfers. I lived there for 16 years. If I wanted to go to the beach, I'd go to Main Beach or further north, The Spit, or I would take my boat and go out to South Stradbroke Island or whatever. I never go to Surfers ... Surfers itself is like Patong here, basically. It's sacrificed to the business ...

(Phuket, 9 December 2013)

NICOLE: ... honestly, I can count on my hand in the last three or four years the amount of times I've been to Surfers Paradise. I don't go there. ... If I go out to dinner I go to Broadbeach or somewhere else, so – it's only if there's something specific, like Ben & Jerry's that I can't get anywhere else – then I will go.

(Gold Coast, 4 November 2014)

Not surprisingly, the desire to avoid the tourist hubs is strongest during peak seasons and major events, when tourist-local tensions are at their highest. This includes famous events such as the Full Moon Parties in Koh Phangan, Spring Break in Miami and Cancún, Schoolies on the Gold Coast, and the summertime clubbing season in Ibiza, as well as times around music, arts and cultural festivals, public holidays and school holidays. During these busy periods, locals alter their everyday routines to avoid the tourist hubs by driving different routes from usual, opting to only go to restaurants in more local areas, and so on. On the Gold Coast, if we must go into Surfers at these times, the experience is usually not a pleasant one, fraught with discomfort, irritation and frustration. This is particularly bad for those who live in or near tourist hubs, since avoidance is not an option. Nicole and Seth explained their experiences of living around Surfers during 'Indy' (the former, and still colloquial, term for an annual car race now named the Gold Coast 600):

NICOLE: I lived on the Indy track in Main Beach, from when I was age, say, 14 to 20, 21. And at one stage we were right on the track and that was full on. It's loud, there's drunk bogans ... I think it just ruins the landscape. There's beautiful beaches and then like 'vroom' [loud car noise] and concrete barriers, and they put fences on the beach – it's shit ... But then we moved to the other side of Main Beach, and while we didn't have the cars going past, it still sounded like they did, and you still had to have a pass to get in and out of your driveway, and if you didn't leave by 7 am, then you couldn't get your car out, so you had to park your car in Fisherman's Wharf [a nearby tavern]. It's just a pain in the fucking ass. And you're not compensated for it, you don't get free tickets to the Indy or anything like that.

(Gold Coast, 4 November 2014)

SETH: I definitely didn't like living at Budd's Beach [a small riverside area in Surfers] while Indy was on. That was really, really bad ... when Schoolies or Indy was on, it impacted the people that lived locally, severely. But you didn't really feel as though once that finished the council or whoever's in charge went back to trying make that place better for you. It wasn't like a case of 'hey, we know you guys live here, sorry we're gonna need to basically take your local area over for the next two weeks and do all these things to service all these tourists, but once they go away we'll do some nice things for you, like put in a park for your kids to play at' or whatever ... It feels very, very weighted towards whatever can be done to create the most amount of money, based on tourism, and probably spend the least amount of money on locals ... if they're gonna fix up the roads, they're doing it for tourist buses, they're not fixing it up for the local people that live there.

(Gold Coast, 24 November 2014)

Besides the obvious disruption caused by the road closures and noise, residents also resent not being compensated for these inconveniences. They are made to feel that tourists have more of a right to city space than they do, and that their needs as residents are secondary to satisfying tourists and generating revenue (see Chapter 6).

In Miami, similar tensions are present. According to Emilio, the Spring Break crowds present when I visited were nothing compared to Urban Beach Week. A highly contentious event, Urban Beach Week is an unofficial hip hop music festival that takes place over the Memorial Day weekend each year in South Beach. It attracts up to 250,000 attendees over five days (de Leon 2016; Smiley 2012), providing a sizeable boost to Miami's tourism industry, especially for hotels and prominent nightclubs. It is also notorious for bad traffic, road closures, public drunkenness, violent incidents, and clashes between police and party-goers (Grieco 2017; Flechas 2016; Benn 2013; Smiley 2012). This causes great disruption for the residents of South Beach, many of whom are known to flee the area for that weekend (Alvarez 2012). The discontent has spread to local businesses as well, with some – such as upmarket restaurants and smaller nightclubs – purposely closing over the weekend to avoid dealing with the disorderly crowds, who also deter patronage from their usual customer base (Pajot 2014; Alvarez 2012; Smiley 2012). As a result, there have been calls to end, or at least extensively regulate, Urban Beach Week (Grieco 2017; Abdill 2011).

Since the event is organised through informal networks like social media, and is not sponsored by the city, there is little that authorities can do to change the event's parameters or participants (Veiga 2016; Alvarez 2012). City officials have, however, begun to schedule a number of parallel cultural activities – which in 2018 included 'a gospel performance, a celebrity basketball game, a movie screening and a barbecue contest' – in an attempt to reterritorialise Miami Beach, and to change the weekend's reputation for partying and violence (Gurney 2018). In recent years, the city has also increased regulation through surveillance techniques including a significant police presence, the implementation of watch towers, DUI checkpoints and license plate checks on the causeways leading to Miami Beach (de Leon 2016; Veiga 2016; Alvarez 2012). These measures have been criticised as racist for unfairly assuming that the event's participants (the majority of whom are black) are more likely to be engaging in criminal activities than Miami's usual throng of tourists (de Leon 2016; Veiga 2016; Smiley 2012).

During our interview, Luciana raised another example of a touristic event with strong local resistance: Ultra Music Festival, held each March at Bayfront Park, Downtown Miami for the past 20 years. Just as with Urban Beach Week, many residents living in close proximity to this 'ultra deafening, ultra intrusive, ultra disruptive' (Robertson 2018) event opt to stay indoors or leave for the weekend. Luciana explained that during the 2013 festival, tensions between residents, party-goers and local authorities were at their worst:

LUCIANA: Last year they actually had it [Ultra] two weekends and people from all over come for that festival. So I remember how it was like a big deal, how they wanted to get it shut down, how they didn't want it here, you know, but they're like, well it brings us a lot of money and we need it. And people were fighting back and forth. At one point, they almost cancelled one of the weekends of the festival. But then they ended up having the two weekends ... But this year they reduced it back to one weekend.

INTERVIEWER: So why was there such opposition to it?

LUCIANA: ... they complained a lot about the kind of people, like a lot of young people, probably going to be using drugs, or the music being super loud, and the traffic, because they block off certain areas over there. So that's what they were complaining about, and they [locals] were like 'no', but they [the local government] were like 'it's gonna bring us a lot of money'.

(Miami, 13 March 2014)

The Miami commissioner at the time, Marc Sarnoff, opposed the addition of a second weekend to the festival, citing concerns over the disruption to local businesses and residents due to noise, disorderly behaviour, drug use and traffic (Duran 2013). His resolution did not pass, with the City Commission voting that the second weekend would go forward, but with a stipulation that Ultra would only take place over one weekend in the future (Tregoning 2013). Only one year later, the mayor called for the end of the event after a security guard was trampled and severely injured by gate-crashers (Fagenson 2014). Nevertheless, Ultra continues to be held in Miami, attracting upwards of 165,000 festival-goers and generating an estimated US$79 million for the county each year (Gonzalez 2012). In such scenarios, it is easy for locals to feel as if their concerns are of secondary importance to profiteering, and that voicing their disapproval is fruitless.

Conclusion

Resorts are constituted by multiplicities, contradictions and competing discourses, which present themselves in their lived spaces. As this chapter made clear, such tensions are reflected in – and provide the context for – the complex relationships that resort residents have to where the live. Residents, like tourists, enjoy the good weather, the beaches, the lifestyle and the diversity and hybridity that flourishes with ongoing, transnational flows of people, products and trends. At the same time, however, they have to deal with a range of negative social, environmental, political and ecological consequences that they may feel are out of their control. These effects manifest differently, and with varying degrees of severity, in each resort, contingent on its local specificity. Despite these differences, a common theme has emerged: that the frustrations of residents are most intensified when they feel that their needs, desires and expectations are peripheral to – and even threatened by – those of tourists and the tourism industry. The next chapter explores this theme further, focusing particularly on how these circumstances influence everyday practices, opportunities and senses of belonging for resort locals.

Notes

1 As epitomised by numerous chain stores, souvenir shops and street vendors selling gimmicky toys.
2 For example – with a few exceptions – restaurants in places like Surfers Paradise and South Beach are notorious among locals for providing poor customer service and poor quality food at exorbitant prices. These establishments need not rely on loyal, regular customers, instead surviving by virtue of their convenient locations for transient visitors.

References

Abdill, R 2011, 'Gunfire, death and crime spur calls for end to Miami Beach's Urban Beach Weekend', *Miami New Times*, 30 May, viewed 29 October 2016, <http://www.miaminewtimes.com/news/gunfire-death-and-crime-spur-calls-for-end-to-miami-beachs-urban-beach-weekend-6561322>.

Agarwal, S & Shaw, G 2007, 'Re-engineering coastal resorts in Mexico: some management issues', in S Agarwal & G Shaw (eds), *Managing coastal tourism resorts: a global perspective*, Channel View Publications, Clevedon, pp. 216–232.

Alvarez, L 2012, 'As hip-hop devotees come in, many Miami Beach residents prepare to leave', *The New York Times*, 25 May, viewed 17 September 2016, <http://www.nytimes.com/2012/05/26/us/as-hip-hop-devotees-come-in-many-miami-beach-residents-prepare-to-leave.html?_r=1>.

Anderson, W 2009, 'Promoting ecotourism through networks: case studies in the Balearic Islands', *Journal of Ecotourism*, vol. 8, no. 1, pp. 51–69.

Baker, S, Bennett, A & Wise, P 2012, 'Living "the strip": negotiating neighborhood, community, and identity on Australia's Gold Coast', in C Richardson & HA Skott-Myhre (eds), *Habitus of the hood*, Intellect, Bristol, pp. 97–120.

Benn, ES 2013, 'Drugs, drinking part of many Urban Beach Week arrests in Miami Beach', *Miami Herald*, 28 May, viewed 17 September 2016, <http://www.miamiherald.com/latest-news/article1951924.html>.

Berger, AA 2007, *Thailand tourism*, Haworth Hospitality & Tourism Press, New York.

Boissevain, J 1996, 'Introduction', in J Boissevain (ed.), *Coping with tourists: European reactions to mass tourism*, Berghahn Books, Providence, pp. 1–26.

Bosman, C 2016, 'Changing landscapes: Gold Coast residents and the impacts of rapid urban development', in A Dedekorkut-Howes, C Bosman & A Leach (eds), *Off the plan: the urbanisation of the Gold Coast*, CSIRO Publishing, Clayton South, pp. 75–83.

Brenner, L, Engelbauer, M & Job, H 2018, 'Mitigating tourism-driven impacts on mangroves in Cancún and the Riviera Maya, Mexico: an evaluation of conservation policy strategies and environmental planning instruments', *Journal of Coastal Conservation*, pp. 1–13, doi:10.1007/s11852-018-0606-0.

Castellanos, MB 2010, 'Cancún and the campo: indigenous migration and tourism development in the Yucatán', in D Berger & AG Wood (eds), *Holiday in Mexico:*

critical reflections on tourism and tourist encounters, Duke University Press, Durham, pp. 241–264.

Cohen, E 1988, 'Authenticity and commoditization in tourism', *Annals of Tourism Research*, vol. 15, no. 3, pp. 371–386.

Cohen, E 2008, *Explorations in Thai tourism: collected case studies*, Emerald, Bingley.

Córdoba Azcárate, M 2011, '"Thanks God, this is not Cancun!" Alternative tourism imaginaries in Yucatan (Mexico)', *Journal of Tourism and Cultural Change*, vol. 9, no. 3, pp. 183–200.

D'Andrea, A 2007, *Global nomads: techno and new age as transnational counter-cultures in Ibiza and Goa*, Routledge, New York.

de Leon, J 2016, 'Miami Beach makes black tourists feel unwelcome during Memorial Day weekend', *Miami New Times*, 25 May, viewed 17 September 2016, <http://www.miaminewtimes.com/arts/miami-beach-makes-black-tourists-feel-unwelcome-during-memorial-day-weekend-8477990>.

Dedekorkut-Howes, A & Bosman, C 2015, 'The Gold Coast: Australia's playground?', *Cities*, vol. 42, pp. 70–84.

Duran, JD 2013, 'Ultra Music Festival 2013: City of Miami to vote on resolution "disapproving" of second festival weekend', *Miami New Times*, 7 January, viewed 16 September 2016, <http://www.miaminewtimes.com/music/ultra-music-festival-2013-city-of-miami-to-vote-on-resolution-disapproving-of-second-festival-weekend-6448643>.

Fagenson, Z 2014, 'Miami officials seek to end annual Ultra music fest, cite "chaos"', *Reuters*, 31 March, viewed 16 September 2016, <http://www.reuters.com/article/us-miami-ultra-idUSBREA2U17H20140331>.

Flechas, J 2016, 'Miami Beach plans for traffic, crowds of Memorial Day Weekend', *Miami Herald*, 18 May, viewed 17 September 2016, <http://www.miamiherald.com/news/local/community/miami-dade/miami-beach/article78279202.html>.

Fortuny, M, Soler, R, Cánovas, C & Sánchez, A 2008, 'Technical approach for a sustainable tourism development. Case study in the Balearic Islands', *Journal of Cleaner Production*, vol. 16, no. 7, pp. 860–869.

Gonzalez, V 2012, 'Ultra Fest generates $79 million annually for Miami economy: can EDM save the country?', *Miami New Times*, 10 October, viewed 16 September 2016, <http://www.miaminewtimes.com/music/ultra-fest-generates-79-million-annually-for-miami-economy-can-edm-save-the-country-6469494>.

Grieco, M 2017, 'Urban Beach Weekend: why it needs to end', *The New Tropic*, 6 June, viewed 25 May 2018, <https://thenewtropic.com/urban-beach-weekend-michael-grieco/>.

Gurney, K 2018, 'What's Memorial Day weekend going to look like this year? Miami Beach has big plans', *Miami Herald*, 6 April, viewed 24 May 2018, <http://www.miamiherald.com/news/local/community/miami-dade/miami-beach/article208128469.html>.

Hall, CM & Lew, AA 2009, *Understanding and managing tourism impacts: an integrated approach*, Routledge, New York.

Henkel, R, Henkel, P, Agrusa, W, Agrusa, J & Tanner, J 2006, 'Thailand as a tourist destination: perceptions of international visitors and Thai residents', *Asia Pacific Journal of Tourism Research*, vol. 11, no. 3, pp. 269–287.

Highmore, B 2005, *Cityscapes: cultural readings in the material and symbolic city*, Palgrave Macmillan, New York.

Hobbs, JD, Na Pattalung, P & Chandler, RC 2011, 'Advertising Phuket's nightlife on the internet: a case study of double binds and hegemonic masculinity in sex tourism', *Journal of Social Science Issues in Southeast Asia*, vol. 26, no. 1, pp. 80–104.

Jones, M 1986, *A sunny place for shady people: the real Gold Coast story*, Allen & Unwin, Sydney.

Kontogeorgopoulos, N 2004, 'Conventional tourism and ecotourism in Phuket, Thailand: conflicting paradigms or symbiotic partners?', *Journal of Ecotourism*, vol. 3, no. 2, pp. 87–108.

Kontogeorgopoulos, N 2009, 'The temporal relationship between mass tourism and alternative tourism in Southern Thailand', *Tourism Review International*, vol. 13, pp. 1–16.

Lawton, LJ 2005, 'Resident perceptions of tourist attractions on the Gold Coast of Australia', *Journal of Travel Research*, vol. 44, no. 2, pp. 188–200.

Lefebvre, H 2004 [1992], *Rhythmanalysis: space, time and everyday life*, trans. S Elden & G Moore, Continuum, London.

McDowall, S & Choi, Y 2010, 'A comparative analysis of Thailand residents' perception of tourism's impacts', *Journal of Quality Assurance in Hospitality & Tourism*, vol. 11, no. 1, pp. 36–55.

McDowall, S & Wang, Y 2009, 'An analysis of international tourism development in Thailand: 1994–2007', *Asia Pacific Journal of Tourism Research*, vol. 14, no. 4, pp. 351–370.

Meethan, K 2001, *Tourism in global society: place, culture, consumption*, Palgrave, Basingstoke.

Minca, C 2000, '"The Bali syndrome": the explosion and implosion of "exotic" tourist spaces', *Tourism Geographies*, vol. 2, no. 4, pp. 389–403.

Mugerauer, R 2004, 'The tensed embrace of tourism and traditional environments: exclusionary practices in Cancún, Cuba, and Southern Florida', in N AlSayyad (ed.), *The end of tradition?*, Routledge, London, pp. 116–143.

Murray, G 2007, 'Constructing paradise: the impacts of big tourism in the Mexican coastal zone', *Coastal Management*, vol. 35, no. 2–3, pp. 339–355.

Pajot, S 2014, 'South Beach clubs closing for Urban Beach Week', *Miami New Times*, 21 May, viewed 17 September 2016, <http://www.miaminewtimes.com/music/south-beach-clubs-closing-for-urban-beach-week-6444916>.

Park, RE 1967, 'The city: suggestions for the investigation of human behaviour in the urban environment', in EW Burgess, RD McKenzie and RE Park (eds), *The city*, University of Chicago Press, Chicago, pp. 1–46.

Pile, S 1999, 'What is a city?', in D Massey, J Allen & S Pile (eds), *City worlds*, Routledge, London, pp. 3–52.

Poon, A 1993, *Tourism, technology and competitive strategies*, CAB International, Wallingford.

Probyn, E 1996, *Outside belongings*, Routledge, New York.

Robertson, L 2018, '"I'm going to Davie": Ultra-annoyed downtown Miami residents plan their annual exodus', *Miami Herald*, 22 March, viewed 1 May 2018, <http://www.miamiherald.com/news/local/community/miami-dade/downtown-miami/article206374469.html>.

Sakolnakorn, TPN, Naipinit, A & Kroeksakul, P 2013, 'Sustainable tourism development and management in the Phuket Province, Thailand', *Asian Social Science*, vol. 9, no. 7, pp. 75–84.

Salazar, NB 2009, 'Imaged or imagined? Cultural representations and the "tour-ismification" of peoples and places', *Cahiers d'Études Africaines*, vol. 49, no. 193/194, pp. 49–71.

Shaw, G & Williams, AM 2004, *Tourism and tourism spaces*, SAGE Publications, London.

Sheller, M 2004, 'Demobilizing and remobilizing Caribbean paradise', in M Sheller & J Urry (eds), *Tourism mobilities: places to play, places in play*, Routledge, London, pp. 13–21.

Smiley, D 2012, '"Success" of Beach's Memorial Day weekend depends on point of view', *Miami Herald*, 28 May, viewed 17 September 2016, <http://www.miamihera ld.com/latest-news/article1940223.html>.

Smith, RA 1991, 'Beach resorts: a model of development evolution', *Landscape and Urban Planning*, vol. 21, no. 3, pp. 189–210.

Smith, VL 2001, 'Tourism change and impacts', in VL Smith & M Brent (eds), *Hosts and guests revisited: Tourism issues of the 21st century*, Cognizant Communication Corporation, New York, pp. 107–121.

Tourism and Events Queensland 2013, *Gold Coast social indicators 2013*, viewed 19 April 2014, <http://www.tq.com.au/fms/tq_corporate/research/destinationsresearch/gold_coast/RegionalSnapshotYESep13-GC.pdf>.

Tregoning, J 2013, 'Ultra Music Festival wins approval to hold second weekend in 2013', *inthemix*, 11 March, viewed 16 September 2016, <http://inthemix.junkee.com/ultra-music-festival-wins-approval-to-hold-second-weekend-in-2013/17955>.

Veiga, C 2016, 'Memorial Day on Miami Beach ends with big crowds, 153 arrests', *Miami Herald*, 30 May, viewed 17 September 2016, <http://www.miamiherald.com/news/local/community/miami-dade/miami-beach/article80802872.html>.

Wise, P 2010, 'Life, style and the capture of code', paper presented at Crossroads in Cultural Studies, Hong Kong, 17–21 June.

6 The right to the city
Stratification and belonging among resort residents

Introduction

How people feel about where they live has significant implications for their daily lives, well-being and trajectories. As discussed throughout this chapter, living in a resort provides a complicated context in which to negotiate senses of belonging to one's locality and ownership over one's everyday spaces. The experiences of residents also have implications for the formation, identity and vitality of the city itself. Extending the discussion of the previous chapter, below I draw connections between local attitudes towards tourism and the broader, more structural consequences of these experiences for the sociality and spatiality of resorts. I consider how infrastructure and developments are often geared towards catering to tourists rather than locals, and how this effects the mobilities and opportunities of residents. Further, I explore the ways in which tourism shapes socio-economic stratification in resorts, and how such inequalities become spatialised.

Tourism: a necessary evil

Local attitudes towards tourists and tourism are considerably more complex than straightforward appreciation or dissatisfaction. Residents of resorts are, as Revels (2011) puts it, 'trained ... to love and hate tourists in relatively equal measure' (p. 3). There exists an ambivalent dynamic of frustration and tolerance, disdain and appreciation, as was evident in my discussions with locals:

JEFF: I get annoyed a bit sometimes, but again, you just have to take a reality check. Just let it go. You can't win ... if they weren't here, we wouldn't have anything to do here either, there'd be no money. So I realise that it has to be here ... It depends on tourism. It's a tourist island and we need tourists here.

(Phuket, 9 December 2013)

EMILIO: We don't like tourists in Miami. That's how I see it – we don't like tourists. And yet we live off of tourism. Highly ironic.

(Miami, 12 March 2014)

JAKUB: I much rather the low season than the high season because of the more peaceful life. But that said, the tourists are the lifeblood of this island, so if there was no tourism, it wouldn't be what it is. ... it's like a necessary evil, let's put it that way.

(Phuket, 9 December 2013)

BRETT: Look, it's a necessary evil. Without tourism, I wouldn't have this job [beach club manager], we wouldn't be here talking right now.

(Phuket, 9 December 2013)

INTEVIEWER: Our version of South Beach, Surfers Paradise – we all hate going there because it's full of tourists and we all hate that, it's a bit strange.

DAMLA: I feel like that about my hometown in Turkey [also a resort] ... it's kind of a double standard, because obviously people make money, a lot of people don't work all winter, they only make money within those three, four months, right? But then they'll talk shit about tourists, like 'oh, we're waiting for October to come so that all these people can leave'.

(Miami, 11 March 2014)

Other people I spoke to informally – transfer drivers, hotel staff, restaurant waiters and other locals – echoed these sentiments. Tourism is accepted as something *necessary*, as vital to a resort's economic prosperity. This is true in many ways, particularly from a macroeconomic perspective – tourism creates and supports jobs in hospitality, retail and construction industries; produces revenue for related businesses through tourism expenditure; incentivises the upkeep and development of infrastructure and public leisure spaces; and so on. However, this does not mean that all residents benefit from tourism, whether directly or indirectly, with income generated by tourism distributed unequally in resorts (Cohen 2008).

Multi-national corporations, foreign investors and land owners reap the largest economic rewards of tourism (Kontogeorgopoulos 2009; Wattanakuljarus & Coxhead 2008; Wilson 2008; Murray 2007; Mugerauer 2004). Even locally owned and operated businesses may not benefit as much from the tourist presence as might be assumed. In Cancún, for instance, the popular all-inclusive style of accommodation means that tourists are less likely to venture beyond their hotels for a meal or for entertainment. This is also similar in Thailand due to the popularity of packaged tourism deals:

JEFF: ... why the Thais get annoyed is basically because they [Russian tourists] don't spend any money either, because they pay for everything before they come – they pay the travel agent. Breakfast is in the hotel; lunch is in the hotel. They don't really come here and get out in the shops and spend.

(Phuket, 9 December 2013)

In addition, among the workforce, opportunities and income can be stratified according to class and ethnicity. As Felipe explained:

FELIPE: It is more competitive and it's less paid than it used to be before … Now, to have a job in the tourism industry, you have to have a degree, a college degree, to make good money; speak at least three languages – *at least*.

(Cancún, 4 March 2014)

As a result, more prestigious, higher-paying positions like managerial, supervisory and front-of-house roles tend to be held by educated, English-speaking workers from overseas or elsewhere in the country (Mugerauer 2004). At my hotel in Koh Samui, for example, I was surprised to find that most of the English-speaking staff at the front desk were not Thai, but Filipino.[1] Similarly, many of the front desk workers at my hotel in Cancún had migrated there from other regions in Mexico. Low-paying, low-status, low-skilled jobs with limited advancement opportunities like janitor, cleaner or kitchen hand are more likely to be occupied by indigenous local people who are less formally skilled or who do not speak English (Castellanos 2010a). As Zukin (1995) observes, this labour force hierarchy is typical in places where the symbolic economy reigns:

> In the symbolic economy, employers hire a work force with cultural capital and higher education to do productive labor and provide a labor-intensive service called fun. Because of language requirements, business establishments use 'European' employees in front regions in direct contact with customers and 'minority' employees in the back. (p. 74)

If minorities or indigenous people *are* involved in front regions, this may be a strategic decision motivated (on behalf of management and other higher-ups in the industry) by a desire to present tourists with the kinds of exoticised appearances they expect.

Therefore, although tourism is often seen as a mechanism for modernising underdeveloped regions and raising standards of living, it may actually function to further marginalise, objectify and exclude local people (Castellanos 2010a, 2010b; Kontogeorgopoulos 2009; Wilson 2008; Mugerauer 2004; Pi-Sunyer, Thomas & Daltabuit 2001; Hiernaux-Nicolas 1999). Not only are the poorest locals restricted in their opportunities for upward mobility, but they also have little power in terms of how their culture and heritage is represented and sold (Evans 2005). As Agarwal and Shaw (2007) point out, despite Cancún's success, 'the Maya people are some of the most economically and socially marginalised people in Mexico' (p. 228), with higher rates of poverty in the Yucatán Peninsula than the rest of the nation. Thus, tourism – this 'necessary evil' – reproduces the kinds of inequalities of wealth that are characteristic of contemporary global capitalism (Wilson 2008), cutting off the most disadvantaged people from its benefits.

Privileging tourists, marginalising locals

In the resorts I have focused on, it was clear from a range of examples that despite opposition, resistance and complaints from residents, little has been done to curtail the negative effects of tourism or compensate for them. Residents commonly get the feeling that their cities – the local government, businesses and other institutions – function to service the needs and desires of transient visitors rather than those who live out their everyday lives there. Whether or not this is accurate is debatable, but that this sentiment is so widespread among locals is in itself significant. When interviewees were asked 'Do you feel the city caters more to locals or to tourists?', they responded:

EMILIO: Tourists … A hundred per cent, yes.

(Miami, 12 March 2014)

LUCIANA: I think definitely more for tourism. I feel that Miami is very underdeveloped for the amount of people that live here. Public transportation sucks, the roads are horrible. So instead of focusing on things like that, they're kind of like, investing in areas like this [downtown]. They just focus on the touristy areas.

(Miami, 13 March 2014)

NICOLE: To tourists. I think it's getting a little better … I'd say it'd be like, 70/30. 70 towards tourists, 30 to locals. They wanna build a casino in my front yard at the moment, it's completely fucked.

(Gold Coast, 4 November 2014)

CORY: … they spend tons of money promoting tourism and business, and certainly residents here feel like they do that at the expense of residents and their needs.

(Miami, 14 March 2014)

SETH: I'd say that's probably the fundamental thing about the Gold Coast, that all decisions made are made based on a tourist need before they're made based on the locals or the homeless … the way I felt living in Surfers was that I was essentially invisible – all my needs as a local were invisible to the people that were in charge, like the council, or even a lot of times the police … And it's maybe starting to cater to locals a little more now ... but only because now there's so many more locals that they can't ignore us anymore.

(Gold Coast, 24 November 2014)

JEFF: It's very seasonal, so the businesses cater to different people at different times of the year. Look, a large part of the year, it's the locals that keep these places going. If it wasn't for us, they'd make no money ... but come high season, particularly places along here [the beach], I think they forget about us ... they forget that we keep them going all year. We get treated a little bit like second class citizens ...

(Phuket, 9 December 2013)

FELIPE: ... they just look after the tourism ... They don't care what they do, as long as they do something for tourism to make money. They don't care if they destroy the environment, like the [Nichupté] Lagoon. This lagoon is dead because they filled it with land to build in some shopping malls, so they have no circulation. So it used to be full of fish and full of animals and wildlife, now they're dying, or dead.

(Cancún, 4 March 2014)

Clearly, the decision makers in resorts – whether government or corporations – are assumed to be motivated by a capitalistic 'dollar-worshipping ethic' (Jones 1986, p. 1) that trumps considerations of community, heritage or environmental preservation (unless these can be strategically packaged for tourist consumption). On the Gold Coast, for instance, with ongoing construction ensuring that tourists have the modern, luxurious facilities that they expect, there is little opportunity for buildings to become old enough to be considered local heritage in the future. This perpetual development is harmful to the environment as well, threatening the integrity of the landscape that so many residents love. Perhaps the most notable and controversial contemporary example of this on the Gold Coast is the proposal for a cruise ship terminal with accompanying casino, hotels and other facilities. Proposed sites have included The Spit (a sand spit with beaches and parks, located north of Surfers Paradise), a popular area among locals for fishing, surfing, swimming and beachside picnics, as well as nearby Wave Break Island, a favourite spot for boaters.

Since the first proposals for development in the early 2000s, there has been strong local resistance to the project, spearheaded by the community action group, the Save Our Spit Alliance. The Alliance has based its opposition on numerous potential impacts, particularly that the development will take away a treasured recreational public space from locals, and that it will have irreversible environmental consequences. The Alliance was successful in applying pressure to quash the original plans, and the Queensland State Government, which first proposed the idea, no longer supports the project (Kane & Rafferty 2016; Potts 2015). Despite the lack of public support and state government backing, local media persistently report that the city is losing millions of dollars in tourism revenue every year because it does not have a cruise ship terminal (see Emery 2016; Pierce 2015). The city council continues to commission new feasibility studies, the latest of which features an ocean-side terminal off Philip Park, Main Beach, just south of the previously proposed sites (Council of the City of Gold Coast 2018).

While there is an apparent overemphasis on developing tourism facilities in resorts, not enough attention is paid to developing infrastructure for locals. This is most clearly observable in Cancún. Buildings, roads and vegetation in the Hotel Zone are fairly well-maintained (save for a few abandoned hotels), but the further you travel from this area, the more you see dilapidated buildings, potholes, cracked sidewalks and unkempt gardens. Maintaining adequate infrastructure and public services in Cancún has been particularly challenging due to its rapid population growth and insufficient levels of ongoing urban planning,[2] which have led to the creation of squatter settlements that lack basic amenities like street lights, potable water or sewerage systems (see Córdoba Azcárate 2011; Castellanos 2010a; Agarwal & Shaw 2007; Mugerauer 2004; Clancy 2001). One interviewee, Felipe, attributed this failing to what he perceives as a corrupt government: 'they don't spend the money in the right way … Locally, federal, state – you name it. It's just a bunch of thieves' (Cancún, 4 March 2014).

An example of how infrastructure is geared towards tourists in resorts can be seen in their public transport systems. The bus system in Ibiza, for instance, predominantly features routes connecting beaches and other tourist areas, and during summer there are additional 'Discobus' services implemented specifically to shuttle tourists between nightclubs across the island. Without a rental car, this makes it difficult to venture beyond the tourist hubs to more rural local areas. Conversely, this also means that it can be challenging for locals – especially those without the economic capital necessary to own or operate a car – to access more built-up zones of the island.

In Miami, all of my interviewees expressed strong dissatisfaction with the public transport system, citing it as one of their least favourite things about living there. When I was staying in Miami Beach, I regularly took the 'SoBe Local', a bus whose route loops around South Beach and costs only a quarter (US25 cents) per trip. Travelling further inland proved considerably less convenient and less affordable – a bus trip to Downtown Miami cost me nine times as much, at a flat fare of US$2.25 each way; and getting to nearby residential suburbs like Brickell or Coral Gables by public transport took three times longer than driving, and required at least one change to another bus or train. There is, however, a free rail service, the Metromover, servicing downtown areas northwards to Omni and southwards to the financial district, stopping at landmarks and attractions like Freedom Tower, the American Airlines Arena, the Adrienne Arsht Center for the Performing Arts, the Pérez Art Museum Miami and the Miami Riverwalk, among others. Nonetheless, travelling to and from areas like Miami Beach and Downtown Miami becomes increasingly difficult the further away one lives from the tourist hubs. This is a significant problem considering Miami's dispersed, sprawling urban formation, in which the poorest residents – those who may be most reliant on public transport – are located on the margins. Thus, the system privileges the interests of tourism, making it easy for visitors to travel within desired zones at the same time that it isolates residents. This gearing of transport systems towards tourism is one of many ways in which tourist hubs like Miami Beach operate as exclusionary spaces.

Stratification, gentrification and ghettoisation

In resorts, as elsewhere, stratification is spatialised (Massey 1994). Unequal power relations contribute to uneven development, creating hierarchical and segregated spaces, centres and margins (Brown 2013; Massey 1998, 1994). Brown (2013) explains the effects of this in places like resorts:

> The evolution of tourist spaces in conjunction with the escalating scale of the tourist enterprise eventually leads to spatial enclosure, heightening the segregation and separation between spaces of leisure and those of work, spaces of consumption and those of production, spaces of the wealthy and those of the poor, spaces of the foreigner and those of the local. This process of dispossession and displacement parallels spatial strategies of settler colonization … (p. 193)

This pattern can be found in each resort, to varying extents. Cancún provides the most obvious example, having been developed with three distinct zones – a tourist enclave on the barrier island, a downtown with local services on the mainland's coast, and a residential area built around the edges with room to sprawl inland (for an in-depth exploration of how this segregation has intensified over time, see Córdoba Azcárate, Baptista & Domínguez Rubio 2014). Miami has a similar arrangement, with tourists, local elites and major businesses located in Miami Beach and downtown, and suburbia and local services spreading outwards from there. The general trend in resorts is that visitors and wealthy residents are located in or close to tourist hubs (the 'centre', in an ideological rather than geographical sense) and middle to lower class residents occupy the spaces extending centrifugally from there (the 'margins'), with many of the poorest locals situated the furthest away. Of course, the existence of such patterns from a macro perspective does not mean that each zone is coherent or homogenous, nor are they completely segregated. Indeed, as discussed below, some of the poorest locals, the homeless, live on the very same streets dominated by affluent residents and tourists consuming in excess. The stratified zones of resorts are interconnected, have shifting boundaries and can bleed into one another, and there are always anomalies and exceptions. Despite the efforts of tourism officials and city planners, tourist and local rhythms inevitably intersect and intermingle.

Nevertheless, the exclusionary nature of tourist hubs keeps them relatively segregated from local lives and movements. Since they are expensive and sometimes difficult to access, locals do not always avoid them simply by choice or out of distaste. For many residents, particularly those who are poor, isolated or otherwise disadvantaged, participating in touristic leisure spaces is not a feasible option. As Jakub explained, most local Thai people who work in tourism and hospitality in Phuket cannot afford to go to the same leisure spaces as tourists: 'They are not going to buy a mojito or whatever you buy, it costs you 200 baht, 300 baht, I'm not sure what, it's a crazy price. They don't even earn half of it on a daily salary' (Phuket, 9 December 2013). The tourism industries of resorts benefit from the exclusion of particular locals – hiding the messiness of everyday life, and the social blights of inequality and poverty, helps to maintain the hedonistic, hyperreal, glamorous imaginaries on which the touristic appeal of resorts depends. In other words, exclusionary techniques ensure that the tourism bubble remains, to an extent, 'a cocooned, sanitized, affluent, and gated space' (Córdoba Azcárate 2011, p. 187).

With tourists increasingly seeking affordable accommodation outside of tourist hubs, the 'centre' is expanding, encroaching on local areas, raising costs of living and pushing the poor further out (Brown 2013; Torres & Momsen 2006; Mugerauer 2004).[3] This is compounded by processes of gentrification, which, while beneficial to middle and upper class residents (at least in the short-term, before becoming popular with tourists), function to displace the poor and migrant communities living in the areas being revitalised (Zukin 2010; Minca 2000). One notable case is in Miami's Wynwood neighbourhood. Formerly a working-class area populated by Puerto Rican and Cuban immigrants and the site of garment factories and warehouses, Wynwood began to transform in the mid-2000s. Today, Wynwood oozes 'hipster charm' (Zukin 2010, p. 8) with the spectacle of colourful, elaborate street art covering its warehouses and streets (see Figure 6.1 and Figure 6.2), complemented by numerous trendy bars, coffee shops, craft breweries and art galleries.

As the resident of a resort, I momentarily found myself wishing there was a place like this on the Gold Coast – an 'authentic' leisure space, positioned away from the tourist hub, that focuses on (high) culture and creativity. Of course, this is because I could afford to go to such a place, and because the 'new' spatiality of Wynwood largely conceals any negative effects its transformation has had. During our interview, which took place in Wynwood, Emilio gave me a brief history of the neighbourhood and insight into how its gentrification, initiated by private individuals, satisfied a larger, more sinister civic agenda:

EMILIO: ... the people that bought the art galleries at first, they bought blocks, entire blocks ... they bought massive amounts of property here in Wynwood and in the Design District in the late '90s and early 2000s. 'They' as in him [Tony Goldman], his investors, his family.[4] And then

Figure 6.1 Street art in Wynwood, Miami

Figure 6.2 A man rides a bicycle through Wynwood, Miami

they started renting them out to local, but mostly New York, galleries, art collectors, to house their collections at a cheap rate and to also open them for exhibition and things like that. And so what that created was a movement toward, basically, them driving the message and the discourse and the policy of what should happen in the neighbourhood, right? And so, like, paving this street is something that took place fairly easily after they moved in ... whereas residents have been trying to pave this street for like 15 years and nothing was getting done ... So the history of Wynwood is incredibly interesting in that you see all the Cuban cafeterias or the Puerto Rican cafeterias that were in the neighbourhood beginning to disappear slowly – rents were driven up, and now this kind of coffee-house [where the interview took place] are the norm rather than the Cuban-owned cafeterias that were here prior to the galleries ... Now it's the bar owners that are beginning to drive the policy ... When you look at it historically, the city of Miami has, historically since the 1950s, late '50s, tried to drive out the lower income communities of Wynwood and Overtown. But specifically though policy, directly through policy. And they have not always been successful at it. At least from city efforts, right? But now when this happens more 'organically' [uses air quotes] – there's nothing really organic about it, but it seems like the change is happening from within – rather than the city being the ones that are sort of like driving the policy that is moving people out, it's really the business owners now in these communities which are doing the work for them.

INTERVIEWER: ... And is it supported by local government policy?

EMILIO: Yeah, and so it plays right into the city's long fight with trying to get rid of these lower income communities out of the city of Miami.

(Miami, 12 March 2014)

Later in the interview, Emilio remarked that he expects the area will not stay very cool for long, and that soon chain stores and high-end retailers would move in, displacing the locally-run coffee shops and galleries. This would follow the typical trajectory of gentrification that Zukin (2010) outlines: 'artists and gentrifiers move into old immigrant areas, praising the working-class bars and take-out joints but overwhelming them with new cafés and boutiques, which are soon followed by brand-name chain stores' (pp. 1–2).

By displacing working class, poor and homeless locals, gentrification can impel ghettoisation, a process which 'position[s] social marginality at a safe or insulated and bounded distance' (Grosz 2002 [1992], p. 302). As lower-class residents are forced to relocate away from revitalised areas due to rising costs of living, they are relegated to living in 'ghettos' with high rates of poverty and crime (Gladstone 1998), and often underdeveloped public services and infra-structure. In Cancún, these ghettos have manifested as shantytowns on the outskirts of the city, which are rife with gang activity (Castellanos 2010a, 2010b; Torres & Momsen 2006). As Torres and Momsen (2006) argue, ghettoisation is not necessarily a major concern for city officials as long as the ghettos are *hidden* from tourists (something that becomes increasingly difficult as they venture away from the tourist hubs). This is why Cancún was designed to have segregated zones in the first place – to 'avoid *Acapulquización*, in which ghettos and their waste-flows intermingle with beach-side resort hotels, resulting in a loss of exclusivity for the resort'[5] (Torres & Momsen 2006, p. 59).

In the case of Miami, while some ghettos are embraced and positioned as tourist attractions (e.g. Overtown), official measures are still in place to sanitise other spaces. During my visit, Downtown Miami featured a number of signs warning that it is a 'no panhandling zone' (see Figure 6.3), signifying official attempts to regulate the presence and behaviours of homeless people and beggars in the area. Over time, this zone had been expanded to include the streets surrounding popular attractions such as the American Airlines Arena and the Adrienne Arsht Center for the Performing Arts (Garcia-Roberts 2010; Mazzei 2010). According to the City of Miami (2010), panhandling 'damages otherwise positive experiences for tourists and general public visiting the area' (p. 1), causing them not to return. As such, the justification for these laws is that they will preserve the 'economic vitality' of the designated areas and 'protect the safety of the general public and protect citizens from … fear, harassment, and intimidation' (City of Miami 2010, p. 1).

When the City speaks of 'citizens' and the 'general public', the homeless are excluded from this rhetoric. These statements, and this legislation, reveal a power structure in which 'residents of the street' (Emilio, Miami, 12 March 2014) are clearly not regarded as residents at all, and not worthy of

Figure 6.3 'No panhandling zone' sign in Downtown Miami

representation and advocacy in local government. In 2017, the panhandling ban was ruled unconstitutional in that it infringed on one's capacity for free speech in public space (Smiley 2017). Nonetheless, this example highlights how the well-being and experiences of tourists are routinely privileged over those of the homeless. Tourists are, in effect, treated as if they have more of a right to occupy city space than the people who actually live there. The homeless, then, are seen as little more than an eyesore and an annoyance that erodes the facade of the tourism bubble, disrupts tourist expectations and exposes the nation's social ills and political failings.[6] Rather than focusing on strategies that might help the homeless, the emphasis is on policy that limits their interactions with others, and that makes them less visible by forcing them to relocate to ghettos where they are 'allowed' to live. In the interests of tourism, the homeless are criminalised and dispossessed, further entrenching their social isolation.

'Who has rights to the city?'

Taking into account the examples and experiences presented throughout this chapter, it is clear that the interests of tourists (as well as developers and businesses associated with tourism) are frequently privileged over the needs, desires and well-being of locals. For me, the most significant questions raised by this phenomenon are those also raised by one of my interviewees: 'Whose city is this? Who has rights to the city?' (Emilio, Miami, 12 March 2014), or, in Sharon Zukin's (1995) words, 'whose city ... whose culture?' (p. 47). These questions echo the sentiments of Lefebvre's (1996, 1974 [1968]) work on 'the right to the city', and the literature that has stemmed from it (e.g. Purcell 2014; Shields 2013; Harvey 2003, 2008; Mitchell 2003). The right to the city is not so much about individual accessibility to spaces and resources, but about the capacity to exercise power, to transform our localities collectively in line with our needs and uses (Harvey 2008, 2003). Typically, one would assume a city 'belongs' to its residents, which include those who comprise local government and local businesses, and that via democratic processes, residents exert the greatest level of influence and control over how the city functions and evolves. It is often the case, however, that the interests of capitalism[7] and the state have dispossessed this right (Purcell 2014; Harvey 2008). In resorts, residents have limited control over processes of urbanisation, with outside influences so prominent that any definitive assumptions about local ownership and belonging would be naïve or at least too simple.

There are multiple processes of territorialisation (Deleuze & Guattari 2004 [1987]) occurring in resort assemblages. Surin (2011) observes that places, or territories, are 'more than just spaces: they have a stake, a claim, they express (my house, their ranch, his bench, her friends)' (pp. 92–93). Our homes, our cities, are spaces that we territorialise, that we make our own. We form affective attachments to the landscape, we take comfort in going to our regular hang outs, and we develop bonds with others who live out their everyday lives in these spaces as well. As we territorialise space, we seek to create a sense of harmony, uniformity and fixity (Hillier 2007), such as through notions of cultural identity and community. This is never necessarily achieved, however, with other forces inevitably disrupting anything approaching stability or coherence. In resorts, attempts by some residents to territorialise space are undercut by other local (and sometimes foreign) entities with competing interests, such as regional governments, entrepreneurs and developers. These groups aim to territorialise space differently, to create uniform, regulated tourism hubs, which also inevitably experience disruption. In Surin's (2011) words, '[t]erritories are not fixed for all time, but are always being made and unmade, reterritorializing and deterritorializing' (p. 93).

If territorialisation refers to processes of ordering, connecting and controlling, deterritorialisation is that which destabilises this, sparking ruptures, disjunctures and changes in nature (Deleuze & Guattari 2004 [1987]; Colebrook 2002). Flows of tourists and other mobilities can deterritorialise local city spaces, temporarily passing through or occupying them, and transforming them as they do so. Brown (2013) argues that this makes the tourist an 'unwitting colonizer' (p. 186) who brings to bear his or her culturally distinct tastes, expectations, behaviours and practices on other places. This means, for example, that the significant presence of American tourists in Cancún has transformed the city through the establishment of facilities and services that cater to the desires of American visitors rather than only Mexican or Maya locals. The same is true for Chinese (and previously, Japanese) tourists on the Gold Coast, British tourists in Ibiza, and so on.

Thus, deterritorialisation introduces new influences, new lines of flight, engendering hybridity in resorts. The presence of tourists in particular areas has impelled the development of hotels, restaurants, bars, nightclubs, retail stores, airport shuttles and tour companies (which are also temporary in the sense that they can only survive so long as the area remains 'cool', iconic or otherwise desirable to visit). Hyperreal spaces like theme parks or packaged heritage sites may provide the most obvious instances of touristic deterritorialisation, Theme parks rely on fantasy, on a sense of detachment from territorial contexts, whereas heritage sites involve the re-working and manipulation of territorial culture and history (Xie 2015). The emergence of these tourism facilities has further transformed the landscape and the lifestyle for locals in resorts, as demonstrated by the impacts of tourism outlined throughout this and the previous chapter.

Tourists, then, can be understood as having reterritorialised some spaces in resorts, particularly the tourism hubs and other entertainment zones. These areas are no longer considered by residents as 'local' spaces, but have been reappropriated as sites that predominantly service tourists. Locals, however, also have the capacity to deterritorialise and reterritorialise these city spaces. This may manifest as: resistances to de/reterritorialisation, such as with the opposition to the Gold Coast's cruise ship terminal; initiatives to reclaim or revitalise portions of space for local use, such as non-mainstream, out-of-the-way venues in the tourist hubs; and the implementation of specific opportunities and events where local identity can be re-asserted and senses of community can be strengthened, such as arts and cultural festivals. Therefore, spatiality and belonging in resorts is constructed by ongoing movements between deterritorialisation and reterritorialisation, mobility and fixity, tourist and local. These relations, as the above discussion made clear, are not equal – those individuals and groups with the greatest amounts of financial and cultural power (Zukin 2010) have the greatest capacity to impose order and provoke change.

The effects of these processes of deterritorialisation and reterritorialisation on local lives are multiple. In addition to, and in response to, macro-level consequences, such as the stratification of wealth and the inadequacies of public infrastructure, there are also more subtle, affective, micro-level impacts of tourism's pervasiveness, such as on residents' subjectivities and belongings. Marginalised by tourism, locals can experience displacement, dispossession and disconnection, feeling like strangers in their own city (see also Revels 2011; Zukin 2010; Holmes 2001; Allen 1999). The experience of being a local in a resort is a liminal one, caught between insider and outsider.

These feelings, while individual and specific, nevertheless have wider implications, particularly in relation to senses of community, civic responsibility and social cohesion. Residents may find it challenging to be invested, as citizens, in their localities when they are so often neglected by their elected governments, excluded from decision-making processes surrounding tourism's future developments, and made to feel that they are politically disempowered to instigate change. Beyond identifications with lifestyle (and the subsequent appreciation of particular landscapes and leisure activities), there is little sense of a cohesive, city-wide collective identity or community in resorts. This fragmentation is not unusual for contemporary urban formations due to their characteristically large populations, cultural and ethnic diversity, structural inequalities and geographic dispersion. However, as Nijman (2011) points out, social capital 'may be scarce in a society at large while abundant within certain smaller social enclaves' (p. 124). This is true in some respects – such as through the existence of family ties and friendships; and in the case of some resorts – such as with Little Havana, Little Haiti and other cultural enclaves in Miami – but not others.

On the Gold Coast, for example, young people can feel that it is difficult to connect with others who share certain identities and affinities based on sexuality, music, style, hobbies, and so on. The city's local cultures are multiple and diverse, but are frequently ignored or marginalised by those in power in favour of focusing on what appeals to, and what can be packaged for, tourists. One of my interviewees expressed frustration over the fact that there was 'no gay scene' (Alyssa, Gold Coast, 24 September 2014) on the Gold Coast, with only one gay nightclub at the time, making it difficult for her to make friends and meet potential romantic partners. Similarly, another interviewee remarked that there was little in the way of alternative nightclubs or live music venues anymore, reflecting on his youth spent at establishments like The Party (an alternative nightclub in Surfers that played punk, rock and metal music, and attracted patrons who typically dressed in styles associated with these genres) and the Chophouse (a bar in Surfers that featured local live bands and DJs remixing vinyl of alternative bands). The lack of physical spaces available to people seeking non-mainstream, non-touristic experiences can significantly impact on their capacity to build important social networks and communities with like-minded people.[8] This may lead to social isolation, and can also motivate young people to move elsewhere to seek out these connections.

Conclusion

The resort residents I interviewed expressed an interesting ambivalence towards their localities, embodying a liminal affective position marked simultaneously by appreciation and resentment, acceptance and frustration. It is apparent that such feelings stem, in part, from the ways in which tourism industries in resorts significantly shape, and constrain, the opportunities, spatial practices, everyday experiences and senses of belonging for residents. I have only explored a select few impacts and experiences in this chapter – emphasising those with spatial dimensions, such as inequalities of wealth, processes of exclusion and feelings of displacement – based on what my interviewees communicated to me, as well as my own experiences as a local on the Gold Coast and a researcher in the field. It would be impossible to offer any kind of comprehensive account of what it is like to live in a resort, given that they are infinitely complex, heterogeneous assemblages that are constantly evolving. Instead, my aim in this chapter (and Chapter 5) has been to capture some of the local experiences and narratives that exist beyond the popular imaginary and the touristic metanarrative. It is clear that tourists and locals perceive and use the same spaces in disparate, contested ways, and it is important to recognise that all of these different understandings and practices comprise the unique lived spatiality of resorts. Moreover, it is essential that local governments, developers and tourism organisations acknowledge and work productively with such tensions if they are to produce sustainable forms of tourism into the future, as well as enhance the well-being of the local communities in which tourism takes place. These concerns form the basis for the following, final chapter.

Notes

1 The Philippines has a significantly larger English-speaking population than Thailand.
2 Although the city was well planned prior to its development, the ongoing management of its growth has been less carefully considered.
3 This is a problem that stems from alternative forms of tourism (e.g. backpacker tourism, ecotourism, and so on) as much as mass tourism. Alternative

accommodation options like Airbnb likely also contribute to this trend in that apartments and houses advertised by hosts are most often located in more local areas.

4 Tony Goldman, along with his family, purchased many of Wynwood's warehouses and pioneered the popular Wynwood Walls art project.

5 This refers to the mistakes in the urban planning of Acapulco, one of Mexico's older major resorts. Acapulco's development was predominantly focused on constructing tourism facilities, and did not adequately account for the local infrastructure that would be needed to support the influx of workers needed to run the resort (Sackett 2010; Hiernaux-Nicolas 1999). As a result, Acapulco suffered due to pollution, hyperinflation, poverty and the rapid growth of shantytowns (Mugerauer 2004; Clancy 2001; Hiernaux-Nicolas 1999).

6 These issues are, of course, not restricted to America. Recently, prior to the commencement of the 2018 Commonwealth Games on the Gold Coast, I witnessed the homeless locals in my suburb being relocated and displaced (e.g. by closures of parks and roads that they occupied) over a number of weeks before the influx of tourists, athletes and other international delegates arrived.

7 Purcell (2014) notes, for instance, that policy and legislation tend to favour property owners (whether local, foreign or otherwise) over city dwellers.

8 This is not to say that communities must be spatially-bounded, but many of us do indeed seek physical spaces for interaction and belonging, in addition to participating in imagined and online communities.

References

Agarwal, S & Shaw, G 2007, 'Re-engineering coastal resorts in Mexico: some management issues', in S Agarwal & G Shaw (eds), *Managing coastal tourism resorts: a global perspective*, Channel View Publications, Clevedon, pp. 216–232.

Allen, J 1999, 'Worlds within cities', in D Massey, J Allen & S Pile (eds), *City worlds*, Routledge, London, pp. 53–97.

Brown, DF 2013, 'Tourists as colonizers in Quintana Roo, Mexico', *The Canadian Geographer*, vol. 57, no. 2, pp. 186–205.

Castellanos, MB 2010a, *A return to servitude: Maya migration and the tourist trade in Cancún*, University of Minnesota Press, Minneapolis.

Castellanos, MB 2010b, 'Cancún and the campo: indigenous migration and tourism development in the Yucatán', in D Berger & AG Wood (eds), *Holiday in Mexico: critical reflections on tourism and tourist encounters*, Duke University Press, Durham, pp. 241–264.

City of Miami 2010, *Legislation: ordinance*, file number 10–01210, viewed 27 September 2016, <http://egov.ci.miami.fl.us/Legistarweb/Attachments/60810.pdf>.

Clancy, M 2001, *Exporting paradise: tourism and development in Mexico*, Pergamon, Oxford.

Cohen, E 2008, *Explorations in Thai tourism: collected case studies*, Emerald, Bingley.

Colebrook, C 2002, *Understanding Deleuze*, Allen & Unwin, Crows Nest.

Córdoba Azcárate, M 2011, '"Thanks God, this is not Cancun!" Alternative tourism imaginaries in Yucatan (Mexico)', *Journal of Tourism and Cultural Change*, vol. 9, no. 3, pp. 183–200.

Córdoba Azcárate, M, Baptista, I & Domínguez Rubio, F 2014, 'Enclosures within enclosures and hurricane reconstruction in Cancún, Mexico', *City & Society*, vol. 26, no. 1, pp. 96–116.

Council of the City of Gold Coast 2018, *Ocean-side Cruise Ship Terminal feasibility study*, viewed 9 May 2018, <http://www.goldcoast.qld.gov.au/ocean-side-cruise-ship -terminal-feasibility-study-37930.html>.

Deleuze, G & Guattari, F 2004 [1987], *A thousand plateaus: capitalism and schizo-phrenia*, trans. B Massumi, Continuum, London.

Emery, L 2016, 'Millions of dollars sailing away from Gold Coast without cruise ship terminal, says expert', *Gold Coast Bulletin*, 13 June, viewed 20 September 2016, <http://www.goldcoastbulletin.com.au/news/council/millions-of-dollars-sailing-awa y-from-gold-coast-without-cruise-ship-terminal-says-expert/news-story/99621ecb99 5374b0fa8d3e543ae0a231>.

Evans, G 2005, 'Mundo Maya: from Cancún to city of culture. World heritage in post-colonial Mesoamerica', in D Harrison & M Hitchcock (eds), *The politics of world heritage: negotiating tourism and conservation*, Channel View Publications, Cleve-don, pp. 35–49.

Garcia-Roberts, G 2010, 'Downtown Miami's no-panhandling zone displaces home-less', *The Miami New Times*, 2 December, viewed 27 September 2016, <http://www. miaminewtimes.com/news/downtown-miamis-no-panhandling-zone-displaces-hom eless-6378832>.

Gladstone, DL 1998, 'Tourism urbanization in the United States', *Urban Affairs Review*, vol. 34, no. 1, pp. 3–27.

Grosz, E 2002 [1992], 'Bodies-cities', in G Bridge & S Watson (eds), *The Blackwell city reader*, Blackwell Publishing, Oxford, pp. 297–303.

Harvey, D 2003, 'The right to the city', *International Journal of Urban and Regional Research*, vol. 27, no. 4, pp. 939–941.

Harvey, D 2008, 'The right to the city', in RT LeGates & F Stout (eds), *The city reader*, 6th edn, Routledge, New York, pp. 270–278.

Hiernaux-Nicolas, D 1999, 'Cancún bliss', in DR Judd & SS Fainstein (eds), *The tourist city*, Yale University Press, New Haven, pp. 124–139.

Hillier, J 2007, *Stretching beyond the horizon: a multiplanar theory of spatial planning and governance*, Ashgate, Aldershot.

Holmes, D 2001, 'Monocultures of globalization: touring Australia's Gold Coast', in D Holmes (ed.), *Virtual globalization: virtual spaces/tourist spaces*, Routledge, London, pp. 175–191.

Jones, M 1986, *A sunny place for shady people: the real Gold Coast story*, Allen & Unwin, Sydney.

Kane, C & Rafferty, M 2016, 'Gold Coast council to explore three cruise ship term-inal options offshore from Southport Spit', *ABC News*, 8 June, viewed 20 Sep-tember 2016, <http://www.abc.net.au/news/2016-06-08/gold-coast-council-to-exp lore-three-cruise-terminal-options/7489258>.

Kontogeorgopoulos, N 2009, 'The temporal relationship between mass tourism and alternative tourism in Southern Thailand', *Tourism Review International*, vol. 13, pp. 1–16.

Lefebvre, H 1974 [1968], *Le droit à la ville: suivi de, Espace et politique*, Anthropos, Paris.

Lefebvre, H 1996, 'The right to the city', in E Kofman & E Lebas (eds & trans.), *Writings on cities*, Blackwell Publishers, Oxford, pp. 147–159.

Massey, D 1994, *Space, place, and gender*, University of Minnesota Press, Minneapolis.

Massey, D 1998, 'Spatial constructions of youth cultures', in T Skelton & G Valentine (eds), *Cool places: geographies of youth cultures*, Routledge, London, pp. 121–129.

Mazzei, P 2010, 'Miami expands no-panhandling zone near popular venues', *Sun Sentinel*, 19 November, viewed 27 September 2016, <http://articles.sun-sentinel.com/2010-11-19/news/fl-miami-panhandling-20101119_1_panhandling-commission-cha irman-marc-sarnoff-beggars>.

Minca, C 2000, '"The Bali syndrome": the explosion and implosion of "exotic" tourist spaces', *Tourism Geographies*, vol. 2, no. 4, pp. 389–403.

Mitchell, D 2003, *The right to the city: social justice and the fight for public space*, The Guilford Press, New York.

Mugerauer, R 2004, 'The tensed embrace of tourism and traditional environments: exclusionary practices in Cancún, Cuba, and Southern Florida', in N AlSayyad (ed.), *The end of tradition?*, Routledge, London, pp. 116–143.

Murray, G 2007, 'Constructing paradise: the impacts of big tourism in the Mexican coastal zone', *Coastal Management*, vol. 35, no. 2–3, pp. 339–355.

Nijman, J 2011, *Miami: mistress of the Americas*, University of Pennsylvania Press, Philadelphia.

Pierce, J 2015, 'Rejection of Wavebreak Island terminal costs Gold Coast millions of dollars a week in lost revenue', *The Courier Mail*, 10 May, viewed 20 September 2016, <http://www.couriermail.com.au/travel/australia/queensland/rejection-of-wa vebreak-island-terminal-costs-gold-coast-millions-of-dollars-a-week-in-lost-revenue/news-story/e788758a63bddfe775ea573a18eba063>.

Pi-Sunyer, O, Thomas, RB & Daltabuit, M 2001, 'Tourism on the Maya periphery', in VL Smith & M Brent (eds), *Hosts and guests revisited: tourism issues of the 21st century*, Cognizant Communication Corporation, New York, pp. 122–140.

Potts, A 2015, 'Gold Coast cruise ship terminal debate a long-running saga', *Gold Coast Bulletin*, 11 August, viewed 20 September 2016, <http://www.goldcoastbulle tin.com.au/lifestyle/gold-coast-cruise-ship-terminal-debate-a-longrunning-saga/news-story/2b6858a1343cc430cfce8b1cece5f790>.

Purcell, M 2014, 'Possible worlds: Henri Lefebvre and the right to the city', *Journal of Urban Affairs*, vol. 36, no. 1, pp. 141–154.

Revels, TJ 2011, *Sunshine paradise: a history of Florida tourism*, University Press of Florida, Gainesville.

Sackett, A 2010, 'Fun in Acapulco? The politics of development on the Mexican Riviera', in D Berger & AG Wood (eds), *Holiday in Mexico: Critical Reflections on Tourism and Tourist Encounters*, Duke University Press, Durham, pp. 161–182.

Shields, R 2013, 'Lefebvre and the right to the open city?', *Space and Culture*, vol. 16, no. 3, pp. 345–348.

Smiley, D 2017, 'Miami's downtown panhandling ban is unconstitutional, court says', *Miami Herald*, 18 August, viewed 26 May 2018, <http://www.miamiherald.com/news/local/community/miami-dade/downtown-miami/article167945127.html>.

Surin, K 2011, 'Force', in CJ Stivale (ed.), *Gilles Deleuze: key concepts*, 2nd edn, Acumen, Durham, pp. 21–32.

Torres, R & Momsen, JH 2006, 'Gringolandia: Cancún and the American tourist', in ND Bloom (ed.), *Adventures into Mexico: American tourism beyond the border*, Rowman & Littlefield, Lanham, pp. 58–74.

Wattanakuljarus, A & Coxhead, I 2008, 'Is tourism-based development good for the poor?', *Journal of Policy Modeling*, vol. 30, no. 6, pp. 929–955.

Wilson, TD 2008, 'Economic and social impacts of tourism in Mexico', *Latin American Perspectives*, vol. 35, no. 3, pp. 37–52.

Xie, PF 2015, *Industrial heritage tourism*, Channel View Publications, Bristol.

Zukin, S 1995, *The cultures of cities*, Blackwell Publishers, Oxford.

Zukin, S 2010, *Naked city: the death and life of authentic urban places*, Oxford University Press, Oxford.

7 Conclusion
Mobilising difference and complexity

Introduction

This book has examined resorts as distinctive kinds of urban assemblages that share a number of commonalities with each other, but nonetheless have their own local particularities. Treated as examples, each resort is interpreted in terms of its singularity as well as its connections to other resorts and to wider social and cultural phenomena, such as the effects of mass tourism and globalisation on urban spatiality. I have considered how resorts are produced through complex arrangements of material and symbolic elements, including popular imaginaries, narratives of identity, representations, built environments, rhythms, social and spatial practices, and lived experiences. In this final chapter, I discuss some of the implications of my findings, the limitations of the project, and possibilities for alternative approaches and future research.

Conceptual and practical implications

Resorts are unusual urban sites for which conventional understandings of cities – how they develop, how they are arranged and how they function – are only partially able to account. My interest in these spaces that are characterised more by transience than by sedimentation required that I start with some fundamental questions about how people use them, what they bring to them, how they experience them and what they take from them – that is, how socio-spatial relations occur. During the research process, I came to realise that my project was not driven only by an interest in resorts *per se*, but in how we conceptualise spatiality. Spaces are assemblages that are open, dynamic, unpredictable and heterogeneous, full of multiplicities and perpetually in process. They are shaped by dominant metanarratives and marginalised rhythms, by global trends and localised expressions, by mobilities and settlements, by the material (the real, the perceived) and the symbolic (the imaginary, the conceived), and by the interconnections and disjunctures between and among each of these.

These relations reveal themselves in the experience of lived spaces and their rhythms. When I walk through unfamiliar urban spaces, I notice the architecture, the movements of people, the quality of the air; I am guided by signage, pedestrian crosswalks and Google Maps on my smartphone; I compare how it looks and feels 'in real life' to the images I saw on television shows, TripAdvisor and Instagram; I reflect on the narratives in my mind of what 'kind' of place this is – hip, or dodgy, or romantic, or kitsch, or cultured, or whatever else; I get caught off guard when observing or feeling things I did not expect; I observe shifts in activity in the transition from day to night and back again; and I continuously interpret what I encounter in terms of what is familiar and common sense to me – my *habitus*, memories and conceptual mappings of home. This embodied, *in situ* experience brings to light the ways in which the material and the symbolic are always folded together, the present is always mediated by the past and the future, and the micro and the macro are always inter-implicated.

It is all too common for the material to be privileged over the symbolic, and the macro privileged over the micro, or vice versa. However, this kind of hierarchical, binary logic does not reflect what is actually going on in lived spaces. Rather than trying to regulate and control the messiness of the urban (Highmore 2005), or attempting to impose coherence on it through overly simplified assessments (e.g. resorts as depthless, hyperreal, homogenous), we must work productively with its complexity and disorder. By taking a cultural studies approach to urban analysis, this book demonstrates the value in noticing specificities and commonalities, attending to relationality and liminality, acknowledging multiplicities and disparities, and embracing openness, fluidity and partiality. Such an approach allows us to rethink conventional notions of authenticity, culture, belonging and community. As is the multidisciplinary 'nature' of cultural studies, this work has been informed by concepts and processes taken from urban studies, cultural geography, cultural sociology and tourism studies. In effect, the work is as much a product of *bricolage* conceptually, theoretically and analytically as it is methodologically.

This book purposely did not develop any kind of universal, overarching model of resorts that can be 'applied' to places for planning, development or management purposes. The complexity of urban assemblages cannot be understood only through models or morphologies. There is no question that such approaches are useful in particular contexts in that they enable planners, policy makers and applied researchers to identify and analyse patterns and networks in order to manage the development of particular settings. However, if not used in conjunction with a range of other methods and concepts, they can function to reinforce sameness, obscure differences and anomalies, and perpetuate binary logics. As explored throughout this book, instead of thinking in terms of 'either/or', we need to develop ways of thinking that account for multiplicity: 'and … and … and' (Deleuze & Guattari 2004 [1987], p. 27).

It is vital to establish more open, flexible and nuanced approaches to conceptualising spatiality. All people are spatially located, and our everyday spatial contexts play a significant part in shaping our subjectivities. In turn, all spaces are produced, to a significant extent, by the people who occupy them. Chapter 6 demonstrates that locals in resorts are conscious of their own marginalisation, and feel that the needs and desires of tourists are privileged over those of residents. This raises several key questions that matter for citizens of resorts as much as they do for citizens of conventional cities: Who has rights to city space? *To whom* do cities belong? Is it the residents, or is it the visitors, the property developers, the foreign investors, the business owners? In reality, it is all of these. But *who belongs to* cities? The answer to this is, overwhelmingly, the people whose lives take place there, who feel attachments to the spaces and people they encounter on an everyday basis. For resort residents, these senses of belonging are complicated by feelings of displacement and resentment, or at least ambivalence, stemming from the tourist-centric nature of their localities.

These insights are useful for urban planners, policy makers, local governments and other bodies involved in tourism development. Too often, the concerns and capacities of residents in relation to their own localities are overridden by the economic and promotional imperatives of tourism and development. This is a problem in any city, but in resorts it is particularly difficult for citizens to resist changes that impact on their quality of life when the counter-argument invariably dwells on how growth and infrastructure for tourism are essential to sustain a regional economy that depends on that tourism. Indeed, virtually all other sectors – even those apparently unrelated, such as education and health services – ultimately depend on the tourism that has driven the urbanisation of the region in the first place, and continues to underpin its growth even as the city matures and diversifies its economic base. Similarly, it is equally difficult for citizens to demand improved infrastructure or new public spaces in local areas when their cities are so caught up in sustaining and nurturing tourism for the very same reasons listed above.

There is a need to consider more deeply the impacts of development for residents and the environment, to actively engage residents in decision-making processes (rather than disseminating information about what has already been decided), and to strategise appropriate ways in which to offset the inconvenience caused by touristic events. Further, while residents in resorts understand the extent to which their cities' and regions' economies depend on the tourism industry, local governments should not abuse that understanding by taking residents for granted or minimising their needs in the priorities of city governance. Government – whether local, state or federal – can and should support policies and planning with the sole aim of benefitting residents, especially those who are disadvantaged. Taking steps to protect and enhance the well-being and interests of residents is necessary to promote social cohesion and civic responsibility, to ensure that the tourism industry remains sustainable as the resident population grows, and to protect the environmental and cultural assets that are both attractions for tourists and central to residents' perceptions of local distinctiveness and lifestyles.

Places across the world are capitalising on their symbolic economies (Zukin 1995), mobilising local distinctiveness and local cultures for monetary gain, as is evident in resort tourism as well as urban tourism, rural tourism, back-packer tourism, cultural tourism and other alternative styles. Tourism and globalisation do not merely erode local cultures, but can transform them and strengthen them, fostering diversity through hybridisation and celebrating difference through cultural attractions. This is, of course, most positive and productive when locals themselves are involved in the creation of such sites; when they are geared to residents and tourists alike (as opposed to models in which non-locals create attractions for other non-locals); and when they are financially and spatially accessible to residents (such as through affordable, efficient public transport networks). These attractions should be designed as *shared* spaces which emphasise local specificity and lifestyles, simultaneously reinforcing collective notions of belonging and local identity while offering tourists the unique experiences they desire. Through working productively with difference, emphasising distinctiveness and multiplying ways of appreciating local cultures, environments and experiences, the benefits of tourism can be spread more widely for tourists and residents.

While over-emphasis on tourism produces particular difficulties for residents of resorts, concerns about misplaced policy priorities are not limited to these places. Tensions between capitalistic pursuits and the needs of the community and environment are central to social and political discourses surrounding many contemporary places, whether urban, regional, rural or in-between. Similarly, a significant proportion of the major social and cultural phenomena discussed in this book are relevant well beyond resorts. For example, the connections between capitalism, tourism, globalisation and postmodernism, and the familiar stereotypes and binaries associated with each, have implications for everyone, wherever they live. As Chapter 4 explains, the manifestations and effects of these forces are anything but straightforward or predictable, and thus cannot be regarded simply as destructive or otherwise inherently negative. With such issues, as with most of the matters I have raised, complex challenges that are playing through in sites characterised by difference, plurality, fluidity and multiplicities, require approaches that eschew the over-simplifications that inevitably attend attempts to think in terms of binary oppositions.

Productive limitations and future potentials

This book – albeit with its years of work organised into chapters, sections and subsections, beginning with an introduction and ending with a conclusion – is necessarily incomplete and open-ended. In saying this, I urge readers to think beyond the scope of this research, and to consider how my work can be adapted and extended. My findings and methods have a number of limitations, and recognising as much elucidates possibilities for future research. For instance, the resorts I chose to focus on, and the issues I became drawn to, were based very much on my own subjectivity – the media I had consumed throughout my life, my research interests and disciplinary background, my position as a young Australian woman, and my spatial context as a Gold Coast resident and long-time local of south-east Queensland. Similar research projects from different perspectives will inevitably raise other important lines of inquiry.

The evolution and effects of tourism in the localities on which I focus may not be generalisable to other places. As I stressed at several points throughout this book, despite their commonalities, each resort has different trajectories, circumstances and social dynamics at play, and their local specificities demand policies and processes that are attentive to their particularities and their livedness. There are a range of other resorts that could have been included and would have offered their own unique insights, such as the Maldives; Rio de Janeiro, Brazil; and the Hawaiian Islands, USA. Further, rather than undertaking a transnational project, as mine was, the multi-sited approach could be narrowed to particular regions to illuminate their specific social, political, historical and ecological/environmental conditions. For example, making use of the bodies of literature already existing on these regions, future projects could examine the spatiality of resorts in the Mediterranean (e.g. Nice, France; Majorca, Spain; Santorini, Greece; and Dubrovnik, Croatia); Southeast Asia (e.g. Bali, Indonesia; Boracay, Philippines; and Pattaya, Thailand); or the Caribbean (e.g. the islands of Jamaica, Barbados, the Bahamas, Aruba and the Dominican Republic). Sites could also be selected for comparative analysis based on certain common factors, like current phase of development (e.g. burgeoning domestic destinations or international destinations experiencing decline), spatial formations (e.g. cities or islands), representations in specific forms of media (e.g. in literature or film), or experiences of and responses to various issues (e.g. environmental degradation, sex tourism, relations between ethnicities or genders).

My choice of applied methods significantly shaped the discussion as well, and different methodological decisions would have yielded different results. As I set out to take a comparative, multi-sited approach with limited financial resources, the amount of time I could spend in each place was limited to a single visit during the peak season. Similar studies of resorts in the future could take a more ethnographic approach, staying longer in each site to observe the ebb and flow of tourist arrivals over time, and undertaking interviews with a variety of stakeholders (not only locals, but also tourists, hospitality workers, local government officials, and so on).

As the resorts covered in this book continue to develop and change, some will decline, while others will grow and diversify, perhaps evolving into quite different urban formations altogether. In any case, these changes will involve different and unpredictable social, cultural, political and environmental effects that will be worthy of further interrogation.

Conclusion

Much like the resorts I have analysed, this book is inevitably connected to what exists beyond it – from the places, experiences and concepts that inspired the research, to its potential implications, future projects and adaptions, and its contribution to broader theoretical, methodological and disciplinary terrains. I have conceptualised resorts in terms of their shared characteristics and their own local specificities, and examined how their spatiality is produced, reproduced and transformed through myriad material and symbolic factors. Treating resorts as examples – occupying the liminal space between universal and particular – my analysis contributes to wider understandings of tourism, globalisation and spatialisation, reimagining how these processes unfold in complex, heterogeneous places. Moving forward, it is vital that we resist models that enforce a sense of sameness, linearity or predictability, instead *working with* the difference, messiness and idiosyncrasies that constitute lived spaces.

References

Deleuze, G & Guattari, F 2004 [1987], *A thousand plateaus: capitalism and schizophrenia*, trans. B Massumi, Continuum, London.

Highmore, B 2005, *Cityscapes: cultural readings in the material and symbolic city*, Palgrave Macmillan, New York.

Zukin, S 1995, *The cultures of cities*, Blackwell Publishers, Oxford.

Index